STUDIES IN HISTORY, ECONOMICS AND
PUBLIC LAW

Edited by the
FACULTY OF POLITICAL SCIENCE
OF COLUMBIA UNIVERSITY

Number 520

PRUSSIAN MILITARY REFORMS 1786-1813

BY

WILLIAM O. SHANAHAN

PRUSSIAN MILITARY REFORMS 1786-1813

BY

WILLIAM O. SHANAHAN

AMS Press, Inc.
New York
1966

Copyright 1945, Columbia University Press
New York

Reprinted 1966
with Permission of Columbia University Press

AMS Press, Inc.
New York, N.Y. 10003

UA
718
.P9S5

CANISIUS COLLEGE LIBRARY
BUFFALO, N. Y.

Manufactured in The United States of America

To

HELEN
AND
MICHAEL

AUTHOR'S PREFACE

ALTHOUGH German militarism is not a new historical phenomenon, its importance in modern history has been made evident by two World Wars in which the German nation has played a prominent part. This circumstance has given the professional historians an opportunity as well as a great responsibility. There may be a few historians who do not search the past for an explanation of events in their own time, but most historians are agreed that the usefulness of their craft lies in the understanding that only an historical perspective seems to provide. Knowledge alone may yield a rich satisfaction for the antiquary, but to be useful, historical knowledge must provide a basis for political judgments and decisions. A monograph such as this is only a small fragment of the historical literature, now written and remaining to be written, that can explain German militarism; still, a profound lesson can be learned from Napoleon's failure to prevent Prussia's military recovery after the crushing defeat of Jena. It is of course the author's hope that his interpretation of those events may help to devise a more certain means of restraining German military ambition.

An historian's work is nourished by libraries and to these institutions and their staffs the author is indebted for the substance of his book: the libraries of Columbia University, the University of Notre Dame, the University of Chicago, the University of North Carolina, Duke University, and the New York Public Library. In Berlin extensive use was made of the erstwhile library of the *Kriegsakademie* and the Great German General Staff, the *Deutsche Heeresbücherei*. Materials were also derived from the *Preussische Staatsbibliothek* and the *Preussische Staatsarchiv*. Among German university libraries that of the University of Leipzig proved most useful.

My first thanks for assistance and guidance in completing this study are due Professor C. J. H. Hayes of Columbia University in whose seminar the work began. His patience and encouragement were a constant source of inspiration to the author.

Mr. T. H. Thomas of Cambridge, Mass., who first suggested the topic, has offered invaluable criticism of the manuscript and has given the author the benefit of his extensive knowledge of armies and warfare. And a permanent debt of gratitude is owed Professor Waldemar Westergaard of the University of California at Los Angeles for directing the author into the rich field of military history. To Professors Charles W. Cole, Robert L. Schuyler, and John H. Wuorinen of Columbia University, who criticized the organization and style of the manuscript, I owe special thanks. I am also grateful to Professor John A. Krout, Chairman of the Department of History, Columbia University, for his kindly interest and helpful suggestions.

A generous grant from the University of Notre Dame has assisted the author in the publication of this book. I especially wish to thank President J. Hugh O'Donnell and Rev. Philip S. Moore, Dean of the Graduate School, for making the grant possible. And to Rev. Thomas T. McAvoy, Chairman of the Department of History, the author is indeed indebted for his never-failing help.

WILLIAM O. SHANAHAN
Lt. (j. g.), USNR

CHAPEL HILL, N. C.
OCTOBER 1, 1944

TABLE OF CONTENTS

	PAGE
Author's Preface	7
Introduction	11

CHAPTER I
Prussian Military Institutions in 1806 17

CHAPTER II
The Development of the Canton System 35

CHAPTER III
Efforts at Reform before 1806 61

CHAPTER IV
The Battle of Jena and the First Reforms 88

CHAPTER V
The Work of the Reformers in 1808 127

CHAPTER VI
Conscription and the *Krümper* 150

CHAPTER VII
Military Training and the *Landwehr* 179

CHAPTER VIII
The Mobilization of 1813 197

Conclusion	225
Bibliographical Essay	235
Bibliography	241
Index	255

INTRODUCTION

HISTORICAL INTERPRETATION OF THE PRUSSIAN *Krümper* SYSTEM

IN the period between the death of Frederick the Great in 1786 and the War of Liberation in 1813 the Prussian army experienced a number of severe trials. The acquisition of Polish territory imposed a reorganization on the army that weakened its fighting power and seriously interfered with its methods of recruiting. Yet this was not as fateful as the tests of strength between France and Prussia. The first clash in 1792 did not offer any direct proof that French military methods were superior to those perfected by Frederick the Great. Only an alert minority of reform-minded Prussian officers were aware that since the Seven Years' War the profound alteration of the French army had introduced a new era of warfare. Except for the increased size of foreign armies and the new problems raised after 1795 by the common frontier with Russia, most Prussian officers were not alarmed by military developments abroad. Their complacence received a rude shock in 1806. At Jena and Auerstädt not only the Prussian army but the state collapsed. A period of political and military reorganization followed that was brightened by the work of Stein and Scharnhorst. Not all of Scharnhorst's military reforms were carried out, but the army shattered in 1806 was rebuilt upon a secure foundation. This army supported by Russian forces confidently offered battle to the French in the spring of 1813.

The historians' interest in this period has been centered principally upon the era of reform that followed the battle of Jena. They have customarily attributed the rebuilding of the Prussian army to the *Krümper* system, which was Scharnhorst's means for outwitting Napoleon's attempt to prevent Prussian military recovery. By the Treaty of Paris the Prussian army was limited to 42,000 men, but Scharnhorst's measures for successively training this number of recruits are supposed to have brought into being a secret army more than three times the size of the one that was permitted. Henderson, an historian of the last generation, offers the traditional explanation of how this was accomplished: " The Treaty of Paris, of September, 1808, had required that the numbers of the army should never exceed forty-two thousand; — a poor showing if we think of the six hundred and fifty thousand men that Napoleon was able to lead against Russia. But the fertile brain of Scharnhorst had evolved a plan by which the letter of the law might be kept, but the spirit evaded. By his famous crimper system (*sic*), so called from the spare horse that was kept in reserve, recruits were given leave of absence after a month of rigid drilling in the most essential points. While the army at any given time might not exceed in numbers the alloted figure, there were thus trained in all some one hundred and fifty thousand men; when the troops marched out to parade, a number of them invariably remained behind in the barracks, so that there might be the less ground for suspicion and inquiry." [1]

The French historian J. M. E. Godefroy Cavaignac was among the first to cast doubt upon the success of the *Krümper* system. His account in *La formation de la Prusse contemporaine* (2nd ed., Paris, 1897-1898), II, 407-15, was more accurate than that of his contemporaries, but the scope of his subject was too great and his acquaintance with the sources too slight for an effective analysis of Scharnhorst's measures. More recent historians have doubted the value of the *Krümper* system without directly challenging the traditional conception of it.[2] This is especially true of historians who have made use of Curt Jany's documentary history of the Prussian army, *Geschichte der Königlich Preussischen Armee* (Berlin, 1928-1933, 4 v.). Jany's treatment of the military reforms carried out under Scharnhorst's direction differs from older historical accounts in

[1] Ernest F. Henderson, *A Short History of Germany* (Rev. ed., New York, 1923), II, 281.

[2] *Cf.* Herbert Rosinski, *The German Army* (Rev. ed., Washington, D. C., 1944), pp. 46-47.

emphasizing the reorganization of the army rather than the *Krümper* system. Material on the *Krümper* system is found in volume three as well as in volume four; but whether this circumstance owes to a want of literary organization or to the author's reluctance to treat the failure of the *Krümper* system as a separate topic cannot be said.[3] A careful reader by noting scattered paragraphs can discover that Jany believes the results of *Krümper* training to have been exaggerated.

No one attempting to write about the Prussian army can deny his debt to Jany; many of the data upon which the author's thesis are based have been obtained from his published works. If the present author has made any contribution to historical literature it is in a systematic presentation of the existing as well as his new evidence for the failure of the *Krümper* system between 1807 and 1813. This is the principal purpose of the present study. It is also intended to explain the relation between the *Krümper* system and the conscription proposals of the military reformers; and to describe in some detail the real basis of Prussia's renewed military strength: the conscripted *Landwehr* of 1813. By an examination of the reform efforts over the span of years from 1786 to 1813, the debt of Scharnhorst and his colleagues to those unsuccessful reformers who tried to remake the Prussian army after the death of Frederick the Great can be understood. Finally, some practical value may adhere to this study for the light it may shed on one of the grave problems of our time: the limitation and control of Germany's armed forces.

Consideration of *Krümper* Training at the Paris Peace Conference

At the Paris Peace Conference in 1919 the Allies' attempts to solve this problem were influenced to a very large degree by their understanding of the Prussian *Krümper* training program of 1807. Preliminary suggestions about the size and composition of the German army were entrusted to the Allied Military

---

3 *Cf.* Curt Jany, *Geschichte der Königlich Preussischen Armee* (Berlin, 1928-1933), III, 465-68, IV, 12-13, 40-41.

Committee with Marshal Foch as presiding officer. This body proposed an army of 200,000 men and 9,000 officers. No restrictions were to be placed on the method of recruitment; either volunteers or conscripts could be used but the term of service for the men was to be limited to one year.[4] The discussion of this proposal revealed a grave difference of opinion between the civilian leaders of the peace conference who feared a rapid expansion of the German army made possible by successive short enlistments, and the professional soldiers who feared the development of German cadres by the thorough training permitted in long enlistments.

The civilians' ideas about Germany's armed forces were expressed in conversations between Lloyd George, Clemenceau, and Colonel House on March 7, 1919, the day after the draft of the Military Committee had been discussed by the Supreme War Council. They drew up a resolution that described a German army of 200,000 volunteers serving for not less than twelve years.[5] Marshal Foch objected to this plan on the ground that the quality of an army was determined by its cadres, that is the framework of officers and trained non-commissioned officers, not merely by the number of men in ranks. His committee would allow the Germans to train 200,000 new recruits annually, but there would be no corresponding cadres since the number of officers and non-commissioned officers would always be small. As long as the Germans were prevented from forming cadres their military preparations would not be dangerous. Foch pointed out that before 1914 the real strength of the German army rested in the 120,000 professional non-commissioned officers. If men were permitted to remain with the colors for a great length of time another mass of capable non-commissioned officers would be trained. These ideas were shared by all the

[4] David Hunter Miller, *My Diary at the Conference of Paris* (N. Y., 1924), XV, 134-36.

[5] David Lloyd George, *Memoirs of the Peace Conference* (New Haven, 1939), I, 187.

allied commanders in chief: Marshals Petain and Haig, and Generals Pershing and Diaz.[6]

For Lloyd George the formation of new cadres did not matter since Germany had numerous experienced officers and non-commissioned officers whose services would be available for at least twenty-five years. By one means or another these men could always form cadres. " He would enquire, therefore, why a present of this great force should be made to Germany. He thought that history would be repeating itself and the Allies would be doing exactly the same thing as Napoleon had done after the battle of Iéna. The annual renewal of the whole army as suggested merely meant in the course of years the creation of an enormous army. That was a mistake which should not be repeated." [7]

Lloyd George's refusal to accept the generals' advice was based on his conviction that a long enlistment was the only guarantee of a small army. Clemenceau also defended the proposals for a small army of long-term volunteers. Although French military experts succeeded in reducing the number of men from 200,000 to 100,000, the civilian leaders determined those clauses of the treaty which restricted the German army to volunteers who enlisted for twelve years. " The object of this proposal was that Germany should not have an annual contingent of recruits, and should not be able to play the same trick on Europe as she had after Jena." [8]

The rebirth of the German army within fifteen years of the peace conference has attached more than academic interest to the military issues debated there. In view of Germany's swift rearmament after Hitler came to power in 1933, it is evident that the Allied military experts had more foresight than the civilian leaders of the Allied governments. The generals' forecast of events in Germany would also have been a sound histor-

[6] Miller, *op. cit.*, XV, 182-83; Lloyd George, *op. cit.*, I, 395-97.
[7] *Ibid.*, I, 397.
[8] Miller, *op. cit.*, XV, 244.

ical analysis of Prussia's military recovery in Napoleon's time. From 1807 until 1813 only a small number of men were trained; on the face of this achievement the *Krümper* system was a failure. It became a danger to Napoleon when these men, and the personnel of the regular Prussian army, were used to form cadres for receiving the conscripts of 1813. In 1807 as well as in 1919 the real threat lay in the use to which trained personnel could be put in order to expand the army rapidly with relatively untrained men. If a nation retains the services of the professional officers and non-commissioned officers, a formidable mass army can be built with incredible speed by filling the ranks with hastily trained conscripts.

CHAPTER I

PRUSSIAN MILITARY INSTITUTIONS IN 1806

THE Prussian army of 1806 was distinguished from all other European armies by the canton system. The principal feature of this system was the recruiting and the training of the reservists by regiments in formally defined areas known as cantons. Service in the reserve was limited to Prussian subjects, who were liable to military duty for twenty years, but were actually trained only several weeks each year. Volunteers who enlisted for ten to twelve years made up the standing units of the army. In the spring, contingents called up from the conscripted native reservists trained and drilled with the professional soldiers. During the remainder of the year the conscript natives remained at their civil occupations in their own districts, or cantons, as a wartime reserve for the regiment in which they had served. These arrangements gave the Prussian army a war strength of trained men distinct from its peace strength. Like modern armies which mobilize trained reserves upon the declaration of war, the Prussian army could increase its armed strength upon the outbreak of hostilities without calling on untrained recruits.

THE INFANTRY

Infantry was the backbone of the Prussian armed forces. After the fashion of the time, the types and functions of infantry were specialized, with units of musketeers, grenadiers, fusiliers, and sharpshooters distinguished from one another in command, uniform, tactics, and drill. Musketeers and grenadiers were known as " infantry of the line," in token of their extended formation in three ranks which was used for both attack and defence. Fusiliers and sharpshooters, on the other hand, were light troops employed mainly in scouting, protecting the flanks, and fighting in open order.[1]

Infantry was organized for administration into regiments, each consisting of two grenadier companies, twelve musketeer companies, and one company of reservists. All grenadier and musketeer companies had the same strength of four to five officers, twelve non-commissioned officers, three musicians (grenadiers five), four artillerists, ten sharpshooters, and 140 men, making a total of 169 combatants, not including the officers. A surgeon and several servants for the officers were normally attached to each company. A reserve company consisted of nine non-commissioned officers, two musicians, and 120 men.[2] Battalions were the tactical units of the army and were formed by four companies. Fusiliers were organized for battle in their own battalions of four companies, each company with five officers and 165 men including twenty sharpshooters.[3] What were known as third battalions were being formed in 1805 and 1806. In an attempt to increase the size of the army, a number of veterans were withdrawn from their own units. Reservists were added to this small nucleus until a strength of 500 men was reached. The third battalions were intended to be mobile auxiliaries to the field army, but in 1806 many third battalions existed only on paper.[4]

---

[1] Colmar von der Goltz, *Von Rossbach bis Jena* (2nd ed., Berlin, 1906), pp. 189-200. On the Prussian infantry before 1806 consult Curt Jany, *Die Gefechtsausbildung der Preussischen Infanterie von 1806* (Berlin, 1903), pp. 19-33, 77 ff. Henceforth this will be cited as *Gefechtsausbildung*.

[2] Jany, *op. cit.*, III, 533. This organization outlined in the Cabinet Order of July 5, 1806 did not differ greatly from the previous organization, except that grenadier battalions remained on a permanent footing instead of being formed only for exercises and mobilization. Cf. *ibid.*, III, 158-59, 373-74.

[3] Ottomar Frhrn. von der Osten-Sacken und von Rhein, *Preussens Heer von seinen Anfängen bis zur Gegenwart* (Berlin, 1911-1914), I, 339-40.

[4] Jany, *op. cit.*, III, 463.

The Cavalry

Cavalry was numerous in proportion to the total strength of the army, and like the infantry was organized in light and heavy units. Hussars and Towarczys (known later as Uhlans) made up the lightly-armed raiding horse, while dragoons and cuirassiers were the shock cavalry used in masses on the battlefield.[5] Cavalry had great prestige in the Prussian army because Frederick the Great had prized that arm. It still enjoyed royal patronage and in the eyes of Europe was the most famous branch of the Prussian armed forces.[6]

Squadrons were the tactical units for cavalry; while regiments were the units of administration. Companies were known only in the king's own *Garde du Corps* which had two companies to each squadron. This elite unit consisted of a regiment of five squadrons, each with seven officers, fourteen non-commissioned officers, two trumpeters, one surgeon, two farrier-sergeants, and 132 men. There were no reserve units for the *Garde du Corps*. Towarczys, made up of the lesser Polish nobility, were organized in a regiment of fifteen squadrons. Other nationalities swelled the strength of this regiment which rested on a Polish complement of fifty-one officers, 100 non-commissioned officers, and more than 1,100 men. There were special articles of war for the Poles and their reserve was drawn from two other cavalry units. Hussar regiments had ten squadrons averaging five officers and 150 men. Cuirassier and dragoon regiments were divided into five squadrons of six officers and 162 men each. Every squadron included ten to twelve carbineers, while each of the reserve squadrons, which were unmounted, had six officers and 182 men.[7]

[5] Curt Jany, *Der Preussische Kavalleriedienst vor 1806* (Berlin, 1904), pp. 6-7. Henceforth this will be cited as *Kavalleriedienst*.

[6] *Ibid.*, p. 1; *cf.* G. von Pelet-Narbonne, *Geschichte der Brandenburg-Preussischen Reiterei* (Berlin, 1905), I, 341-46.

[7] Jany, *op. cit.*, III, 378-79; Osten-Sacken, *op. cit.*, I, 340.

ARTILLERY AND TECHNICAL TROOPS

Artillery had been a neglected branch of the Prussian army since the time of Frederick the Great who had underestimated its importance. Middle class officers served in this arm, while the transport of the guns was not entrusted to soldiers but to non-military conscripts called *Knechte*. The tactical organization was backward; many guns were scattered among the battalions of infantry, where a contempt for gunnery prevailed. Mounted batteries of six-pound cannon were the main reliance of the field artillery. Fortress artillery, also supposed to be available for field service, was old and ineffectual and could hardly be relied on to fire a shot.[8]

On August 20, 1805 the mounted artillery regiment had been given a new organization. Its ten companies averaged five officers, four master gunners, ten corporals, twenty-two bombardiers, two trumpeters, a surgeon, and 172 cannoneers. Two batteries each with six six-pound field pieces and two seven-pound howitzers made up the armament of each company. Unmounted artillery was more numerous and was organized in four regiments each of ten companies. The complement of these companies was the same as that of the mounted artillery, except that there were only 160 instead of 172 cannoneers. The number of batteries in an unmounted artillery company varied, but the armament of a battery approximated six twelve-pound cannon and two ten-pound howitzers. Fortress artillery personnel served the heavier cannon and was organized in fourteen companies plus some smaller formations distributed among the important Prussian fortifications. Each company averaged four to five officers, eight to eleven non-commissioned officers, several arsenal officers, a surgeon, ten to fifteen bombardiers, and from 100 to 130 cannoneers.[9] Prussian artillery in 1806 had altogether 7,059 available guns.[10]

---

[8] Goltz, *op. cit.*, pp. 210-11; K. von Schöning, *Historisch-biographische Nachrichten zur Geschichte der Brandenburgisch-Preussischen Artillerie* (Berlin, 1844-1845), III, 43-60.

[9] Jany, *op. cit.*, III, 377-78, 392-94.

[10] *Ibid.*, III, 382.

Technical troops played only a small part in the Prussian army. A pontoon unit of two and a half companies numbering about 150 men had the equipment for bridging the Elbe, the Oder, and the Vistula rivers. Four companies of miners totaled about 400 men. Miners and pontoons were commanded by graduates of the Royal Engineering Academy who also supervised the construction and repair of fortresses. There were about a dozen important fortifications which were designed to serve as magazines of food and munitions for the army as well as centers of resistance. In addition to the specialized troops, a non-military personnel numbering 34,074 served in the artillery and baggage trains when the army took the field. These *Knechte* were conscripted from among Prussian subjects only on the outbreak of war and hence received no training in peacetime.[11]

TRAINING AND DRILL

The training and organization of the Prussian army developed many smart and well-drilled regiments without bringing together in peacetime units as large as divisions or corps. It was impossible for the several arms to train with one another. Commanding officers were therefore inexperienced in handling large bodies of troops, and the men were unaccustomed to any drills or exercise that involved more than one regiment. The principal training period occurred in the spring when the conscripts were taken from the cantons and sent to the regiments. For about six weeks there was an intense drill period in which the recruits were taught the military postures and the complicated parade maneuvers of the Prussian army. As long as the cantonists reported annually it was possible for provincial garrisons to drill as smartly as the regiment of Potsdam. After 1798, however, annual training was provided only in the Brandenburg regiments, which were personally inspected by the king. All other regiments trained their cantonists every other year.[12]

11 *Ibid.*, III, 349-50, 382; *cf.* Goltz, *op. cit.*, pp. 211-12.

12 *Aus dem Garnisonleben von Berlin und Potsdam 1803 bis 1806* (Berlin, 1906), pp. 6-9, 37-42, has the detailed training instructions for the Potsdam Inspection. Jany, *op. cit.*, III, 446.

The emphasis on smartness and correctness of drill went hand in hand with the tactics of the Prussian army. The tactics of the thin line used by the army of 1806 derived from the time of Frederick the Great. To achieve fire power, as many men as possible were crowded into the line of battle. This deployed the troops in great breadth and reduced the battle order to three ranks. Precise alignment, speed of fire, and maintenance of discipline even in the heat of battle were the three objectives of training.[13] When these were attained it was possible to form the long battle line quickly and at a moment when the enemy could be attacked in the flank instead of frontally. This was the favorite battle tactic of the Prussians. The men were drilled endlessly in the art of forming a line of battle out of an echelon of battalions, which could advance on the enemy diagonally and overwhelm him with fire directed on a segment of his line.[14]

Soldiers were as carefully trained in musketry as in drill. A volume of fire was preferred to accurate shooting; therefore, quick-loading and firing rather than target practice were stressed. Double-ended iron ramrods, large funnel-shaped charge holes in their flintlock muskets, and careful rehearsal of the movements of loading, gave the Prussians a speed of fire that exceeded that of any other European army. With the new muskets in use in 1806 the infantry could fire six shots a minute in practice, but only two and a half shots were expected on the battlefield. Most of the artificial styles of shooting that had been common under Frederick the Great, such as fire by companies or sections of companies, had been abandoned by 1806 in favor of battalion salvos.[15]

The light infantry troops of the Prussian army were among the best trained units. Experience in Poland and in the Rhine campaigns of 1792-1795 had shown that the thin lines of infantry required protection in front and on the flanks. Sharp-

[13] *Gefechtsausbildung*, pp. 4-16.

[14] Reinhard Sautermeister, *Die taktische Reform der preussischen Armee nach 1806* (Tübingen, 1935), pp. 7-8.

[15] *Gefechtsausbildung*, pp. 4, 33-45; G. von Berenhorst, *Betrachtungen über die Kriegskunst* (3rd ed., Leipzig, 1827), pp. 295, 304-05.

shooters and the type of light infantry known as fusiliers had been developed to supply this need.[16] By all accounts they were well versed in their art of deploying, fighting from irregular positions, and repelling attacks of enemy light horse. Accurate shooting was particularly stressed and they were armed with a rifle instead of the smoothbores carried by the other foot soldiers. Yet the Prussian light infantry was not numerous enough to meet the army's requirements, and like other units, had perfected individual training at the expense of cooperation.[17]

The cavalry of the Prussian army was less thoroughly trained than the infantry. For about ten months of each year cavalry mounts were sent to graze on the peasants' fields or along the public highways. There were no mounts at all for the reserve units, as the competition of other armies in the purchase of horses had depleted the European supply. Cavalry was placed on the wings of the infantry line to neutralize the opposing horsemen, or to assist the infantry in throwing the enemy lines into disorder. The cooperation that this entailed was never practiced in time of peace, so that on the battlefield of Jena the Prussian cavalry fought individual actions without regard for the objectives of the infantry. On the march the cavalry was not trained to range far ahead. There was no cavalry screen and reconnaissance was unknown.[18]

Artillery was the least trained branch of the Prussian army. Although Scharnhorst was an artillerist who had been in Prussian service since 1801, his influence was confined to academic instruction rather than the practical training of the army.[19] Practice firing at unknown ranges was rarely attempted in peacetime, for the state's supplies of powder and shot were lim-

[16] Goltz, *op. cit.*, pp. 192-94.

[17] Pascal Bressonnet, *Études tactiques sur la campagne de 1806* (*Saalfeld-Iéna-Auerstedt*) (Paris, 1909), pp. 370-74, 378-79.

[18] *Kavalleriedienst*, pp. 2-5, 32, 50-54, 65.

[19] Carl von Clausewitz, *Nachrichten über Preussen in seiner grossen Katastrophe* (*Kriegsgeschichtliche Einzelschriften*, II, Heft 10, Berlin, 1888), p. 443.

ited and had to be conserved for a more serious use. Drill engaged as much of the artillerists' time as it did that of the infantrymen. Batteries were judged by the speed of unlimbering and the smartness of appearance rather than the rate and accuracy of fire. Even less attention was paid the technical troops, whose training was not undertaken very seriously.[20]

The final element in the training of the Prussian army was the review of the type that had become famous under Frederick the Great.[21] Originally there had been a spring review in every province at the conclusion of the cantonists' period of service. Owing to lack of funds most regiments by 1806 were holding reviews only every other year. None was held in 1806 because a third of the reservists had been retained with the regular troops for additional training. From the fall of 1805 the army had been kept on a partial war footing because of the French threat to Prussian neutrality. The reviews were entirely formal with all the maneuvers specified in advance, and with emphasis placed upon the perfection of the parade drill.[22] If a sham battle were fought, it became a theatrical event and the side commanded by the king always won. The fixed program accustomed the officers to having everything arranged; instead of developing commanders the reviews brought into being a corps of automatons.

Discipline and Punishment

Rigorous discipline was as much a part of the training as the drill, for it was felt that the precise evolutions and the fire power of the infantry line depended upon the automatic response of the soldier to his officer's command.[23] It was an established prin-

---

[20] Jany, *op. cit.*, III, 500-05. On the contemporary use of artillery see David G. von Scharnhorst, *Handbuch der Artillerie* (Hanover, 1804-1814), I, 1-9, III, 215-36.

[21] Jean Réné de Toulongeon, *Une mission militaire en Prusse en 1786* (J. Finot and R. Galmiche-Bouvier, eds., Paris, 1881), pp. 241-53.

[22] *Aus dem Garnisonleben von Berlin und Potsdam*, pp. 26-32 for the detailed program of a review held at Berlin on May 21-23, 1804.

[23] *Cf.* J. A. H. de Guibert, *Bemerkungen über die Kriegsverfassung der Preussischen Armeen* (Cologne, 1778), pp. 100-01.

ciple that the soldier had to fear his officer more that the enemy. The basis of the army's discipline was found in the Articles of War which were read at least once a year to the men.[24] There were no corresponding articles for the officers, but they were bound by the traditions and honor of the Prussian officers' corps.

Non-commissioned officers were subject to the Articles of War and could be reprimanded, degraded, or deprived of their pay. They were allowed to use a cudgel on the men for minor offenses. Serious crimes, such as theft, mayhem, or murder, were tried formally. The most brutal penalty was known as *Spiessruthenlaufen,* or *Gassenlaufen,* literally " running the gauntlet." It was carried out in the streets, where about 200 soldiers were provided with birch rods and lined up in a double row facing inward. The culprit was stripped to the waist and he was led down the line the men were expected to beat him with all their strength. Minor offenders were led back and forth six times, while thirty-six times were ordinarily sufficient for a criminal sentenced to die.[25]

Military Administration

The Prussian army had a decentralized and even chaotic administration.[26] Frederick the Great had directed the army in person, but neither Frederick William II nor his successor, although they were both interested in the more spectacular aspects of the army, had any taste for the actual routine of military administration. Their indifference for work of this character had resulted in the creation of a number of offices which were without order or plan in their division of business. The lack of inte-

---

[24] "Entwickelung der Preussischen Kriegsartikel," *Militär-Wochenblatt,* Beiheft 1890, pp. 381-84.

[25] F. Schulze, ed., *Die Franzosenzeit in deutschen Landen 1806-1815* (Leipzig, 1908), I, 19; Max Lehmann, *Scharnhorst* (Leipzig, 1886-1887), II, 100-01.

[26] *Cf.* R. de Courbière, *Grundzüge der Deutschen Militärverwaltung* (Berlin, 1882), pp. 15-24; and Joseph M. C. Vidal de la Blache, *La régénération de la Prusse après Iéna* (Paris, 1910), pp. 30-35.

gration reflected the absolute monarch's practice of creating administrative organs from time to time and fitting them haphazardly into the framework of government. And by 1806, offices which had only a cursory significance under Frederick the Great, had become under his successors centers of independent authority.

This was especially true of the office of General Adjutant, which acquired considerable influence in military matters during the reigns of Frederick William II and Frederick William III.[27] The basis of the General Adjutant's authority was the privilege unique among the military officials of holding direct audience with the king. As the trusted confidant of the monarch the adjutant influenced royal decisions and acted as an emissary to the officers of the army and the heads of the administrative bureaus. All important business required the king's approval and in practice this meant that the adjutant closely scrutinized military administration. Since the adjutant was invariably a courtier, the army's affairs were conducted in the same spirit of intrigue and cabal that characterized the Prussian government during these two reigns.[28]

The remaining offices of administration were purely clerical in function and were so engrossed in their own bureaucratic procedures that years often elapsed before the simplest suggestion was adopted by the army. Two bureaus, the Military Department and the High Council of War, had overlapping authority with respect to the training, mobilization, magazines, pay, armament, and provisioning of the army.[29] In 1806 the Military Department was the more important of the two as it

[27] R. Schmidt-Bückeburg, *Das Militärkabinett der preussischen Könige und deutschen Kaiser 1787-1918* (Berlin, 1933), pp. 4-9. From the office of the General Adjutant developed what was called after 1865 the "secret military cabinet."

[28] Jany, *op. cit.*, III, 400-01. *Cf.* M. Philippson, *Geschichte des Preussischen Staatswesens vom Tode Friedrichs des Grossen bis zu den Freiheitskriegen* (Leipzig, 1880-1882), II, 171-72.

[29] C. Bornhak, *Geschichte des Preussischen Verwaltungsrechts* (Berlin, 1884-1886), II, 318-19; Courbière, *op. cit.*, pp. 22-23.

formed a section of a principal governmental organ, the General Directory.[30] Since the Military Department and the High Council of War lacked a large staff of bureaucrats, many details of military administration were turned over to other government bureaus. Recruiting, for example, was supervised by officials of the royal tax administration. General Inspectors were another element of the military bureaucracy. They ascertained in the name of the king whether the drill was being carried out with the degree of exactness that had come to characterize the Prussians.[31]

Supply Services

Neither a Minister nor a Ministry of War guided the administration of the army. Large commands were never formed in time of peace, hence the administration and supply of the army were carried out by companies within each regiment.[32] This circumstance gave the regimental colonels the nominal supervision of the "housekeeping" details of their troops. They had to abide by general rules in selecting officers and in conscripting native reservists, but a large discretion was allowed in handling money. There was no formal auditing and the Inspectors made only routine inquiries, so that each colonel was free to make a full or partial return for the money and supplies advanced his regiment by the state. Because of the low salaries and the inadequate pensions most officers felt justified in making a profit out of the military pay and supply system.[33]

Within the regiment the actual work of supplying small stores and paying the men was handled by company and squadron captains. Each regimental colonel was normally the head of

[30] On Prussian administration in the eighteenth century, consult W. Dorn, "The Prussian Bureaucracy in the Eighteenth Century," *Political Science Quarterly*, XLVI (1931), 403-23, XLVII (1932), 75-94, 259-73.

[31] Courbière, *op. cit.*, p. 21.

[32] Bornhak, *op. cit.*, II, 68-69, 196.

[33] Vidal de la Blache, *op. cit.*, pp. 34-35 describes the opportunities for graft; see Apel, *Der Werdegang des Preussischen Offizierkorps bis 1806 und seine Reorganisation* (Oldenburg i. Gr., n. d.), p. 78.

a company or squadron in order to participate in their profit-making opportunities. In 1806 no money was being paid directly to the captains for recruiting long service professionals as these were supplied by royal recruiting agents.[34] Before that date the company captains had absorbed from one-third to one-half of the appropriation. Pay accounts were another source of revenue for them. The soldiers' pay was specified in exact grades, but if men were sent on leave to their homes, or if they were freed of watch duties, the captain was permitted to keep their pay. Extra revenue was derived from the sale of shirts, leggings, belts, pouches, and insignia to the men. A daily bread ration was provided by the government and it was possible in some cases for the officers to make a profit on its distribution. These practices added 1,200 to 1,600 thalers to the captain's normal income of 800 thalers a year.[35]

The provision of material supplies for the garrisons, providing the horses for the cavalry and artillery, as well as forage, required the cooperation of the circle and provincial governments. Costs of all these were borne by the army's budget, but the officials were considered part of a dual civil-military administration, some of whom were put under military jurisdiction upon mobilization of the army.[36] When on a war footing the army was supplied from magazines by its own bread trains.[37] Although there was a department of supply in the High Council of War, food and munitions for the army in the field were gathered and stored by three War Magazine Administrations, which were not only independent of the central authorities but had their own treasuries. A General Intendant was empowered in the summer of 1806 to bring order into these arrangements, but

[34] Jany, *op. cit.*, III, 435-36.

[35] *Ibid.*, III, 186-87, 423, IV, 18-19. *Cf.* Berenhorst, *Betrachtungen*, pp. 293-94.

[36] Courbière, *op. cit.*, pp. 16, 26-27.

[37] Max Jähns, *Geschichte der Kriegswissenschaften vornehmlich in Deutschland* (Munich and Leipzig, 1889-1891), III, 2185-87.

the organization not only for equipping the army for mobilization, but for maintaining the army in the field, remained inadequate as the events of that year showed. Covering the financial cost of the mobilization of 1806 proved especially difficult, and it was met only by demanding contributions from the provincial governments and from the various estates of the Prussian lands.[38]

THE OFFICERS' CORPS

The officers' corps of the Prussian army in 1806 was still composed largely of aristocrats from Brandenburg, Pomerania, and East Prussia. Of a total number of 7,166 officers some 700 non-aristocrats served in the arms that afforded less prestige, the hussars, fusiliers, artillery, or the technical troops.[39] The professional qualifications of most officers were adequate according to the standards of the time, but few had been formally trained in military academies. About half had entered the army at the age of twelve or fourteen and had been educated by army chaplains and instructed in the art of war by the company officers. Their education could continue in a scattered group of military schools, but except for the Academy for Officers under Scharnhorst's direction, the standards were low. An alert minority of officers kept informed of new developments in warfare by joining military societies and reading military periodicals.[40]

The most serious shortcoming of the Prussian officers' corps was the advanced age of its personnel. In the absence of an adequate pension system, most officers felt obliged to remain on the active list until actually infirm. Among 244 senior officers in 1806, not less than 166 had passed their sixtieth year. More than half were over sixty-five, and only thirteen were under fifty. Of

---

38 Jany, *op. cit.*, III, 403-09.

39 K. von Schmidt, "Statistische Nachrichten über das Preussische Offizierkorps von 1806 und seine Opfer für die Befreiung Deutschlands," *Militär-Wochenblatt*, Beiheft 1901, pp. 432, 437.

40 Vidal de la Blache, *op. cit.*, pp. 17-21; A. von Boguslawski, *Armee und Volk im Jahre 1806* (Berlin, 1900), pp. 14-15, 18-20.

fifty-four infantry colonels, forty-two were over sixty, and twelve were more than seventy. Infantry majors were also over-aged. Among 281, only eighty-five were under fifty. In the cavalry, where physical vigor was especially necessary, the situation was worse. There, of forty-four colonels only six were under fifty, and twenty-six of the twenty-seven major generals were between fifty-four and seventy. No artillery regiment had a commander less than sixty-five, and this was equally true of the colonels in the fortress artillery. Technical troops had the same kind of leadership with two commanders of seventy. More than half of all the majors in the army were past fifty-five, and many were beyond sixty. Such elderly leaders could hardly be expected to equal the dashing young marshals who served Napoleon.[41]

An officer's age tended to determine his attitude toward the army and military life. On this basis General von Boyen discerned three general types. There were the old campaigners of the Frederician era who revered all the antiquated tactics and drill. A second group of officers had entered the army after the Seven Years' War and by 1806 had become colonels. They were engrossed in the economy of their regiments and fearful lest the outbreak of war ruin their chance of making money. A younger group of officers had tasted war in Poland and along the Rhine and from this experience judged the Prussians to be invincible. Yet a fourth category might be added: it consisted of all those officers who realized that the Prussian army needed reforms to keep pace with the progress made by the French. Scharnhorst was the spokesman of this group, and his enthusiasm and ability had brought together a reform-minded circle of officers who were ready for the great responsibility thrust upon them after 1806.[42]

41 Schmidt, *op. cit.*, pp. 439-44; Goltz, *op. cit.*, pp. 125-27.

42 Hermann von Boyen, *Erinnerungen aus dem Leben des General-Feldmarschalls Hermann von Boyen* (Friedrich Nippold, ed., Leipzig, 1889-1890), I, 215-16.

Life of the Men

Except for the spring training period when the native reservists were with the colors, the ranks of the Prussian army were filled with professional soldiers.[43] Their life was not an easy one, with interminable drill in the spring and summer, and throughout the rest of the year a hard struggle for existence in some non-military occupation. These conditions encouraged desertion, and it was said that half the army had to take turns watching the other half. Gates of garrison cities were always locked at night. Newly enlisted men were forced to bunk with veterans, and on those infrequent occasions when the troops bivouacked, loyal soldiers formed a chain of posts around the camp.[44] Economic misery was probably the main cause of desertion. Although prices had risen enormously the pay had not been increased, with the result that most of the professional soldiers were forced to eke out a living by practicing another trade.[45] All manner of shops were set up near the garrisons, while the barracks resembled factories with spinning wheels and looms being operated by the soldiers. Others wandered through the town looking for work. Civilians disliked the soldiers as they competed with the guilds, but a garrison was of some service as it policed the town and acted as a fire brigade.[46]

Soldier tradesmen were a development of the furloughing practiced in the Prussian army. Originally the working soldier was a recruit who was to remain in the garrison but be free of watch duty. For this privilege the *Freiwächter* (a man freed of

---

[43] The number of men in the standing army in 1806 was 128,916. Jany, *op. cit.*, III, 445. *Cf.* F. von Kleist, *Über die eigenthümlichen Vollkommenheiten des Preussischen Heeres* (Berlin, 1791), pp. 46-48.

[44] E. Babel, *Die alte Preussische Armee vor 1806* (Oldenburg i. Gr., n. d.), p. 25.

[45] *Cf.* F. Meusel, "Die Besoldung der Armee im alten Preussen und ihre Reform 1808," *Forschungen zur Brandenburgischen und Preussischen Geschichte*, XXI (1908), 243-49.

[46] L. von Scharfenort, *Kulturbilder aus der Vergangenheit des altpreussischen Heeres* (Berlin, 1914), pp. 11-15, 22-24; Jany, *op. cit.*, III, 447 footnote 77.

watch duty) granted the company captain most of his pay, but continued to receive the other military emoluments, clothing, shoes, and bread.[47] Only professional soldiers were so furloughed in 1806. The practice was popular since it increased the revenue of the captains and provided the *Freiwächter* with the security of army life together with the possibility of an artisan's income. Tools and raw materials were often supplied by the company chiefs who were entrepreneurs on a small scale. While advantageous for the individuals, the system was destructive of training and made the army resemble a guild enterprise.

Nor did the presence of soldiers' wives in the garrisons add to the military atmosphere. But they could prepare food for an army that had neither cooks nor field kitchens. Indeed, foreign mercenaries were urged to marry local women in order to lessen the temptation to desert. Extra bread portions for the soldiers' families and the cost of educating their numerous children were included in the military budget.[48] But the army was not always so paternal. Many old soldiers were simply given the king's *Gnadenthaler* and dismissed. Another recourse was colonization on the newly acquired lands in the east, or employment in the school system or in the royal tobacco administration. More often, after a lifetime of service the veterans were placed in *Invaliden* companies, where they received pay and rations but were freed of active duties. In every regiment there were one or more companies of aged soldiers who were kept in uniform although their military careers had long since ended.[49]

STRENGTH OF THE ARMY IN 1806

Such arrangements reflected the poverty of the state and the excessive size of the army which was maintained in spite of financial limitations and the small population of Prussia. For

[47] The practice of freeing men from watch began in the time of the Great Elector. *Gefechtsausbildung*, p. 27.

[48] Scharfenort, *op. cit.*, pp. 16-17, 24-30. In 1802 there were in the army quarters 95,761 wives and 130,056 children. Jany, *op. cit.*, III, 448.

[49] E. Schnackenburg, *Das Invaliden und Versorgungswesen des brandenburg-preussischen Heeres bis zum Jahre 1806* (Berlin, 1889), pp. 118-42; Philippson, *op. cit.*, I, 413-17.

PRUSSIAN MILITARY INSTITUTIONS IN 1806

the test of war in 1806 Clausewitz' estimate of the actual military resources of the kingdom is available. He based his calculations on the fact that not every unit had its full war strength and that most of the new reserve formations planned in 1805-1806 existed only on paper. Third battalions alone among the newly planned reserves were included by Clausewitz. His was, however, an estimate of what the state would actually have been able to accomplish if its available military resources were mobilized.[50]

THE STRENGTH OF THE PRUSSIAN ARMY IN 1806 AS ESTIMATED BY CLAUSEWITZ

INFANTRY

116 Battalions of Musketeers	99,760
29 Battalions of Grenadiers	19,952
24 Battalions of Fusiliers	16,512
3 Battalions of Sharpshooters	1,800
5 Battalions of Royal Guards	3,440
Total infantry effectives	141,464

CAVALRY

60 Squadrons of Cuirassiers	7,920
80 Squadrons of Dragoons	10,560
95 Squadrons of Hussars	15,390
15 Squadrons of Towarczys	2,430
Total cavalry effectives	36,300

ARTILLERY

10 Companies of Mounted Artillery 4 Regiments of Unmounted Artillery	8,000
Total Field Troops	185,764

RESERVE TROOPS

58 Third Battalions	29,000
58 Companies of Pensioners	2,900
Total Reserve Troops	31,900
Grand Total of Field and Reserve Troops	217,664

50 Clausewitz, *Nachrichten*, pp. 471-72. Clausewitz estimated the actual strength at one-twelfth less than the established complement. Osten-Sacken indicates that in 1806 the field and reserve troops actually at hand totaled 216,900 men. *Op. cit.*, I, 370.

The reserve troops in the third battalions, numbering 29,000, existed mainly on paper as their formation had been decreed only in 1805. Pensioners in the *Invaliden* companies numbered 2,900 but they were useless for war. It was not considered expedient, even in view of close relations with Russia, to leave the eastern frontier unguarded. Hence the strength of the army placed in the field in 1806 was further reduced when 21,424 men in East Prussia were not mobilized. And, while not less than 10,320 troops were left in South Prussian garrisons to police the Polish population, an additional 4,300 men were sent to Silesia to prevent disturbances there. Besides, recent changes in the organization of the artillery which had eliminated some of the heavier guns left about 2,000 artillerists behind.[51] All these shortages reduced the strength of the mobile forces from an estimated 185,764 to 147,720 men.[52]

What might still have been a formidable army lost its effectiveness by the unhappy decision to divide the command and to create several smaller armies. In the campaign of 1806 these were attacked separately and destroyed before they could unite for mutual support. Even on the field of battle the Prussians fought as a poorly coordinated mass of troops. It was as if the battalions of each regiment waited their turn to challenge the entire French army only to be annihilated. Thus the fatal defect of the Prussian army became clear: the absence of great corps and the dependence upon masses of battalions which did not cooperate with one another.

51 Clausewitz, *Nachrichten*, pp. 472-74.
52 Jany gives a total of 147,290 combatants. *Op. cit.*, III, 540.

CHAPTER II
THE DEVELOPMENT OF THE CANTON SYSTEM

THE reserves of native Prussians trained for service in a particular regiment gave the army a unique composition. Although other European armies had adopted various forms of compulsory service, the Prussian system was the most complete and effective method for training civilian reserves. These reservists only supplemented the standing army, however, for by 1806 the use of a professional soldiery had long been established in Prussian military practice. Yet by the use of subjects in the reserves the size of the army had been increased far beyond what Prussia could afford if only mercenaries had been hired. The type of service demanded of the subjects remained distinct in both law and practice from that of the paid professionals who were, theoretically, volunteers. Recruiting of the professionals continued until 1806 along the traditional lines. But the presence of trained reserves made possible a rapid expansion of the army in case of war and eliminated expensive wartime recruiting in competition with other armies. To understand the operation of the system whereby natives were trained in the reserves, an explanation of its historical evolution is necessary.[1]

At the end of the seventeenth century every army, including the Prussian, was made up of professional soldiers who were recruited and enrolled directly by the captains under whom they served. Many abuses were associated with this system, since the captains competed for recruits and often resorted to violence or kidnapping in order to obtain men.[2] Frederick I and Fred-

[1] See Kurt Wolzendorff, *Der Gedanke des Volksheeres im Deutschen Staatsrecht* (Tübingen, 1914), p. 14. A penetrating discussion of the politico-military nature of the Prussian army in the eighteenth century is found in Ernst Huber, *Heer und Staat in der deutschen Geschichte* (Hamburg, 1938), pp. 85-92.

[2] W. Rüstow, *Untersuchungen über die Organisation der Heere* (2nd ed., Basel, 1868), pp. 38-58; P. Kalkoff, *Die Vorgeschichte der allgemeinen Wehrpflicht in Preussen* (Breslau, 1913), pp. 10-11.

erick William I had been the first Prussian monarchs to alter the system. Their regulation of recruiting activities contributed to the growth of absolute government in Prussia, although they had been concerned only with immediate practical problems such as the demands of war or the shortage of money. Changes in the method of recruiting had begun under Frederick I because his policy of alliances kept the state almost constantly at war and the wastage of men could not be replaced in the normal way. Moreover, during the latter part of the seventeenth century, the size of armies had increased to such an extent that the monarch of Prussia had been forced to economize by compelling his own subjects to serve in the army.[3]

PRUSSIAN EXPERIENCE WITH A MILITIA

There was a good precedent for this practice in Prussia for on various occasions in the seventeenth century, particularly during the Thirty Years' War, a peasant militia had been formed to repel invaders. The legal obligation to serve in the militia was not without significance for the subsequent development of the canton system.[4] Yet it was not an easy matter to conscript native subjects for the standing army's reserves. The distinction between the standing army and a militia was only too clear to the populace who loathed any kind of military service. In fact, enrollment in the militia had come to be regarded as a means of escaping the demands of the regimental recruiting officers.[5] Moreover, in the development of royal absolutism the militia had tended to be slighted in favor of the standing army, for the popular forces had long been associated with feudal privilege and provincial rights.[6] Despite these limitations the

[3] Robert Freiherr von Schrötter, "Die Ergänzung des preussischen Heeres unter dem ersten Könige," *Forschungen zur Brandenburgischen und Preussischen Geschichte*, XXIII (1910), 81-83, 124-25.

[4] F. Schwartz, *Organisation und Verpflegung der Preussischen Landmilizen im siebenjährigen Kriege* (Leipzig, 1888), pp. 2-5.

[5] Jany, *op. cit.*, I, 552; also see Schrötter, *op. cit.*, p. 122.

[6] W. Gragert, *Allgemeine Wehrpflicht und Staatsverfassung* (Düsseldorf, 1937), p. 18. *Cf.* Otto Hintze, "Der österreichische und der preussische Beamtenstaat im 17. und 18. Jahrhundert," *Historische Zeitschrift*, LXXXVI (1901), 407-08.

THE DEVELOPMENT OF THE CANTON SYSTEM 37

first Prussian king on several occasions resorted to a militia made up of his own subjects. An elaborate militia regulation in 1701 made the entire male population of Prussia liable for military duty. While this principle of service had been understood for centuries, there had never been any attempt to enroll the civil population in a standing army. Hence the effort of Frederick I evoked the strenuous opposition of the estates and the patrimonial landowners.[7]

Conscription for the Regular Army

More important than Frederick I's militia was the practice of forced recruiting for the royal army that developed during the war years from 1688 to 1697 and from 1703 to 1713. As early as 1693 efforts were made to limit recruiting by the king's regiments to definite areas but a system had never been developed. In some provinces civil officials were instructed to provide men for the army, but usually the regimental officers obtained recruits themselves.[8] The confusion and the abuses attached to this method were so great that from time to time a formal register of able-bodied men was demanded; and in 1703-1705 the officials of Frederick I made a fairly thorough listing of the male inhabitants. A decree of November 26, 1705 established the size of the contingents to be drawn from each province, but the project never seems to have been completed. By 1708 recruiting officers were seizing men again, although in 1711 definite recruiting and assembly places were allocated once more to each regiment.[9] There was never any semblance of

---

7 Schrötter, *op. cit.*, pp. 100-01, 104-05. Frederick I's militia regulation of Febr. 1, 1701 is found in Eugen von Frauenholz, ed., *Das Heerwesen in der Zeit des Absolutismus* (Munich, 1940), Beilage XII, pp. 160-63. This will be cited henceforth as *Heerwesen des Absolutismus*.

8 Jany, *op. cit.*, I, 546-58. The Prussian army by the end of the War of Spanish Succession consisted mainly of native subjects, who were not volunteers but were serving on the basis of a universal service that had not yet been formally decreed in law. *Ibid.*, I, 562.

9 Schrötter, *op. cit.*, pp. 85, 106-07, 133-35, 139. Frederick I's decree of Nov. 24, 1693 is given in *Heerwesen des Absolutismus*, Beilage X, 158-59; other regulations of enrollment in 1704, see *ibid.*, Beilage XVI, pp. 167-68,

order in the completion of Frederick I's regiments from native subjects. It was this chaos that eventually induced Frederick William I to regularize the procedure. During his reign the obligation to serve in the old militia was subtly interwoven with a new concept of a national army.[10]

In 1713 a formal demand was made upon the Prussian subjects to serve in the armed forces. In that year Frederick William I brought the militia experiments of his predecessors to an end.[11] His decision implied, however, that the obligation of his subjects to defend the land in a militia was to be carried over to the regular units of the royal army. This change was symbolized by a decree altering the legal name of the army. It had been called a *regulated militia,* in token of its princely origin, as distinct from the popular levy, or land militia, which was the concern of the provinces and the diets. Henceforth, the terms, *militia* and *soldiery,* were forbidden in connection with the royal regiments. Frederick William I's decree of October 17, 1713 by declaring that whosoever left the land for fear of military service would be considered a deserter, made it clear that every man was in the army by virtue of being a subject.[12]

Unregulated attempts by the army captains to put this principle into effect led to grave abuses and pointed the way for necessary modifications. When in 1714 the king tried to increase his army from 38 to 66 battalions, and from 53 to 114 squad-

Beilage XVII, pp. 168-70, Beilage XVIII, pp. 170-71; the Patent of Nov. 26, 1705 in Beilage XX, pp. 180-84, instructions for recruiting in 1708, Beilage XXI, pp. 184-87.

10 Gragert, *op. cit.,* pp. 2, 18-19; Bornhak, *op. cit.,* II, pp. 66, 192 ff.

11 Schrötter, *op. cit.,* p. 135. Frederick William's order of Mar. 7, 1713 in *Heerwesen des Absolutismus,* Beilage XXIII, p. 194. Notwithstanding, the militia remained a last resort of defence and considerable use was made of it during the Seven Years' War. The temptation to use militia remained strong because it was cheaper than a regular army. Schwarz, *op. cit.,* pp. 25-27.

12 Max Lehmann, "Werbung, Wehrpflicht und Beurlaubung im Heere Friedrich Wilhelm's I," *Historische Zeitschrift,* LXVII (1891), 265-66. The edict of Febr. 14 and Apr. 8, 1718 forbidding the use of the words, *militia* and *soldiery,* in *Heerwesen des Absolutismus,* Beilage XXXVII, pp. 231-32.

THE DEVELOPMENT OF THE CANTON SYSTEM 39

rons, a man-hunt ensued. So exacting were the royal officers, that in many places the landowners armed their peasants for resistance. This turbulence and the flight of the serfs into other countries convinced Frederick William that the land might be ruined, and the basis of the army destroyed, if conscription were to continue without royal supervision. New edicts attempted to stop the migration of youth, and landowners were reassured by forbidding the enrollment of their peasants.[13] Foreign mercenaries remained expensive, however, while the use of natives was simpler and cheaper. Officers continued to conscript natives, and the king permitted it on assurance that no force would be used. Out of custom, a kind of military obligation for the lowest class of peasants came into being. The use of foreign mercenaries was not discontinued, but natives of the Prussian lands were called on for a larger share of the recruits.[14]

Because the conscription of natives still tended to be both arbitrary and cruel, landowners as well as peasants complained loudly. Their pleas were less important to Frederick William I than the serious disturbance already evident in the national economy. In the western provinces young men were migrating to escape conscription, and in the east enough serfs were being taken to impair the harvests, while diets and royal officials could show that the ground tax and the excises were diminishing.[15] Some relief was afforded by the practice which began about 1720 of selecting as youths the peasants who were to perform military service. When these boys were chosen by the regiment they were given either a soldier's red scarf or a regimental hat band, and occasionally even part of an old uniform, as a token of their obligation. In the great army expansion of 1727, how-

[13] Kalkoff, *op. cit.*, pp. 9-10. On the impressment of foreigners see W. von Schultz, *Die preussischen Werbungen unter Friedrich Wilhelm I. und Friedrich dem Grossen* (Schwerin, 1887), pp. 8-18. An edict of Oct. 17, 1713 forbidding migration, in *Heerwesen des Absolutismus*, Beilage XXX, p. 223.

[14] *Ibid.*, Beilage XXXII, pp. 225-27, an edict prohibiting forceful recruiting of native Prussians. See Schrötter, *op. cit.*, pp. 144-45.

[15] Lehmann, "Werbung, Wehrpflicht und Beurlaubung," *op. cit.*, pp. 262-63.

ever, the old harsh methods reappeared, and Frederick William I was moved once again to regularize the procedure of adding men to his army.[16]

Frederick William I Regulates Conscription

The monarch realized that an increase in the size of the army would be easier for both the army and the populace if there were accurate lists of the able-bodied men, and if the regimental conscription were limited to well-defined areas. Following the example of his predecessor, Frederick William I in September, 1732 commanded that a census be made of the hearths, dwellings, and villages in the eastern provinces. This listing became the basis for the organization on May 1, 1733 of cantons, as the regimental conscription districts came to be known. Western provinces were divided into cantons by 1735. The size of the cantons varied; they averaged 6,000 to 8,000 hearths for an infantry regiment, and from 1,400 to 3,500 hearths for each cavalry squadron. Artillery cantons were much smaller.[17]

The orders issued in 1732-1733 outlined the principal features of what came to be known as the Prussian canton system. The long years of peace of Frederick William I's reign had permitted the regularization of the type of conscription begun under Frederick I. Like the bureaucracy and the structure of government the Prussian army gained a better organization during the reign of the Soldier King.[18] The order of September 15, 1733 which is sometimes singled out as the legal basis of the canton system had actually no special significance. It was merely one in a series of orders issued to clarify problems arising out of the

[16] Jany, *op. cit.*, I, 687-88, 691. Consult *Heerwesen des Absolutismus*, Beilage XXXVIIII (*sic*), pp. 233-35, Beilage XXXXII, p. 238, and Beilage XXXXIII, p. 239.

[17] Jany, *op. cit.*, I, 692-93. The Cabinet Order of May 1, 1733, in *Heerwesen des Absolutismus*, Beilage XXXXVIII, pp. 243-45, the Cabinet Order of Nov. 10, 1735, Beilage LII, p. 250. Consult Curt Jany, " Die Kantonverfassung Friedrich Wilhelms I.," *Forschungen zur Brandenburgischen und Preussischen Geschichte*, XXXVIII (1925), 225-72.

[18] Jany, *op. cit.*, I, 679 ff.; Lehmann, " Werbung, Wehrpflicht und Beurlaubung," *op. cit.*, pp. 279-82.

THE DEVELOPMENT OF THE CANTON SYSTEM 41

territorial division of the previous year.[19] The canton system was not created by a particular edict or administrative order. By 1732-1733 the Prussians had gained enough experience to regulate effectively the conscription of royal subjects for the army. Perhaps the inaccurate accounts of the origin of the canton system have arisen because the early orders were secret and were circulated in manuscript form. Orders were issued in 1714, 1718, 1726, 1743, 1750, 1757, and 1773 in addition to those that have been mentioned. Officers dared not show them to unfamiliar colleagues or to persons outside the service, and when new regulations were issued the old ones were returned to the central authorities and destroyed.[20]

THE LEGAL BASIS OF CONSCRIPTION

Military service for the Prussian peasant class was an accepted obligation by 1733. It is impossible to speak of universal conscription in eighteenth century Prussia, although broad and all-inclusive phrases describing every subject's obligation to do military service can be found in most of the militia regulations and even in the canton orders.[21] These statements were nothing more than legal rhetoric introducing practical instructions for singling out the lower and unpropertied classes in the actual enforcement of the law. Yet by repetition of the idea the claim of the state upon all its subjects became established in customary law. This accepted convention of a universal obligation to render military service was to prove very useful to the later re-

19 *Ibid.*, LXVII, 259-60. The order of Sept. 15, 1733, in *Heerwesen des Absolutismus*, Beilage LI, pp. 247-49, dealt with sixteen administrative problems.

20 Lehmann, "Werbung, Wehrpflicht und Beurlaubung," *op. cit.*, p. 257. Details of the orders issued from 1708 to 1713 are summarized in Schrötter, *op. cit.*, pp. 139-44. As a basis of the canton system Schrötter places considerable emphasis upon the regulation of Nov. 20, 1693, which was the first to assign each regiment in the army a definite area for recruiting native subjects. See *ibid.*, XXIII, 85-86.

21 See the broad statement of military service cited in Robert Ergang, *The Potsdam Führer Frederick William I, Father of Prussian Militarism* (New York, 1941), p. 76.

formers of the Prussian army. Hence it is impossible to speak specifically of the order of September 15, 1733 as if it were the legal cornerstone of universal service in Prussia. This erroneous belief was widely accepted among historians because a bureaucrat writing in 1788 wrongly attributed a clause establishing universal service to the law of 1733.[22]

Prussia could not afford a system of universal conscription nor was the social structure of the state adapted to it. The nobility had been freed of military obligation by a decree of 1717,[23] and the middle classes had been granted exemption in 1726 if they possessed property worth 10,000 thalers. Then too, the skilled workers whom the king had induced to settle in Prussia or had trained with great difficulty, were exempted by a series of decrees beginning with the exemption of the weavers in 1717.[24] For reasons of economy or statecraft each Prussian monarch of the eighteenth century added to the list of exemptions so that universal service never existed in fact. Their action is understandable, for the canton system of recruitment rested

[22] Jany, *op. cit.*, I, 697-98. The following clause establishing universal service was erroneously attributed to the law of 1733: "Every inhabitant of the land is born to arms, and is obliged to serve in the regiment to whose canton district his native hearth belongs. From this universal enrollment, only the sons of nobles, and those of middle class parents who possess real property worth 10,000 thalers are exempted. In the future, no regiment shall recruit a man born in the canton district of another regiment." Arnim, *Über die Canton-Verfassung in den Preussischen Staaten* (Frankfort and Leipzig, 1788), p. 7. Arnim also asserted that the canton system came into existence only in 1733. The work of Ordensrath König, *Versuch einer historischen Schilderung der Residenzstadt Berlin* (Berlin, 1796), also maintained that view. It is noteworthy that in Frederick the Great's *Oeuvres* the whole concept of military service is allowed to slip out of sight. For him the entire matter seems to be only a small part of the history of recruiting. *Cf.* Lehmann, "Werbung, Wehrpflicht und Beurlaubung," *op. cit.*, pp. 258-59.

[23] Feudal service had been set aside for money payments under the Great Elector. Edicts issued by Frederick William I in 1717 ordered the allodification of all feudal obligations, and with them disappeared the possibility of a feudal service army. Bornhak, *op. cit.*, II, 66, 68. *Cf.* Otto Hintze, *Die Hohenzollern und ihr Werk* (4th ed., Berlin, 1915), pp. 282-83.

[24] Lehmann, "Werbung, Wehrpflicht und Beurlaubung," *op. cit.*, pp. 269-70.

THE DEVELOPMENT OF THE CANTON SYSTEM 43

on the concept of distinct classes in society, rather than on nineteenth century notions of civil equality.[25]

THE REGULATION OF FURLOUGHING

Another feature of the Prussian army, the *Beurlaubung* of recruits, or the granting of furloughs that lasted the greater part of the year, was regulated under Frederick William I. It would have been ruinous to have kept a large part of the native population continually under arms, since this made it impossible for them to engage in any productive enterprise. Furthermore, the captains needed additional revenues to meet the heavy cost of recruiting the professional soldiers. Frederick William's well known preference for giant soldiers necessitated money gifts by the captains in order that they might hire at least a few tall men for their companies.[26] Since the pay accounts of the company were handled by the captains, by furloughing some of the men after the review and keeping their pay of two and a half thalers a month, enough money could be realized to meet the recruiting expenditures. The monarch regularized the practice by stipulating that full complements need be maintained only during the review which occurred in April and May.[27]

This system of furloughing eased the burden of service for nearly everyone. By retaining only professional soldiers with the colors, the landowners' interests were safeguarded, since the peasant conscripts were released after a two months' drill period every spring.[28] Company captains gained needed revenue and

[25] Hintze, *Die Hohenzollern*, p. 285. From time to time handbooks were written for guiding officials through the administrative maze of the canton system. Notable ones included Arnim's, cited previously, and Ribbentrop, *Verfassung des preussischen Canton-Wesens* (Minden, 1798), and F. Wilke, *Handbuch zur Kenntnis des preussischen Cantonwesens* (Stettin, 1802).

[26] *Cf.* Ergang, *op. cit.*, Chapter VI, " The Regiment of Giants," pp. 84-102.

[27] See Max Lehmann, " Eine militärische Verfügung Friedrich Wilhelm's I," *Historische Zeitschrift*, LXVIII (1892), 83-84; Kalkoff, *op. cit.*, pp. 13-14, 19; Jany, *op. cit.*, I, 707-09.

[28] This point is stressed by Hintze, *Die Hohenzollern*, p. 284. The influence of the estates on the furloughing and enrollment practices of the army is indicated in Paul von Schmidt, *Der Werdegang des preussischen Heeres* (Berlin, 1903), p. 98.

kept a supply of men available to complete their units either for the review or war. The professional soldier who was furloughed was relieved of his military duties and was free to earn his living as he wished. For the parsimonious king the costs of the army were lowered and his soldiers' productive work through ten months of the year helped the national economy. As time went on the furloughing was more precisely regulated, but the practice of releasing both the native conscripts and many of the professional soldiers after a brief annual training continued until the War of Liberation in 1813.[29]

Evolution of the Canton System

Throughout the eighteenth century the canton system underwent a continuous evolution. The practices sanctioned by Frederick I and Frederick William I made the claim of the state on the military service of the lower classes more effective. In token of their obligation to serve, what had previously been known as recruiting now became known as conscription.[30] Under Frederick William I and until the Seven Years' War the actual conscription of natives remained in the hands of regimental officers, who were only partly assisted by civil officials.[31] Military administration of the law proved a heavy burden as the officers were exacting and too narrowly insistent on their own privileges. Not only were the subjects hard pressed under their regime, but the land suffered because the military officials ignored the needs of agriculture.[32]

During the Seven Years' War the extraordinary losses suffered by the army brought ruthless conscription by the military authorities.[33] It became impossible for a regiment to obtain

---

29 The furloughing practiced by the Prussian army was, of course, the origin of what became known late as *Krümper* training.

30 Schrötter, *op. cit.*, pp. 144-45.

31 Lehmann, "Werbung, Wehrpflicht und Beurlaubung," *op. cit.*, pp. 271-72.

32 Jany, "Die Kantonverfassung Friedrich Wilhelms I.," *op. cit.*, pp. 246-47.

33 Jähns, *op. cit.*, III, 2224.

THE DEVELOPMENT OF THE CANTON SYSTEM

replacements from its own district, and order vanished completely when the lists of available men were lost. Subalterns began to seize men indiscriminately, acting without information, or solely on the basis of cheapness and expediency, taking all the men in some villages and none in the next. The crown then became convinced that the civil bureaucracy should have more influence, and conscription under civilian control was inaugurated by the canton regulation of September 20, 1763.[34] Until 1813 conscription of native subjects remained a function of the civil bureaucracy.[35] Furloughing of both native reservists and professionals, as well as the recruiting of mercenaries, was at all times subject to military control.

ATTEMPTS TO REFORM THE CANTON SYSTEM

Persistent attempts were made after the Seven Years' War to reform the canton system and to extend the obligation of military service beyond the peasant class. To equalize the burden it would also have been necessary to introduce conscription in Silesia where the entire population had always been exempted. But annexation of Polish territory beginning with the first partition of 1772 made any approach to general conscription impossible. The new subjects were too unreliable to conscript and they required constant policing. The need for garrisons in the new lands terminated for some regiments the peculiar feature of the canton system, namely the connection of the troops with a recruiting and mobilization area. Territorial expansion thus tended to weaken the army's organization, and by scattering the troops, their efficiency was reduced and they were

[34] Arnim, *op. cit.*, pp. 10-12, 24, 27-29. Changes in the canton system after 1763 are summarized in Jähns, *op. cit.*, III, 2225-30. The revised canton regulations of Sept. 20, 1763, in *Heerwesen des Absolutismus*, Beilage LXXI, pp. 281-87, and the instructions of Oct. 24, 1764, Beilage LXXII, pp. 287-93.

[35] David G. von Scharnhorst, *Auszug aus den Verordnungen über die Verfassung der Königlich Preussischen Armee* (Berlin, 1810), pp. 34, 95. This will be cited henceforth as Scharnhorst, *Auszug*. See *Heerwesen des Absolutismus*, Beilage LXXI, pp. 284-85.

slower to mobilize.³⁶ A general revision of the canton system was decreed by Frederick William II in a Cabinet Order of April 20, 1788, which named Field Marshal von Möllendorf and Minister von Gaudi to serve with other officials on a reform commission. Strangely enough the problem created by the acquisition of Polish territory was not taken into consideration.³⁷

By June 6, 1788 Möllendorf had issued his first report which described some abuses of the existing military system: the conflict between the civilian and military classes, the threat to family unity and the prosperity of the trades, and finally, the widespread abuse of exemptions. His report was notable for its general restraint although it did raise the delicate question of the injustice done the peasant class by the canton conscription system. In order to ease the burden Möllendorf recommended that the reservists' term of service be less than twenty years, but that a larger number of persons be enrolled. No doubt existed in his mind about the right of the state to claim military service from every subject. It was significant that in Prussia during the eighteenth century the idea of universal military service had not been forgotten. It was assumed to be the basis of the canton system, and jurists accepted it as a fact.³⁸ In time of war, Möllendorf wrote, every true subject was bound to serve the Fatherland as long as his strength and health would permit.³⁹

THE CANTON LAW OF 1792

Despite the sincere efforts of the commission, the canton regulations adopted on February 12, 1792 bore the same stamp as their predecessors, with exemptions for the privileged classes

---

[36] Hermann von Boyen (Max Lehmann, ed.), "Boyen's Darstellung der preussischen Kriegsverfassung," *Historische Zeitschrift*, LXVII (1891), 61, 63-65. *Cf.* Jähns, *op. cit.*, III, 2250.

[37] Kriegsministerium, *Mittheilungen aus dem Archiv des Königlichen Kriegsministeriums* (Berlin, 1891-1895), II, 82-83. This will be cited hereafter as *Archiv des Kriegsministeriums*. See Hans Helfritz, *Geschichte der Preussischen Heeresverwaltung* (Berlin, 1938), pp. 161-64.

[38] *Archiv des Kriegsministeriums*, II, 83-95.

[39] *Ibid.*, II, 86. The Duke of Brunswick's ideas, *ibid.*, II, 97-101.

THE DEVELOPMENT OF THE CANTON SYSTEM 47

and conscription for the non-propertied serfs.[40] Universal service was reiterated as a principle: " The obligation of military service is incumbent on our loyal subjects, for whose prosperity, and the security of whose goods and property, as well as the maintenance of the state, we require a numerous army." [41] And again: " The obligation to defend the state is an inborn duty of every subject who enjoys the protection of the state." [42] These introductory declarations were followed by qualifying clauses. " Lucky are the Prussian states, where beside the mightiest and most formidable army, all the arts of peace bloom, where the compulsion of conscription is moderated as much as possible and many classes of subjects are hardly disturbed." [43] Justification for exemption from military service was based on the assertion that, " All members of the state are not useful for this purpose; further, other functions are at hand which are not less important for the support of the body politic, so exemptions from this rule exist, dependent upon the decision of the representatives of the state, who consider which classes will serve the defence of the land, and which are qualified for exemption."[44]

The law of 1792 did not establish universal service; instead, the generous exemptions emphasized the importance attached to the use of mercenary soldiers. An army of professionals was not only sparing of the national man power, but was a more convenient adjunct of diplomacy. Hence more foreigners were enlisted, while the king's subjects were furloughed. Before 1813 all attempts to change or alter the canton edict failed, and the basis of conscription in the Prussian lands remained as it had developed under Frederick William I and his son. Even through the period of active reforms, 1807-1813, natives of Prussia

---

40 The canton regulation of Febr. 12, 1792, in *Heerwesen des Absolutismus*, Beilage LXXXIII, pp. 309-36. Summary of the law, in Jähns, *op. cit.*, III, 2248-50.

41 *Heerwesen des Absolutismus*, Beilage LXXXIII, p. 309.

42 *Ibid.*, Beilage LXXXIII, p. 311; also Wilke, *op. cit.*, p. 134.

43 *Ibid.*, p. 135.

44 *Ibid.*, p. 134.

were conscripted for the army under the provisions of the canton law of 1792.⁴⁵

OPERATION OF THE CANTON SYSTEM

Although the Prussian standing army and most European armies of the eighteenth century were made up mainly of mercenaries, in almost every nation some form of conscription had been tried. No other army had an administrative device as efficient as the Prussian canton system for training civilian reservists. The operation of the canton system remained, then, the most characteristic mark of the Prussian armed forces. Each canton consisted of a specified number of hearths, with a regimental headquarters near the center of the district so that furloughed men might be spared long journeys to their homes. Along the frontiers where peasants could easily flee from the conscription officials, cantons had to be larger to make up the regimental quota of men. Quarrels between colonels over the boundaries of cantons were settled before the High Council of War or the Military Department, to which all cases involving an interpretation of the canton regulations had to be referred. Disputes between regiments also arose from the law that canton duty was determined by place of birth rather than residence. If the family moved, a son still served in his native district, although children born in the new residence belonged to the regiment of that canton. Other complications arose when more than one family lived in the same house, since the hearth or dwelling with a single entrance was the basis for distributing cantons among the regiments. Rather than let a single family escape,

---

45 For the Cabinet Order of Nov. 20, 1807 declaring the canton law of 1792 still in effect, see Scharnhorst, *Auszug*, p. 95. See also *Das Preussische Heer im Jahre 1813* (Berlin, 1914), Anlage I, p. 335. In 1798 Ribbentrop sent the king a draft of a revised canton law in his *Verfassung des preussischen Canton-Wesens* (Minden, 1798), approving freedom for the wealthy but eliminating many other exemptions. Leopold Krug, a leading statistician, also published his analysis of the canton system in 1798, " Über das preussische Kantonwesen," *Jahrbüchern der preuss. Monarchie* (April, 1798). Cited in Jähns, *op. cit.*, III, 2253-54.

THE DEVELOPMENT OF THE CANTON SYSTEM

many colonels were willing to spend years in proving their claims.[46]

Man power was distributed among the regiments by the use of the canton list, or census of male inhabitants.[47] It contained the names of all men between the ages of sixteen and twenty-five. Each entry was retained for twenty years under the heading of cantonist or enrollee. Under the heading of cantonist were included all men who belonged legally to the canton, while enrollee was a provisional designation for those of indefinite status. At that period there was no administrative office for drafting the list except the church which supplied vital statistics. Clergymen at christening were to note the name of the father and his class, the number of his sons, both legitimate and illegitimate, their names and ages, and finally, their place of residence. To prevent errors, clergymen were forbidden by an order of July 23, 1767 to baptize more than one son in a family with the same Christian name.[48]

Each year there occurred a correction and an examination of lists by the Commission of Canton Revision, which also supervised recruiting, investigated cases of exemption, tested the qualifications of the recruits, handled releases from the army, gave out the necessary passes and documents, and considered anything having to do with the canton regulations. The Commission of Canton Revision was made up of civil bureaucrats, primarily the Land and Tax Councillors.[49] During the spring

---

46 *Heerwesen des Absolutismus*, Beilage LIIII, p. 252, for the regulations in case of recruiting disputes between regiments. Wilke, *op. cit.*, pp. 48-49, 56-59. Sons of soldiers belonged to the regiment and not to the cantons. Since most of the soldiers' sons followed their fathers' occupation, this source of replacement for the regiment was not inconsiderable. Although born in Prussia soldiers' sons were listed as foreigners. *Ibid.*, pp. 64-65.

47 Typical lists are found in *ibid.*, pp. 122, 125.

48 *Ibid.*, pp. 53-54, 120-22, 295, 329-30; Ribbentrop, *op. cit.*, pp. 82-83. Duties of pastors in the canton administration are listed in *Heerwesen des Absolutismus*, Beilage LXXXIII, pp. 326-27. *Cf.* A. Lyncker, *Der altpreussische Armee 1714-1806 und ihre Militärkirchenbücher* (Berlin, 1937).

49 Arnim, *op. cit.*, pp. 24, 28-30; Wilke, *op. cit.*, pp. 37-38.

the Commission visited each canton district, gathered up the rolls provided by the local clergymen, and revised them in conjunction with the Chambers of War and Domains (*Kriegs und Domänen Kammern*) and the Inspectors of the regiments.[50]

The regiments could inform the Chambers after the review period of their recruiting needs, although their demands were usually presented in the fall of the year. After the Chambers had approved the requests, they forwarded the certified lists to the Land and Tax Councillors who proceeded to get the men. If the number of conscripted men was insufficient, the regimental commanders had to await the action of civilian officials since army officers could not select men directly. Thus the Commission of Canton Revision was interposed as a civilian authority between the subject and the claim of the regiment. The actual selection and mustering of peasant conscripts was in the hands of the Land and Tax Councillors. In case of a serious shortage of conscripts the Chambers hastily communicated with one another, and by transfers from other regiments and by additional levies made up the deficit.[51]

After the spring training period the regiments drew up specific lists of the men who had been sent on furlough. These lists were then forwarded to the revision authorities who tried to keep the proper ratio between foreign mercenaries and natives. From time to time after the reign of Frederick II, the number of foreign mercenaries and conscripted natives was stipulated. The correct proportion was never maintained because captains preferred to furlough the natives and retain only the foreigners under arms. And until 1792 it was legal for an officer to accept a fee from a native who provided a foreigner to take his place.[52]

50 *Ibid.*, pp. 284-87; Ribbentrop, *op. cit.*, pp. 83-84, 137.

51 *Ibid.*, pp. 84-87; Wilke, *op. cit.*, pp. 300-05. See *Heerwesen des Absolutismus*, Beilage LXXXIII, p. 325, for paragraphs 46 and 47 of the canton law of 1792 forbidding direct conscription by the regiments. See *ibid.*, Beilage LXXXIII, pp. 324-26, 328-31, 332-35, for other administrative details.

52 Arnim, *op. cit.*, pp. 14-15; Wilke, *op. cit.*, pp. 302-03, 307-08.

The Commission of Canton Revision also provided *Knechte,* or conscripted laborers who did the manual work of transport, supply, fortification and the like. These men were listed in the canton rolls and were mustered with the regular recruits; they had to be strong of body, and for the transport service skilled in the handling of horses. Ordinary *Knechte* went to the infantry while the more competent serfs were sent to the artillery and food trains. In every case the choice was made by the Land and Tax Councillors, and when a *Knecht* was assigned he was assured of freedom from molestation by any other regiment. They were subject to call for twelve years but received very little training in peacetime. Because it was desirable to have a reserve, they were chosen and then furloughed under the jurisdiction of the local authorities.[53]

The Basis for Exemption From Military Service

Exemptions also came within the authority of the Commission of Canton Revision. While it had nothing to do with the general policy of exempting subjects, it administered the law in specific cases. There were five or six conditions for exemption: foremost among them was the royal prerogative. Entire provinces, cities, occupations, or classes could be exempted from military duty by the monarch. Ordinarily the individual was exempted on the basis of occupation, property, religion, physical defects, or for miscellaneous reasons. The names of exempted persons were not listed in the rolls but were kept in special records. Parents of exempted youths were held responsible for providing documentary proof of the conditions necessary for exemption.[54]

A royal decree might extend freedom to persons, towns, or even entire provinces. All foreigners and their sons engaged in new arts and crafts were free from canton service, while all who

---

[53] Ribbentrop, *op. cit.,* p. 89; Wilke, *op. cit.,* pp. 126-29.

[54] *Ibid.,* pp. 122-23, 137-39, and particularly the list on p. 125, and the tabulation of exemptions on p. 283. Regulations of Dec. 19, 1742 concerning only sons in *Heerwesen des Absolutismus,* Beilage LX, p. 257, and Beilage LXI, pp. 258-59.

settled on new lands in the east, or built houses "where there was none before," were free, and their sons with them. Freedom for foreigners was extended only to the first and second generations, however.[55]

Executive order granted freedom from military service to the whole or part of the population of many districts and cities, including the provinces of East Frisia and Silesia, and the cities of Berlin, Potsdam, Brandenburg, Magdeburg, Danzig, and Thorn. Some of these places had a double freedom, since the merchants and their sons, property owners, and guild members were beyond the domain of the army. But in Thorn the day laborers did not possess the freedom enjoyed by their fellow residents. In other cities there were legal obstacles to prevent a cantonist from acquiring burgher status. No man could become a burgher, or achieve master's standing in the guilds, unless he had documents asserting his freedom, and could afford to give from twenty to two hundred thalers to the poor. Pastors in canton-free cities kept the rolls of baptized male children exactly as in the case of clergymen in the cantons. Nevertheless, canton officials were warned that many persons were settling in the cities where they and their sons were beyond the reach of the army. Consequently the exemption of the urban classes did place a heavier burden on the rural population.[56]

Occupational Deferments

Profession or occupation provided other categories for exemption. Thus, all civil servants were free as well as their sons.

---

[55] Wilke, *op. cit.*, pp. 140-41, 144-49; Ribbentrop, *op. cit.*, pp. 38-40. Exemptions by executive decree are listed in *Heerwesen des Absolutismus*, Beilage LXXXIII, pp. 311-12.

[56] Ribbentrop, *op. cit.*, p. 33; Bornhak, *op. cit.*, II, 193-94; Wilke, *op. cit.*, pp. 150-61, 301. The head of the civil administration in Silesia petitioned Frederick the Great for canton freedom that the industry and commerce of the province might be spared; instead of cantonists a militia of several thousand men was offered. This petition was granted on Dec. 4, 1743 and the canton regulations were never extended to Silesia. Schwarz, *op. cit.*, pp. 15-17. The regulations concerning the payment of money as a qualification for military exemption are given in *Heerwesen des Absolutismus*, Beilage LXXXIII, p. 323.

THE DEVELOPMENT OF THE CANTON SYSTEM 53

Professors were free, but students were exempted only if they showed proficiency in their studies. If students failed their examinations or led a " riotous life," they were disciplined by being compelled to join the army. Sons of peasants could not easily acquire student exemption since they were not admitted to higher studies without express permission. Military freedom was conferred on a large group of professional men and public employees as well as their sons: doctors, inspectors, tax collectors, judicial officials, magistrates, coinage officials, royal charcoal officials, postmasters, surgeons, teachers, registrars, and the like. Sons born before the father entered an exempt class were not themselves free, however.[57]

A large group of skilled workers, many of whom had been brought to Prussia at great expense, were put in the non-military class. For in the words of a canton official, " While the state needs soldiers for its defence, it also needs burghers, artisans, and peasants for its inner support."[58] Indispensability to the state, and the usefulness of the individual within the larger framework of the mercantile economy, were the tests that determined whether or not freedom would be granted. For owners of small establishments the amount of business, the availability of raw materials, and the number of persons employed were taken into consideration. Urban merchants whose business exceeded 5,000 thalers a year, and their sons if they were studying or assisting in the business, acquired a conditional exemption, and with them all entrepreneurs who gave employment to at least twelve workers. Small manufacturers, particularly damask weavers, silk workers, weavers in wool and cotton, bleachers, dyers, and printers of cloth were free and had the right to claim freedom for their sons if they were being taught the trade. Workers in many other industries were exempt, as

[57] Wilke, *op. cit.*, pp. 162-73, 176, 182, 253-61; Arnim, *op. cit.*, pp. 24-25. Exemptions conferred on students of theology, in *Heerwesen des Absolutismus*, Beilage LV, pp. 252-53; exemptions for royal officials and students, *ibid.*, Beilage LXXXIII, pp. 312-13.

[58] Wilke, *op. cit.*, pp. 188-89.

well as their sons if they followed the same occupation, and all the officials directing the enterprise. This was especially true of the makers of iron, steel, and copper. Whole groups of factory workers in Danzig, the County of Ravensberg, and the important Bielefeld linen establishments were exempted. All miners, whether native or foreign born, and almost all seafarers and fishermen, were exempt. Shipowners and those following trades connected with the sea, including the herring fishers among the inhabitants of East Frisia who were already free, were excused from military service. Persons engaged in transportation, especially the owners of boats or barges operating on inland waters, were free. If they had many craft, their sons were free up to the number of craft their fathers possessed. Even in time of great need it was forbidden to take seafarers into the artillery or train service, on the ground that they knew nothing of horses.[59]

EXEMPTIONS BASED ON PROPERTY, RELIGION, AND PHYSICAL DEFECTS

Exemptions conferred on property owners were prominent in every canton regulation. The original valuation of 10,000 thalers was lowered to 6,000 in 1763, only to be restored again in 1792. To qualify for this exemption the man and his wealth had to remain in Prussia, but the loss of property also meant the loss of freedom. Working plots of land of a certain size liberated the peasants, but the amount varied from province to province. It was for the Land and Tax Councillors and the Chambers of War and Domains to decide whether a profession or a trade was useful to the nation. If they decreed favorably the re-

---

[59] Ribbentrop, *op. cit.*, pp. 58-60, 62-64; Wilke, *op. cit.*, pp. 187-92, 194, 199-203, 249, 251. Artisans who wandered about the land received a pass which all royal officials, innkeepers, and peasants had the right to demand. Magistrates communicated the lists of wander-passes to the Commission of Canton Revision. In case of death, the pass was to be returned by the relatives. Clergymen were not permitted to baptize the children of itinerants unless their travel permits were shown. *Ibid.*, pp. 313-17. The classes of exempted workers are listed in *Heerwesen des Absolutismus*, Beilage LXXXIII, pp. 314-18.

THE DEVELOPMENT OF THE CANTON SYSTEM 55

lease of the individual followed, but no one could expect to escape duty merely by learning a trade. Dwellers of peasant descent on the *platte* land might not learn a trade without the permission of a judicial authority. This provision was intended not only to preserve recruits for the army, but also to prevent the tillers of the soil from becoming unemployed artisans in the cities. It is further to be remarked that the canton officials charged no fees for the drafting of the myriad documents and passes, or for the minute investigations that preceded their decisions, and that the administration of their offices was comparatively free from graft. The basic question for them was: where is the individual most useful to the state?[60]

Exemptions were also conferred on various religious groups. Moravian Brethren and Jews, and their sons, were free from canton service and also from entry in the rolls. The Mennonites were exempted by a decree of July 30, 1789 on condition that they pay a tax of 5,000 thalers. Neither Moravian Brethren nor Jews could inherit land if it carried canton duty, nor could they live on it and remain free.[61]

Physical defects freed many from the claim of the army. Short men were generally considered unfit for military service, although they were sometimes recruited as *Knechte*. Those who were ill at the time of mustering were exempted temporarily; if an indigent cantonist fell ill the War Treasury paid for medical care. Sometimes an eligible subject would mutilate himself in the hope of getting a release, but if the subterfuge were discovered the punishment was the *Spiessruthenlaufen* twenty times.[62] All the penalties for evasion of canton duty were heavy. Men who ran away suffered confiscation of their property; actual deserters who had taken the oath to the colors could be sent to

---

[60] Wilke, *op. cit.*, pp. 207, 227, 232-33, 240, 242, 269-71, 334; Ribbentrop, *op. cit.*, pp. 73-74. Land regulations concerning the peasants, in *Heerwesen des Absolutismus*, Beilage LXXXIII, pp. 320-22. The prohibition of fees, *ibid.*, Beilage LXXXIII, paragraph 117 of the law of 1792, p. 336.

[61] Wilke, *op. cit.*, pp. 272-75; Ribbentrop, *op. cit.*, pp. 53 ff. On the Mennonites, see *Heerwesen des Absolutismus*, Beilage LXXXIII, p. 320.

[62] Ribbentrop, *op. cit.*, pp. 51-52, 117; Wilke, *op. cit.*, pp. 280-82.

the firing squad by a military court. Anyone assisting deserters or fugitives was punished by a fine or death, or was arrested and held until the runaway was found.[63]

Although the civil and military officials were instructed to cooperate with one another, there was a conflict between them over the army's exorbitant demands. Civil bureaucrats frequently complained about officers who were willing to release cantonists for a fee. These men were recorded in the lists as trained and others were called up from the canton to take their places. Some regiments specified the size of the men to be enrolled, and it was irksome for both civil bureaucrats and cantonists when substitutes were refused because they were not of unusual size.[64]

Recruiting the Mercenaries

Though the canton system of conscripting native reservists was peculiarly Prussian, the army's means for obtaining replacements for the mercenaries in the ranks were similar to those of other armies that still hired professionals. In the Prussian army some of these were native born but in 1802 not less than 80,496 were foreigners, although they were mainly of German origin.[65] Recruiting professional soldiers was an important task of the military officials. Prussian enlistment headquarters in the Empire had been at Frankfort on the Main, but as a result of the Treaty of Lunéville (1801) Prussian recruiting activities had been restricted to their own borders.[66] Regulations

[63] *Ibid.*, pp. 313, 324-26. Cantonists could not leave their village without permission from the Land Councillor or the Magistrate, nor go out of the province without informing the Chamber. Persons who moved about were held responsible for the necessary passes and documents. If none was presented to the authorities for absentees, they were presumed to be in flight and their property was confiscated. *Ibid.*, pp. 308-12.

[64] Arnim, *op. cit.*, pp. 13-20; Wilke, *op. cit.*, pp. 307-08.

[65] Jany, *op. cit.*, III, 436.

[66] *Ibid.*, III, 437. The King of Prussia in his capacity as an Elector of the Holy Roman Empire had the right to recruit in all the small German lands, whether the rulers permitted it or not. Scharfenort, *op. cit.*, p. 2. *Cf.* Stetten-Buchenbach, " Rekrutenwerbungen in reichsritterschaftlichem Gebiet im 18. Jahrhundert," *Militär-Wochenblatt*, Beiheft 1903, pp. 451 ff.

THE DEVELOPMENT OF THE CANTON SYSTEM 57

of 1787-1791 set forth only general rules for recruiting foreigners; however on May 15, 1798 the enlistment of Frenchmen was forbidden, and on August 12, 1800 the prohibition was extended to all who had served with the French.[67]

Hiring new recruits was a picturesque and colorful aspect of contemporary life. Instruction books for recruiting officers listed the towns and provinces that were most favorable and gave advice on luring men into the army. Taverns or fairs were generally sought out as places in which numbers of young men might be found. Informers were also used to locate likely youths. An attractive picture of army life was painted for them; the glory of the profession and the elegance of the king's uniform were set before easily tempted country boys. Other prospects could not be induced to make their mark on the enlistment paper until drunkenness had obliterated any remembrance of the common soldiers' misery. Candidates were also attracted by an announcement in the public square accompanied by much fanfare, rolls on the drum and trumpet flourishes, that His Majesty the King of Prussia offered honorable careers in his armed forces to grenadiers, hussars, and the like. Unwary youths drawn to this display could be taken aside to the taverns for more private persuasion. Needless to add, once the recruit had signed, all pleasantries ceased and the iron discipline of the Prussian army began. Numerous precautions were taken by the officers to insure arrival at the regiment. The newly enlisted men were watched constantly, and if the recruit brought his wife special care was taken. Very often the mercenaries were transported to the regiments like prisoners in a chain gang. Neutral territories were frequently violated in search of fugi-

[67] Jany, *op. cit.*, III, 437-38; *cf.* B. von Poten, "Das Preussische Heer vor hundert Jahren," *Militär-Wochenblatt*, Beiheft 1900, p. 26. The recruiting regulations of Febr. 1, 1787, in *Heerwesen des Absolutismus*, Beilage LXXX, pp. 298-308.

tives, and there were many instances when the subjects of small states were impressed.[68]

Until the Peace of Basel (1795) recruiting the professionals had been the affair of the regiment though actually handled by the company captains; but political changes in Europe gradually brought about more state control. The increase of French influence in south Germany and the final partition of Poland in 1795-1796 drove Prussian recruiting agents from some of their best territories. By 1799 it was necessary to place the army on a royal recruiting basis, and the funds formerly sent to the regiments were combined in a General Recruiting Treasury. Through the mobilization of 1805 and the campaign of 1806 the recruits were provided by royal officials.[69]

Prussian Man Power Resources

Despite the difficulty of recruiting during the French Revolution no attempt was made in Prussia to extend conscription of the natives, though there were enough inhabitants to ease the burden. In 1804 there were 9,752,731 subjects in the Prussian lands, including 4,860,747 men, at least half of whom were liable.[70] Men liable to military service in 1799 numbered 2,056,978; in 1802, 2,156,812; and in 1805, 2,320,122.[71] Exemptions on the basis of territorial privilege accounted for 1,170,000 men, while 530,000 men were freed because of estate, profession, religion, or property. It is to be noted that 230,000 of these had acquired exemption under the generous provisions of

[68] Schultz, *op. cit.*, pp. 10-18, 32, 47, 76-84; Stetten-Buchenbach, *op. cit.*, pp. 459-61; Scharfenort, *op. cit.*, pp. 2-7.

[69] Jany, *op. cit.*, III, 435-36. The annual cost of recruiting amounted to 441,235 thalers, but an additional fund was necessary as the mercenaries expected a tip when they signed the muster roll. In the infantry a heavier tip was demanded, consequently there were always shortages of recruiting money in that arm. *Ibid.*, III, 436-37.

[70] *Ibid.*, III, 442-43.

[71] *Ibid.*, III, 443.

THE DEVELOPMENT OF THE CANTON SYSTEM 59

the law of 1792.[72] Conscripting Prussian subjects for the army would not have imposed many hardships after 1798 when the canton districts were enlarged. In the older parts of the monarchy, each regiment had over 20,000 men at its disposal, and some of the new lands in the east had cantons with as many as 58,000 men. Both regiments in Ansbach-Bayreuth had more than 50,000 men each. Large canton areas were not an advantage, however, since the furloughed men lived far from regimental headquarters and the speed of mobilization was slower.[73]

When the troops were established in their cantons a mobilization in the modern sense, with cadres filled by drafting trained reserves, could occur. Preparation for the mobilization was the work of the General Quartermaster and his staff; intendants in the mobilization districts handled local details, and commissariat officers directed the assembly of supplies and forage.[74] Mobilization was not by corps or divisions, since the army had none, but by battalions in each arm. Infantry, cavalry, and artillery had their own assembly points and time tables, the guns normally a week slower than the rest. Sometimes a double mobilization was allowed for artillery, with only light guns in the first phase. Supplying horses, transporting artillery, and gathering food were the main technical problems facing the military bureaucracy.[75] Although reservists could be called up within two or three weeks, in periods of great emergency (during 1805-1806) both reservists and professionals were kept under arms to facilitate rapid and complete mobilization.[76]

[72] Data from Krug, "Über das preussische Kantonwesen," cited in Jähns, *op. cit.*, III, 2253-54.

[73] Jany, *op. cit.*, III, 442.

[74] *Ibid.*, III, 403.

[75] *Archiv des Kriegsministeriums*, III, 153-66. Cf. Gossler, "Beitrag zur Geschichte unserer Heeresverfassung," *Militär-Wochenblatt*, Beiheft 1885, pp. 277-78.

[76] Cf. *Die preussischen Kriegsvorbereitungen und Operationspläne von 1805* (1st ed., Berlin, 1883).

The Idea of Universal Service

After the expansion of the state into the Polish lands conscription of the new subjects proved impossible. Because of this circumstance and the lethargy of the bureaucracy and army, as well as the demands of a mercantile economy and the class nature of society, a military obligation for all the dwellers in the Prussian lands remained a legal fiction.[77] But in the Prussian canton system, which became merely an administrative device for selecting reservists from the lowest classes of the population, both territorial conscription and the idea of universal service persisted. In the era of the great military reforms, 1807-1813, both of these traditions were to find an important place in the reestablishment of the armed forces.

[77] See Wolzendorff, *op. cit.*, pp. 8-9.

CHAPTER III
EFFORTS AT REFORM BEFORE 1806

NEITHER of the successors of Frederick the Great was inclined to make radical alterations in the government or the armed forces.[1] Only because it was customary Frederick William II and Frederick William III began their reigns with investigations of the army. It might be said of Frederick William II that though he showed an interest in military affairs it was perfunctory and casual. Minor details and uniforms were particularly fascinating for Frederick William III, but only great events or eloquent appeals seemed able to arouse his interest in the serious needs of the army. More important than the indifferent leadership provided by the crown was the critical reforming spirit in the leading circles of the army. This manifested itself not only in official documents,[2] but also in numerous unsolicited manuscripts, and particularly in the active and voluminous military journalism that supplied a forum for discussion.

MILITARY PUBLICATIONS IN GERMANY

From the military periodicals came the basic ideas that influenced the officers and statesmen who were to carry out the subsequent reform of the Prussian army. Military periodicals

---

[1] The statement of a Prussian minister to the French ambassador concerning Frederick William III may have been made in half seriousness, but it illustrates what was at first expected of his government: " The revolution which you are making from the bottom toward the top, will perfect itself in Prussia slowly from top to bottom; the King is essentially a democrat, and in a few years there will be hardly any more feudal privileges." Max Lehmann, " Ein Regierungsprogramm Friedrich Wilhelm's III," *Historische Zeitschrift*, LXI (1889), 441.

[2] *Cf.* Max Lehmann, " Das alte Preussen," *Historische Zeitschrift*, XC (1903), 402-03. *Cf.* Georg Winter, ed., *Die Reorganisation des Preussischen Staates unter Stein und Hardenberg. Vom Beginn des Kampfes gegen die Kabinettsregierung bis zum Wiedereintritt des Ministers vom Stein* (Publikationen aus den Preussischen Staatsarchiven, Leipzig, 1931, XCIII), pp. 17-20, 21, 37. This will be cited henceforth as *Preuss. Archiv*, XCIII.

were first published in the eighteenth century, but unlike most military literature which was still being written from a French point of view, they were mainly German in origin and outlook.[3] In the last quarter of the century a literal eruption of military writing occurred, books sharing popularity with magazines. A bookseller's list of 1802 cited fifty-seven titles in German, and forty-three in French on military subjects, and hundreds of copies of the books of well-known theorists, such as Berenhorst or Bülow, were sold. Periodicals were the unique contribution of the German lands, and though short-lived, they testified to the eagerness of officers, officials, and the public for information about armies and warfare.

A partial list bears witness to the amount of writing and the extent of the interest in military affairs during the latter part of the eighteenth century in Germany. Scharnhorst's first effort, the *Militair-Bibliothek* (Hanover, 1782-1784), deserves first mention; it had 670 subscribers. His second attempt, the *Bibliothek für Offiziere* (Göttingen, 1785), lasted only one year. The *Neues militärisches Journal* (Hanover, 1788-1795) was his third venture, with contents rich in the moving spirit of the time.[4] Georg D. von dem Groeben's *Der Veteran* (Breslau, 1782-1783) was made up of anecdotes and accounts of the social life of officers; F. K. Schleicher's *Neues militärische Bibliothek* (Marburg, 1789, 4 v.) provided a lexicon of current books. Valuable accounts of tactics and organization were to be found in the *Militärische Monatschrift* (Berlin, 1785-1787), edited by H. W. von Stamford. Narratives of contemporary campaign experiences and articles about the French armies and their methods of war distinguished the *Magazin der neuesten merkwürdigen Kriegsbegebenheiten* (Frankfort on the Main, 1795-1796). For engineers the *Magazin für Ingenieur und Artilleristen* (An-

[3] Jähns, *op. cit.*, III, 1769-70, 1812. Boguslawski, *op. cit.*, pp. 18 ff., considers the relation of military journalism to military reform before 1806.

[4] For a critique of Scharnhorst's early military writing, see Jähns, *op. cit.*, III, 1816-1818.

EFFORTS AT REFORM BEFORE 1806 63

dreas Bohn, ed., Giessen, 1777-1789; Leipzig, 1795) was significant. Under the title of *Neue Kriegsbibliothek* (Georg D. von dem Groeben, ed., Breslau, 1774-1781) appeared a new edition of an older magazine, founded by the same editor in 1755 and known as the *Kriegsbibliothek oder gesammelte Beiträge zur Kriegswissenschaft* (Breslau, 1755-1771).[5] *Der Soldat* (Buchenröder, ed., Hamburg, 1772-1782) was a weekly intended for the middle classes as well as officers. Excellent articles were published in the *Bellona: Ein militärischer Journal* (K. von Seidl, ed., Dresden, 1781-1787), which introduced experiences, discussion of training, and criticism, thus making it an important source for the military theory of this period. *Bellona* (Hanover, 1794), a second version of this magazine, dealt with the history of war with emphasis on famous personalities. The *Archiv für Aufklärung über das Soldatenwesen* (Leipzig, 1792-1793) was important as it favored the standing army and opposed the militia.[6]

There were also single publications such as the *Militärisches Taschenbuch* (Berlin, 1801), and Scharnhorst's *Handbuch für Offiziere* (Hanover, 1787-1790, 3 v.), as well as many other technical works. To these purely professional accounts must be added the theoretical discourses of Berenhorst, Bülow, Venturini, Decken, and Miller among the Germans, and translations of important books by such foreign commentators as Sylva, Guibert, and Lloyd, which brought the latest European developments to the attention of Prussian readers.

[5] This was the first military periodical in Europe. Other magazines including some published after 1800 were: *Mars. Eine allgemeine militärische Zeitung* (Berlin, 1804-1805); *Militärische Denkwürdigkeiten unserer Zeiten* (Hanover, 1799-1805); *Neue Bellona, oder Beiträge zur Kriegskunst und Kriegsgeschichte* (Leipzig, 1801-1806); *Neues militärisches Magazin* (Leipzig, 1798-1805); *Neue militärische Zeitung* (Marburg, 1789); *Pallas, eine Zeitschrift für Staats- und Kriegskunst* (Tübingen, 1808-1810).

[6] The resources of the *Deutsche Heeresbücherei* in Berlin comprised the richest collection of military periodical literature of the eighteenth century. It should be noted that the *Minerva* (Hamburg, 1792-1854) and other contemporary periodicals of a general nature contained many articles on military subjects. The *Militär-Wochenblatt* was not founded until 1816.

Spirit of the Reform Movement

A critical tone was evident in the periodicals, and since they escaped the scrutiny of the censors there were also articles on matters of general political interest. This literary activity provided the military reformers, both before and after 1806, with the historical examples and the arguments to confound their opponents. For aiding the work of reform the writers and theorists deserved praise second only to that of the important military figures who were responsible for the development of the army.

Military societies were equally significant, and of these the *Militärischen Gesellschaft,* founded by Scharnhorst, was the most important.[7] His prestige as a staff officer and head of the Academy for Officers enabled him to preside over a series of discussions which eventually led to the formal establishment of a society on January 24, 1802. Weekly meetings were held, devoted to the discussion of papers, analysis and review of current military literature, and study of military problems.[8] Not less than 160 meetings were held before 1806, with an average attendance of 188 members, including such prominent officers of the army as Rüchel, Lecoq, Phull, Massenbach, Hake, Kleist, Lottum, Borstell, Valentini, Rühle, Grolman, and Müffling. All of the more valuable papers were published in the *Denkwürdigkeiten der militärischen Gesellschaft* (Berlin, 1802-1805, 5 v.); Scharnhorst was naturally the most frequent contributor. For the general public a lively popular journal was issued. In both publications comparisons were drawn between armies of the Seven Years' War and those of the revolutionary era, and there was a discussion of universal service as it affected the German

[7] G. H. Klippel, *Das Leben des Generals von Scharnhorst* (Leipzig, 1869-1871), III, 30. Max Lehmann, *Scharnhorst* (Leipzig, 1886-1887), I, 320, dates the founding from July 2, 1801 when the discussions began.

[8] Article one of the society's constitution asserted: "The purpose of the society is to provide instruction in all the branches of the art of war by cooperative investigations which encourage the discovery of truth and are best adapted to the avoidance of the narrowness of individual study, and finally to set theory and practice in their proper relationship." Klippel, *op. cit.,* III, 255; the entire constitution, *ibid.,* III, 255-62.

lands. Articles and reviews provided detailed information about French organization, tactics, and campaigns, as well as the effect of new military methods on the Prussians, whose army was not considered beyond reproach simply because it had been developed by Frederick the Great.[9]

Within the circle of officers with literary and intellectual pretentions there raged a pamphlet war on the relative value of the old and new military systems. Shortly after Frederick's death, Templehoff, the artillerist, had ridiculed his formal style of warfare, and in 1790 the king's own adjutant, Karl Friedrich von Lindenau, wrote his brilliant book, *Ueber die höhere preussische Taktik* (Leipzig, 1790). His attack on the unreality of maneuvers was the opening skirmish in a war of pens.[10] Leipziger joined the attack on Lindenau with his *Kritische Beleuchtung der Lindenauschen Bemerkungen* (Breslau, 1793).[11] But none of these writers was as significant for his criticism of the Frederician methods as Berenhorst.

Berenhorst and Bülow

Georg Heinrich von Berenhorst and his pupil, Heinrich Dietrich von Bülow, were the prophets of the new era. Berenhorst's

[9] Cf. *Denkwürdigkeiten der militärischen Gesellschaft in Berlin* (Berlin, 1802-1805), I-IV. Among the more notable articles was one by Scharnhorst, "Ueber die Schlacht bei Marengo," *ibid.*, I, 52-59; his review of Champeaux's *État militaire de la République Française pour l'an X* examined the administration of the French army, composition of the corps, and other matters. *Ibid.*, I, 123-33. Reviews were given a prominent place in the society's publication; frequent mention of French books provided Prussian officers with information about Napoleon's army. Cf. *ibid.*, III, 212-20, 396-97.

[10] K. F. von Lindenau, *Ueber die höhere preussische Taktik* (Leipzig, 1790), p. xxxii. Cf. *Beleuchtung der Anmerkungen eines Ungenannten* (Leipzig, 1790), by the same author. Notice Rohde, *Ueber die Schrift des k. k. Oberstleutnants Herrn von Lindenau* (Potsdam, 1791).

[11] Scharnhorst in the *Neues militärisches Journal*, III (1790), 239-65, agreed that Lindenau had some basis for his criticism of the Prussians, but Scharnhorst remained a resolute defender of Frederick the Great. See *ibid.*, IV (1790), 262-67, for the review of *Anmerkung zu der Schrift des Herrn von Lindenau* (Berlin, 1790), another book which attempted to evaluate Frederician tactics.

most important work, *Betrachtungen über die Kriegskunst* (Leipzig, 1798 and 1799), denounced the existing tactics as artificial and decried the veneration for Frederick the Great. He placed more stress upon the moral and spiritual values of the army than a formal drill learned by repetition. In terse fashion Berenhorst struck at the dominant theorists of the day, Saldern, Massenbach, and Venturini.[12] Saldern's ideas were typical of the strenuousness and pettiness in training that prevailed in the army. Though Saldern's work, *Taktische Grundsätze* (Dresden, 1786), contained many practical suggestions, it was dominated by the narrow outlook of the exercise ground.[13]

Massenbach and Venturini based their military theories on an army's need for supplies, but their system of war had little value for armies having methods of subsistence that supplemented the customary fortresses and magazines.[14] Berenhorst criticized them for regarding the army as a machine, and war as an operation that followed immutable rules, much like the cosmos subject to mathematical order that Newton had described. The emphasis on formulae and the attempt to reduce war to a system was characteristic of much military writing during the eighteenth century. Jomini was the last great representative of this tradition.[15]

[12] Berenhorst, *Betrachtungen*, pp. 225-28, 237. Rudolf Bahn, *Georg Heinrich von Berenhorst der Verfasser der 'Betrachtungen über die Kriegskunst'* (Halle a. S., 1911), pp. 48-50, 65-68; F. von Meerheimb, "Berenhorst und Bülow," *Historische Zeitschrift*, VI (1861), 55-56, 59-60.

[13] Note the oft-quoted observation of Saldern: "Indeed, it is prescribed that in marching there shall be seventy-six steps per minute, but after considerable reflection and much observation, I have concluded that seventy-five steps in a minute are much better." *Die Franzosenzeit in deutschen Landen*, I, 18.

[14] *Cf.* G. Venturini, *Lehrbuch der angewandten Taktik* (Schleswig, 1798-1801, 5 v.). In addition to his articles Massenbach contributed *Betrachtungen über einige Unrichtigkeiten in den Betrachtungen* (Berlin, 1802) to the controversy over military methods. In this work he attacked Berenhorst.

[15] Meerheimb, *op. cit.*, pp. 58-60; Bahn, *op. cit.*, pp. 66-67. *Cf.* E. von Bülow, ed., *Aus dem Nachlasse von Georg Heinrich von Berenhorst* (Leipzig, 1845-1847). Berenhorst's assumption that war could not be reduced to

Heinrich Dietrich von Bülow, the pupil of Berenhorst, spoke appreciatively of his master, but surpassed him in clarity of ideas and power of expression. Through his works, *Neue Taktik der Neuern, wie sie seyn sollte* (Leipzig, 1805), and *Der Geist des neueren Kriegssystems* (Hamburg, 1799), he cleared the air for contemporaries by criticizing the practices and principles of Frederick the Great. He warned officers of the Prussian army that the echelon attack of Frederick's day might be useless against an enemy with the flexibility of Napoleon's troops, or against an enemy that was arrayed in depth with a formidable reserve. Another of Bülow's great services was his recognition before 1806 of the power, both physical and moral, that France had won by making war a matter of national concern. His famous dictum that the " battles of the future will be decided by *tirailleurs*," identified his concept of battle.[16]

Leadership and Military Reform

Berenhorst and Bülow were not without military experience but they could propose reforms only as civilian publicists. Scharnhorst, however, was able to combine the careers of writer and public servant. His ability as an editor and writer had made him famous as a military scholar long before he entered Prussian service in 1801. At twenty-seven he had been the editor of the *Militair-Bibliothek* and at thirty-two his reputation insured a wide sale for the *Handbuch für Offiziere*. In Prussia his work as a staff officer and director of military schools, as well as his great prestige as an authority on military science, gave him the opportunity to expound his ideas before an influential audience.[17] Scharnhorst believed in the soundness of Frederick's

---

rules contrasted with the views of F. von Miller, whose *Reine Taktik* (Stuttgart, 1787-1788, 2 v.) developed a mathematical interpretation of war.

16 Meerheimb, *op. cit.*, pp. 61-63, 65-71; Jähns, *op. cit.*, III, 2133-43. *Cf.* E. Bülow and W. Rüstow, eds., *Militärische und vermischte Schriften von Heinrich Dietrich von Bülow* (Leipzig, 1853). Another stream of enlightened opinion came from the men returning to Germany from the wars in America, among whom was Gneisenau.

17 Scharnhorst's reaction to the critics of the Prussian army is manifested in a letter to Lt. Col. von Lecoq of Nov. 20, 1800 in *Scharnhorsts*

methods when modified to meet the new conditions, but he frankly admitted the advantage won by the French national army with its divisional organization and flexible tactics. By publicly advocating these reforms Scharnhorst convinced many Prussian officers of the need for change before it was so forcibly demonstrated at Jena.[18]

Though the king and his immediate advisers were stirred into action only by that debacle, the reform movement that was sanctioned after 1806 owed much to the previous efforts. Popular military service had been discussed in official circles since the 1790's and there was a well-established practice of entrusting reform suggestions to a special military commission. The members of these commissions were invariably professional officers and though they frequently consulted civil bureaucrats about financial and organizational problems, civilians were not allowed to tamper with the army. This did not mean that reform leadership was entirely absent. There was always a group of line officers, few in number to be sure, who were ready to plan and direct the reorganization of the army.[19] That these officers who finally assumed control in 1807 profited from the previous reform efforts is undeniable. It would be correct to say that the attempts to reform the Prussian army only began to yield tangible results after the battle of Jena.

The long period of peace in Prussia from 1795 to 1806 offered a great opportunity for military reform. Except for a few

Briefe (Karl Linnebach, ed., Munich and Leipzig, 1914), I, 212-14. While in a memorial of November, 1800 addressed to Frederick William III, he wrote: "Never have I written anything detrimental to the Prussian army, I have always been because of conviction its greatest partisan and eulogist." *Ibid.*, I, 214.

18 For Scharnhorst's literary activity see the main bibliography, and also the anthology edited by Colmar von der Goltz, *Militärische Schriften von Scharnhorst* (Berlin, 1881).

19 Jähns indicates that, "After Frederick II's death a strong reform movement began in the leading circles of the Prussian army...." *Op. cit.*, III, 2245. Reinhard Höhn, *Verfassungskampf und Heereseid* (Leipzig, 1938), pp. 3-8, points out the constitutional problems of military reform in an absolute state.

EFFORTS AT REFORM BEFORE 1806   69

minor changes the Prussian military institutions dating from the time of Frederick the Great remained much the same. It is almost unbelievable that a state which owed almost all its fortune to the excellence of its army could watch with complacence the transformation of the French republican armies into a formidable military machine. This lethargy was almost entirely due to the timorous and procrastinating character of the monarchs. If they had been so inclined a reorganization by the reform-minded officers might have kept the army abreast of the French and Austrians.[20] The Archduke Charles of Austria was a zealous reformer whose work had made the Austrian army one of the most powerful in Europe.[21] Almost continuous service in foreign wars gave the French valuable experience that enhanced the superiority of their organization and military methods. In comparison with these armies the Prussians showed few innovations.

The importance of light infantry had been recognized somewhat tardily in 1787 when fusilier battalions were created. And in the same year orders were issued to train ten men from each infantry company in sharpshooting, patrolling, and skirmishing.[22] Neither these reenforcements from the companies nor the twenty-four fusilier battalions that had been erected by 1806 were numerous enough to satisfy the army's light infantry requirements. Some officers recognized this fact and abolished the third rank in order to gain additional man power for the light troops. This practice was eventually sanctioned by a royal order of October 5, 1805 to form the men from the third rank in separate battalions. General mobilization in 1805 interfered with this plan, however.[23]

The initiative of progressive officers who prepared unofficial training instructions for their own commands did not influence

[20] *Cf.* Goltz, *op. cit.*, pp. 96-97.

[21] Oskar Criste, *Erzherzog Carl von Österreich* (Vienna and Leipzig, 1912), II, 391-412.

[22] *Archiv des Kriegsministeriums*, III, 92.

[23] Jany, *op. cit.*, III, 495; Bressonnet, *op. cit.*, pp. 375-77.

the tactical doctrines of the army as much as the accounts of sympathetic German historians would lead us to believe. These individual manuals were recapitulated from time to time after 1798 but they could not offset the great emphasis of the revised infantry regulations of 1787 on line tactics. Since the standards of tactical training were left to the discretion of each commanding officer, and close adherence to the official regulations was not demanded, some units did find it possible to practice skirmishing and *tirailleur* fighting.[24] For most officers the old methods of forming a firing line three ranks deep and advancing in close order on the enemy's flank seemed perfectly adequate. A few officers were skeptical of this traditional style, however, so that the trend toward the use of extended order, the most important tactical development in the era between Frederick II and Napoleon, did not go entirely unnoticed in Prussia.[25]

Frederick William II and his heir took a personal interest in the well-being of old officers and men. Several alms houses intended for soldiers as well as vagabonds were built, but funds sufficient for pensioning old soldiers could not be provided. If an aged veteran did not wish to become a public charge in an institution he was usually permitted to draw army pay and allowances in an *Invaliden* company. For want of a pension system retired officers literally invaded the lower ranks of the civilian bureaucracy. Frederick William III particularly encouraged this practice and by a decree of July 30, 1799 made the lesser posts a monopoly of military invalids. The use of army officers in what had become a highly skilled profession naturally tended to lower the standards of Prussian administration.[26]

24 Cf. *Gefechtsausbildung*, pp. 16-19.

25 Consult Sautermeister, *op. cit.*, pp. 10-14, 16-20; *Gefechtsausbildung*, pp. 60-94. See G. T. von Faber, *Bemerkungen über die französische Armee der neuesten Zeit 1792-1807* (Königsberg, 1808), pp. 110-11.

26 Dorn, *op. cit.*, XLVII, 267-69; Philippson, *op. cit.*, I, 413-18, II, 176-77. Consult Schnackenburg, *op. cit.*, pp. 118-42.

EFFORTS AT REFORM BEFORE 1806

Education of the officers had also been furthered before 1806 by the founding of engineering and artillery academies. Despite the monarch's attention the Prussian military schools were not reorganized until 1810, when Scharnhorst's plan for an integrated system of military education was put into effect.[27] Little was done to improve Prussian armament before the catastrophe at Jena except for the adoption of the Nothardt musket in 1801. Only 45,000 pieces of this new model had been manufactured by 1806, however.[28] Many trivial changes in uniforms and drill were made before 1806 but not one increased the fighting power of the armed forces.

BETTER TRAINING FOR STAFF OFFICERS

An improved training for staff officers which began in 1803 was a reform of great promise. In this way staff officers took their first step, faltering and hesitant to be sure, toward that prominence which they were to enjoy in the Prussian army by mid-century. But in 1803 staff officers did not have any special prestige as they were still few in number and lacked an organization comparable to a modern General Staff. As a distinct organ of the army the General Staff did not begin to function until 1821. That date should make it evident that Scharnhorst was not, as many popular writers suppose, the founder of the General Staff. Although he was called after 1810 the Chief of the General Staff, the title was purely honorary since it did not refer either to an office or to a rank.[29] And in the period of military reforms associated with Scharnhorst's name, 1807-1813, there were no important changes in the duties of staff officers as set forth in the orders of 1803.[30]

27 L. von Scharfenort, *Die Königlich Preussische Kriegsakademie 1810-1910* (Berlin, 1910), pp. 2-3, 6 ff.

28 *Das Preussische Heer im Jahre 1812* (Berlin, 1912), pp. 129-30. This will be cited henceforth as *Preuss. Heer 1812*. There were five types of infantry muskets in use in 1806-1807. Only seven battalions used the Nothardt musket. *Ibid.*, p. 129.

29 See F. von Cochenhausen, ed., *Von Scharnhorst zu Schlieffen* (Berlin, 1933), pp. 9, 16-17, for the popular conception. Jany, *op. cit.*, IV, 36, 122-23.

30 Reform suggestions made in 1807-1808 are listed in R. Vaupel, ed., *Die Reorganisation des Preussischen Staates unter Stein und Hardenberg.*

Staff officers had existed in the Prussian army for some time before that date. They had served Frederick the Great and his brother, Prince Henry, as orderlies, adjutants, or technical assistants, especially in matters of topography. In time of peace they also studied fortification, siegecraft, reconnaissance, and espionage.[31] Until new instructions were provided by Lieutenant Colonel von Lecoq in 1800 Prussian staff officers had not been formally charged with many operational duties. Lecoq believed that staff officers should lead columns, conduct troops into camp, organize foraging expeditions, lay out intrenchments, reconnoiter positions, gather information of all kinds, and give advice to the commanding officer if he asked for it. Little was accomplished by these instructions though they did point the way for the reforms of Colonel von Massenbach. He was the first in Prussia to insist that the technical training of staff officers was indispensable for the command of the army. In four memoirs written for Frederick William III between January, 1802 and April, 1803 Massenbach outlined an improved training course for staff officers and proposed that staff training become an advanced school for commanding officers. He also asked the right of direct audience with the king for the leading staff officer, a right which Scharnhorst obtained only at Stein's insistence in 1808.[32] The later history of this

Das Preussische Heer vom Tilsiter Frieden bis zur Befreiung 1807-1814 (Publikationen aus den Preussischen Archiven, Leipzig, 1938, XCIV), pp. 205-18. Hereafter this collection of sources will be cited as *Preuss. Archiv*, XCIV.

31 Jany, *op. cit.*, III, 411; Scherbening and Willisen, eds., *Die Reorganisation der Preussischen Armee nach dem Tilsiter Frieden* (Berlin, 1862-1866), I, 236-52. This source collection will be cited henceforth as *Reorganisation der Preuss. Armee*.

32 *Ibid.*, I, 252-62. Some patriotic German historians are inclined to overlook Massenbach's part in the reform movement because of his disgraceful conduct in the campaign of 1806. For a more impartial account, and a reference to Lecoq's suggestions, see General Paul L. Bronsart von Schellendorff, *The Duties of the General Staff* (3rd ed., London, 1895), pp. 16-23. For evidence of Massenbach's interest in military reform, see *Preuss. Archiv*, XCIII, 15-17, *Immediateingabe des Oberst von Massenbach*.

EFFORTS AT REFORM BEFORE 1806   73

privilege forms one of the most important chapters in the relations of the Prussian military and civil constitutions.[33]

On November 26, 1803 appeared the royal *Instruktion für den General-Quartiermeister-Stab* (Instruction for the General Quartermaster Staff), incorporating the ideas Massenbach had suggested. Officers were to be selected for staff training by examination, and they were to return to their commands occasionally in order to temper theory with practice. No seniority was recognized and advancement depended upon success in competitive tests. The preparation of war plans became the principal duty of the staff groups and to this end maps were made and collected, the probable theaters of war reconnoitered, and the fortifications and natural defences of the land were studied.[34] But a reform set forth on paper could not be achieved immediately in an army so bound by tradition as the Prussian. It is not surprising therefore that in 1806-1807 the Prussian generals were not inclined to accept advice from their staff officers.

PLANS FOR THE EXPANSION OF THE ARMY

Before 1806 the most serious and sustained reform efforts were associated with attempts to expand the army. With the final partition of Poland in 1795, the new common frontier between Prussia and Russia made evident the need of a larger army. When makeshift attempts to strengthen the eastern defences failed, a general expansion of the army was decreed and an earnest attempt at reform was begun.[35] Both the problems of expansion and reform were entrusted to a commission created on November 30, 1795. Its members were drawn from the High Council of War and Field Marshal von Möllendorf was made its " president," or chairman. This Emergency Commission for Military Organization (henceforth called the Emergency Com-

33 Consult G. Wohlers, *Die staatsrechtliche Stellung des Generalstabes in Preussen und dem Deutschen Reich* (Bonn and Leipzig, 1921).

34 *Reorganisation der Preuss. Armee*, I, 265-77. Clausewitz, *Nachrichten*, pp. 441-42. The rich collection of maps used by staff officers formed part of the archives of the *Deutsche Heeresbücherei* in Berlin.

35 Goltz, *op. cit.*, pp. 244-46.

mission) enjoyed a long life which lasted until the mobilization of 1805.[36] The task of the Emergency Commission was set forth in General von Rüchel's suggestion that a militia be adopted for coast defence. More concrete proposals came from President Schroetter of East Prussia for a popular levy to augment the army, a method which had been used in Lithuania in 1757.[37] His plan appears to have been approved on paper in 1796 without the universal service feature that he had suggested. For a decade the reformers were to grapple with the problem of a militia,[38] while for the immediate increase of the army it is significant that resort was made to the old system of furloughing natives as rapidly as they could be trained.[39]

Under Frederick William III who succeeded to the throne in 1797 the work of the Emergency Commission continued. Much was expected of this monarch who had been closely associated with the army, and who was aware of the reform spirit abroad in it. Though he had worked with the Emergency Commission as Crown Prince, Frederick William's recommendations were not equal to the need of the army.[40] Trivialities of regimental names, uniforms, and a wrangle over the advisability of five instead of four companies to the battalion occupied the monarch's time. Five valuable years were wasted before Frederick

---

36 *Ibid.*, pp. 246-47; R. de l'Homme de Courbière, *Geschichte der brandenburgisch-preussischen Heeresverfassung* (Berlin, 1852), pp. 137-38. This work will be cited henceforth as Courbière, *Heeresverfassung*. The Emergency Commission also attempted to end the confusion in military administration but no real improvement was effected. *Cf.* Jany, *op. cit.*, III, 339-40.

37 *Cf.* Schwarz, *op. cit.*, pp. 25-27.

38 Goltz, *op. cit.*, pp. 249-51.

39 Jany, *op. cit.*, III, 450-51. *Cf. Archiv des Kriegsministeriums*, III, 92-93.

40 Hintze, *Die Hohenzollern*, p. 425; Alfred Herrmann, "Friedrich Wilhelm III. und sein Anteil an der Heeresreform bis 1813," *Historische Vierteljahrschrift*, XI (1908), 490-91. Frederick William III did show an interest in the general problem of reform; at first his efforts were directed toward ending serfdom, reducing aristocratic privileges, and revitalizing the bureaucracy. *Cf.* Lehmann, "Ein Regierungsprogramm Friedrich Wilhelm's III," *op. cit.*, pp. 441 ff. See the discussion of the king's role and the continuity of military reform in Helfritz, *op. cit.*, pp. 221-22.

William III was stirred to consider seriously the task of military reform.

KNESEBECK'S PROPOSED UNIVERSAL SERVICE ARMY

Recommendations of the Duke of Brunswick in 1802 gave rise once more to the militia idea. Though his plan for National Regiments did not prove practical in every detail,[41] the king's interest was aroused and he asked General von Rüchel to prepare a plan for enlarging the army. Rüchel turned to Major von Knesebeck for suggestions and provided him with an elaboration of the Duke's ideas and his own.[42] By the end of 1803 Knesebeck had finished his all-embracing plan, *Ideen über Errichtung einer Vaterlandsreserve und der Provinzial oder Ehrenlegionen* (Ideas concerning the Development of a Fatherland Reserve and the Provincial or Honor Legions), which was the greatest reform proposal to be made before 1806.[43] It is evident that Scharnhorst's prominence has tended to obscure Knesebeck's significance for the reforms before 1806, although the latter's proposals were both practical and farsighted.[44]

[41] Jany, *op. cit.*, III, 453-54. Nelson's victory at Copenhagen in 1801 opened the Baltic to the English fleet; Prussia was forced to strengthen the troops occupying the Pomeranian and Prussian coasts. See *ibid.*, III, 385-86.

[42] Goltz, *op. cit.*, pp. 280-81. *Cf.* Herrmann, *op. cit.*, p. 492.

[43] Goltz, *op. cit.*, p. 281; Jany, *op. cit.*, III, 455-56. Karl Friedrich Freiherr von dem Knesebeck, *Brückstücke aus den hinterlassenen Papieren* (Magdeburg, 1850), contains personal and diplomatic papers for the most part.

[44] Largely because of the historical interpretations of Max Lehmann, a great admirer of Scharnhorst, Knesebeck has been doomed to obscurity. Yet Knesebeck's proposals actually bore more relation to the eventual form of universal service in Prussia than those of Scharnhorst. *Cf.* J. Ziekursch, "Die preussischen Landreservebataillone 1805/06 — eine Reform vor der Reform?" *Historische Zeitschrift*, CIII (1909), 85-94, for belated recognition of the pre-1806 reformers. Goltz praises Knesebeck but keeps to the established interpretations of Prussian military figures, although his study evaluates the old army in striking fashion. Lehmann's best known work is his biography of Scharnhorst. An earlier book, *Knesebeck und Schön* (Leipzig, 1875), presented the dubious thesis that Scharnhorst's militia of 1807 was the prototype of the *Landwehr* of 1813. Older biographies of Scharnhorst, such as that of Klippel, also adhere to the hero-worshipping

Knesebeck's manuscript vigorously defended the popular levy and compared the existing army to a citizen militia affecting only a part of the population. If real universal service were to be applied, Prussia would have in the old practice of holding short annual training periods a means of increasing its military strength.[45]

Other than this demand for universal service Knesebeck proposed no radical alteration of the military system. In fact, his plan was nothing more than the elimination of the exemptions and the lessening of the military burden that had been borne by a single class. At the next canton revision the men should be put into three groups: those suited to the standing army, those indispensable in industry and agriculture for the Fatherland Reserve, and the last group, the unfit, old soldiers, and the like, to comprise the Provincial or Honor Legions. Every year the army should discharge 128,397 men and replace them with recruits chosen from the first category. These would be trained for six weeks during the spring exercise period and then released to the Fatherland Reserve for further drill. In the event of war the Fatherland Reserve would function as a true reserve, strengthening the field forces and providing training cadres. Reservists could be incorporated in the regular army, used in separate formations, or added to the provincial garrisons. Underlying the program was the assumption that war was a matter of national concern, and that the roles of citizen and soldier were interchangeable.[46]

After receiving the plan from General von Rüchel, in whose name it had ostensibly been worked out, the king gave it to the Emergency Commission on July 25, 1803. After three weeks'

formula, and the publications of the General Staff never seek another originator of the military reforms. Otto Hintze, however, believed that the civil reforms were continuous through the late eighteenth and early nineteenth centuries, and without undertaking research, suggested that this was also the case for the military reforms. See Otto Hintze, "Preussische Reformbestrebungen vor 1806," *Historische Zeitschrift*, LXXVI (1896), 413-43.

45 Jany, *op. cit.*, III, 455; Goltz, *op. cit.*, pp. 281-83.
46 Jany, *op. cit.*, III, 455-56; Goltz, *op. cit.*, pp. 283-89.

EFFORTS AT REFORM BEFORE 1806   77

consideration it was flatly rejected.⁴⁷ There was general pessimism over the practical task of eliminating exemptions, for in 1792 the army had found that they were not to be done away with so lightly. Möllendorf raised strong objections to the plan and as a hero of the Seven Years' War his opinion carried great weight.⁴⁸ Guionneau, another expert on the commission, believed that the Fatherland Reserve would endanger the supply of replacements for the regular army, and that the training of such large masses of reserves was useless. Experience during the Seven Years' War had shown that a depleted regiment could train as many as 800 recruits while in winter quarters. Guionneau also objected to the use of the militia in the field rather than in the fortresses, since he doubted whether a militia having only six weeks' training could take the field against a major foe. Knesebeck's proposal to intensify national patriotism among the troops appeared dangerous to the commission. As a substitute for the existing patriotism to the Mark, Pomerania, East Prussia, or other provinces, it might shatter the basis of the army and the state.⁴⁹

OTHER PROPOSALS FOR STRENGTHENING THE ARMY

The discussion was not without effect, however, for the Emergency Commission returned to Rüchel's original proposal, and that of Schroetter of 1796 and 1799, to form a militia of about 50,000 men for coast and home defence. Lest the spread of rumors create a bad impression among the privileged classes the discussions were carried out in secret. While the Emergency Commission was working on the new project, General von Courbière's memoir arrived and its author's prestige assured

47 *Ibid.*, p. 290.

48 Möllendorf's text is given in Courbière, *Heeresverfassung*, pp. 140-41; E. von Conrady, *Leben und Wirken des Generals der Infanterie Carl von Grolman* (Berlin, 1884-1896), I, 36-37, for Möllendorf's letter of July 27, 1803.

49 Courbière, *Heeresverfassung*, pp. 141-43, has the commission's report on Knesebeck's plan. Goltz, *op. cit.*, pp. 289-92. Guionneau was the only member to give his full time to the commission's work. Conrady, *op. cit.*, I, 37.

its immediate consideration. Indeed, a Cabinet Order of April 16, 1804 brought it to the commission's attention. Because Courbière particularly feared an attack by Russia he proposed to strengthen the eastern troops by twelve battalions, increase the complements of all companies to 160 men, eliminate two companies of the Third Musketeer Battalions and use them as cadres for expansion with trained natives.[50] It was but a variation of the *Beurlaubung* system and peacetime reserve characteristic of the Prussian army. Both Möllendorf and Guionneau approved these suggestions enthusiastically, but the king's timidity barred their adoption. Prussian neutrality might be endangered if Napoleon learned of any extraordinary military preparations. Möllendorf, however, was delighted with Courbière's proposal and spoke of it in glowing terms; not only was it practical but it followed Frederick the Great's system of training twenty to forty extra cantonists and holding them in reserve.[51]

The discussion of the militia was suspended while the Emergency Commission investigated the new plan. Cabinet Orders of Frederick the Great concerning popular defence measures were examined for suggestions and precedents. All the various proposals and discussions culminated on August 17, 1805 when royal approval was granted for the development of a militia called the Land Reserve Troops; but ten years had elapsed since the Emergency Commission had begun its work. Rüchel's organization was followed. There were twenty-six brigades, each consisting of three battalions making a total of seventy-eight, with an armed strength of 51,324 men. The Chambers of War and Domains were to select the men from among the cantonists who had served twenty years, able-bodied pensioners, conditionally exempt cantonists, and young men in the canton-free cities and provinces. The last were to be taken only under special conditions, but as the administration of the law in Silesia showed, the local officials were reluctant to conscript anyone exempted by the canton regulations. Officers were to be chosen

50 Courbière, *Heeresverfassung*, pp. 145-46.
51 *Ibid.*, p. 146; Goltz, *op. cit.*, pp. 294-96.

from the *Invaliden* lists, or from among the subalterns and non-commissioned officers of the regular army. Simple uniforms, old muskets, and banners bearing the name of the province were to be provided for the Land Reserve Troops.[52]

More significant was the adoption of the suggestion made by Knesebeck and Courbière that there should be a successive increase in the number of natives in the regiments, and that the third battalion of each regiment also be constituted so as to be able to take the field. From August 17, 1805 each company and third battalion in the East and West Prussian and Warsaw Inspections would train five men over its established strength for four years, alternating them with the other reservists during the exercise period. In four years 320 men would be gained without any foreigners among them. When war broke out these men would form the depot, that is, a regimental reserve for the replacement of casualties. They would, however, compose the the third battalion if it were made mobile, and the infirm soldiers normally in that unit would be shifted to the Land Reserve Battalions. On October 24, 1805 the system was extended to the forty-two third battalions of the army, while the sixteen regiments in the east began to train ten men over the regimental *Etat* (complement), in addition to the ten men over the complement of each battalion. So satisfied was the king with this arrangement, that the Emergency Commission was instructed to study means of applying it in the provinces not included in the canton system.[53]

If all the units of the regular army were at full strength, 192,908 men could be added to the reserves, making the number of effectives 314,380. Out of the total number, 212,372 men, less the officers, were natives.[54] None of these figures represented

---

[52] *Ibid.*, pp. 297-300; Courbière, *Heeresverfassung*, pp. 146-50, has the text of the order. The plan had been submitted to Frederick William III on Sept. 27, 1804 but he had allowed almost a year to elapse before the threat of war in 1805 aroused his interest. Jany, *op. cit.*, III, 460-61.

[53] *Ibid.*, III, 463; Goltz, *op. cit.*, pp. 300-01.

[54] Jany, *op. cit.*, III, 462-63; data in *Die preussischen Kriegsvorbereitungen und Operationspläne von 1805*, pp. 34-35, 50, shows that 161,645 combatants were mobilized in 1805 although part of the army remained in its garrisons.

RESERVE FORMATIONS PROPOSED IN 1805

STANDING TROOPS IN RESERVE

58 Third Battalions	32,248
58 Regimental *Invaliden* Companies	3,596
17 Provincial *Invaliden* Companies	2,529
18 Garrison Artillery Companies	2,351
4 Companies of Miners	403
Total	41,127

SECOND LINE TROOPS IN RESERVE

Land Reserve Troops	51,324
Augmentation of the Third Battalion	19,720
Fusilier Depots	2,568
Artillery Depots	1,112
Cavalry Depots	5,621
Total	80,345
Grand total of reserves	121,472

the actual strength of the troops. All the data were qualified in some way: the reserve training program had hardly begun in 1805 when the outbreak of war in 1806 brought it to an end. Of 192,908 regulars it might have been possible to place at least 185,764 in the field, but political requirements both domestic and foreign reduced this total to 147,720 men for the army's great test in 1806.[55]

REFORM MEASURES OF 1805

Despite a limited success the measures proposed by Knesebeck and Courbière for training additional man power might be called the Reform of 1805. Of particular importance was their emphasis upon an increased number of trained cantonists. Rüchel also contributed important ideas but only Knesebeck and Courbière were able to visualize a cadre army.[56] It is evi-

[55] See Clausewitz, *Nachrichten*, pp. 471-74, and Jany, *op. cit.*, III, 540.

[56] *Cf.* Herrmann, *op. cit.*, p. 491. Jàny concludes, " The central idea of the Courbière proposal, 'the successive enlistment and training of young men,' five per company annually, was begun. *This is the basic idea of the later Krümper system.*" *Op. cit.*, III, 460; italics in the text.

EFFORTS AT REFORM BEFORE 1806

dent that on the eve of the campaign of 1806-1807 the training of *Krümper* had begun in a program that clearly anticipated what Scharnhorst and his circle were to attempt after 1807.

A different fate awaited the Land Reserve Battalions: the mobilization in the fall of 1805 dissolved the Emergency Commission and the work of developing these units passed to the High Council of War. This authority tried to overcome the opposition of the civil bureaucrats, who fulfilled Brunswick's prophecy in opposing the land militia. They entangled the formation of the Land Reserve in red tape until July 24, 1806 when a new Cabinet Order commanded the reexamination and revision of the entire plan. Fourteen days before the battle of Jena the first order for assembling the militia was sent to the Chambers of War and Domains. By dilatory tactics based on a stubborn opposition to the expansion of the army the civil bureaucracy made it impossible to carry out a much-needed reform.[57]

Only in Silesia which was free from the conflicting tendencies of the General Directory was a serious attempt made to create the Land Reserve. This experience brought to light the several weaknesses of the plan. Officers on the inactive list were reluctant to re-enter the service, especially if they had married heiresses or had retired to their estates. Only poor officers were willing to serve. Among the pensioned officers an alarming lack of patriotism was discovered. It was equally difficult to provide non-commissioned officers, since fifteen Silesian battalions required sixty sergeants and 480 corporals. The battalions, which had a complement of 9,120 men, were never assembled: the civil officials followed the canton regulations to the letter and exempted all land-owning peasants, as well as artisans and government employees, which left only 3,300 available men.[58]

Although Scharnhorst was aware that plans for a national militia had been drawn up, he offered a militia plan of his own in April, 1806. His manuscript contained more than a technical

[57] Ziekursch, *op. cit.*, pp. 86-87.
[58] *Ibid.*, CIII, 87-94; *Preuss. Archiv*, XCIII, 418-19.

description of a militia; it described the peril of the impending battles which would decide Prussia's fate, and the army's need of the moral power that came from a nation fighting for its existence. To the regular army Scharnhorst would add only 25,000 men, but he would arm the masses for a people's war by forming a popular militia. Scharnhorst never altered his conception of a militia distinct from the line, even after 1807; whereas Knesebeck and Courbière visualized a cadre army with militia reserves. Scharnhorst, however, recognized in the militia the army of the future, made up not of cosmopolitan fragments but of conscripted national elements.[59]

INCREASING THE ARMY'S MOBILITY

With the resumption of the Napoleonic wars in 1805 the formal attempts to change the relation of the subjects to the army had come to an end. Henceforth, the defence of Prussian neutrality took precedence over the need for reorganization and the troops were maintained on a war footing. Nevertheless, the mobilization of 1805 proved useful in revealing the army's defects.[60] The troops had been slow to assemble and it was evident from the army's sluggish movements that it would lack mobility both on the march and on the battlefield. Mobilization districts prepared in advance with war material and supplies were proposed in order to speed the concentration of troops, but it was easier to sketch such changes on paper than to carry them out. Mobilization was the concern of the civil as well as the military bureaucracy, and this division of responsibility made

[59] Lehmann, *Scharnhorst*, I, 378-81. Scharnhorst's plan was submitted to the Duke of Brunswick and the General Adjutant von Kleist; whether Frederick William III saw it remains unknown. See Jany, *op. cit.*, III, 532-33.

[60] *Die preussischen Kriegsvorbereitungen und Operationspläne von 1805*, pp. 14-20. The mobilization of 1805 was intended to safeguard Prussian neutrality in the war between France and Austria. Demobilization did not immediately occur in Prussia and the army remained on a war footing. Meanwhile, the military authorities made an investigation and embodied their recommendations in a *Promemoria* of May 16, 1806. *Archiv des Kriegsministeriums*, III, 146-86.

necessary a reorganization of the administrative bureaus in the proposed districts. Naturally the old antagonism between the civil bureaucracy and the army sprang up and the attempt to improve the mobilization perished.[61]

Two burdens reduced the mobility of the armed forces: artillery and an excessively heavy train. Artillery was lightened by eliminating some of the heavy pieces from the field equipment. Reserve cannon were reduced in numbers and were allocated to the fortresses lying along the anticipated lines of operations, which was a useful arrangement since the Prussian artillery reserve was mainly a replacement depot. The exchange of sixteen batteries of heavy six-pounders for light six-pounders and the elimination of the howitzer, mortar, and fusilier batteries completed the list of very practical measures for ridding the army of some of its dead weight.[62]

Mobility was still restricted by the great masses of baggage and the extra horses that were included in the train of the army. Any attempt to simplify the train not only violated cherished traditions but raised the larger question of the supply of the army in the field. Prussian operations were based on the assumption that the army could be supplied from fortresses or magazines that would be stocked in advance of the war. A massive train shuttled supplies back and forth from these places to the front. Requisitions were not ordinarily used and if a rapid advance were necessary, enough bread was baked beforehand to supply the troops. Reliance on cantonments instead of bivouacs was a further handicap to rapid movements.[63]

The entire subject of supply in the field was raised when the reformers asked the elimination of the numerous personal horses of the officers, and the abandonment of the wagons that bore the luxury articles officers believed necessary for their com-

61 *Ibid.*, III, 146-63.

62 *Ibid.*, III, 167-96, 225-26, 230-35.

63 Jähns, *op. cit.*, III, 2184-88; *Archiv des Kriegsministeriums*, III, 218-21. Administrative aspects of the supply problem are treated in Helfritz, *op. cit.*, pp. 173-77.

fort.[64] The extra pack and riding horses for each officer were not only a burden for the train personnel, but with a general shortage of horses in Europe the question of remounts was complicated. Both the king's adjutants proved sympathetic to the spirit of the suggested reforms. Kleist, though often a determined foe of change, thought that a reduction of the baggage would help in a war with the French. But loyalty to tradition led Field Marshal Brunswick to oppose the elimination of bread trains. His attitude may have been determined by the failure of the supply trains in his command at Valmy in 1792.[65]

Nevertheless, strong measures were taken to cut down the baggage and eliminate much of the heavy artillery. Actually, the munitions trains were reduced too much. Supply trains were still used, though requisitions were approved in certain circumstances. The impression that the Prussians had as much baggage as an oriental army arose mainly from the confusion of the retreat in the autumn of 1806. But the king's expressed wish, " To make our army more like the French," came too late to be carried into effect.[66]

[64] *Archiv des Kriegsministeriums*, III, 167, 208, 214. In 1806 York took into the field two extra uniforms, ten pairs of gloves, four pairs of trousers and vests, an extra hat, cloaks, personal clothing in great abundance, four pairs of leather breeches, fifteen pairs of stockings, eight nightgowns, five night caps, three table cloths, thirty-six napkins, a mattress, five pillows, a red silk bed cover, two bed pans, a set of china and silver, cooking utensils, a coffee grinder, eight razors, twelve glasses, and twenty-five bottles of liquor. This collection was carried in a wagon and a light chaise. *Ibid.*, III, 139-40.

[65] *Ibid.*, III, 197-206, 218-21.

[66] Goltz, *op. cit.*, p. 307; Jany, *op. cit.*, III, 530-31. Failure to adopt the French foraging methods was not serious. For the campaign of 1806 it is noteworthy that the French developed great magazines in Bamberg and Kranach; there was never any lack of attention to trains and the transportation of food and material in the French army. Finally, in evaluating the Prussian insistence on magazines, it ought to be remembered that Napoleon's disaster in retreating from Moscow resulted from his decision to cut off from his bases in East Prussia, Poland, and Lithuania. See Liebert, " Die Rüstungen Napoleons für den Feldzug 1812," *Militär-Wochenblatt*, Beiheft 1888, pp. 355-92, especially pp. 367-75.

EFFORTS AT REFORM BEFORE 1806 85

REORGANIZATION IN DIVISIONS

The same judgment could be passed on the decision in 1806 to organize the army in divisions. Scharnhorst had long urged that the Prussians adopt the divisional organization of the French army. In 1801 he had called the king's attention to divisions,[67] but Frederick William saw no need then for arraying the army in anything more than the van, the mass, and the rear guard.[68] Royal approval for divisions was obtained only in the eleventh hour when the troops had set off for the theater of war; while on the march they were reorganized in combat units made up of the several arms. In the main army of the Duke of Brunswick there were six, while Prince Hohenlohe had four. Each division consisted of two brigades of infantry, each numbering four to five battalions, a cavalry brigade, ten to fifteen squadrons strong, a battery of unmounted artillery, and another of mounted artillery. A fusilier battalion and five to ten squadrons of hussars and dragoons supplied the light troops for each division. The divisions were manifestly weak in artillery, and further, by scattering the cavalry it became impossible to use the shock tactics for which the horsemen had been trained.[69]

These measures imperiled the fighting power of the armed forces, for the Prussians had an insufficient number of commanders capable of leading divisions. Training was one-sided and few officers knew the technical nature of the other arms.[70]

---

[67] See Scharnhorst's letter to Frederick William III in 1801, *Scharnhorsts Briefe*, I, 241-42.

[68] Lehmann, *Scharnhorst*, I, 237-40, 299-300, 306-07, 375, and Beilage II, pp. 527-30, *Die ersten preussischen Armee-Divisionen*. Klippel, *op. cit.*, III, 577-81, has Scharnhorst's plan for divisions in 1811. His early recommendation of divisions had been presented in an article in the *Denkwürdigkeiten der militärischen Gesellschaft*, II (1803), 91-96. For the French ideas about the combination of arms see R. Villate, " Le mouvement des idées militaires en France au XVIIIe siècle," *Revue d'Histoire Moderne*, X (1935), 255-56.

[69] Lehmann, *Scharnhorst*, I, 412-13; Conrady, *op. cit.*, I, 45-46.

[70] Schmidt, *op. cit.*, pp. 433-35. Gneisenau commented that the Prussians tried to imitate the French without thinking about the generals capable of commanding divisions. *Reorganisation der Preuss. Armee*, I, 8.

The sudden adoption of divisions thus gave rise to problems which neither the experience nor the training of the army could solve. The episode well illustrates the charge that Scharnhorst was often moved by academic rather than practical considerations. There can be no question that in other armies divisions developed more power than the customary organization. Still, Scharnhorst did not consider the inopportune time for reorganizing the Prussian army or its lack of trained divisional officers.[71]

The Problem of Military Reform Before 1806

The reform efforts before 1806, although undertaken seriously, faltered before the indifference of the crown and the hostile attitude of the political and military advisers. Frederick William III was not inclined to assume responsibility and remained timid and hesitant. His esteem for the military technicians was unfortunate and none of his military aides could be called a radical reformer.[72] Brunswick, Möllendorf, Kleist, and all the others were steeped in the spirit of the mercenary army. Nor was the king's cabinet government adapted to the cause of reform. The General Adjutants were sycophants who agreed with the king and avoided discussion of such unpleasant topics as military reorganization.[73] No minister of war stood at hand to guide the evolution of the army; military and civil administration was a many-headed hydra.[74]

---

[71] See Boyen, *Erinnerungen*, I, 216-17. Scharnhorst seems to have believed that more effective staff work could compensate for the inexperience of the division commanders. At such a late hour it was impossible to change the traditional Prussian methods of conducting operations merely by issuing new instructions to the staff officers. *Cf.* Lehmann, *Scharnhorst*, I, 410-11.

[72] Conrady, *op. cit.*, I, 41. Helfritz' conclusion is more favorable to Frederick William III and his military advisers. *Op. cit.*, pp. 222-23.

[73] The storm over the adjutants broke before 1806. See *Preuss. Archiv*, XCIII, 10, 18-19, 21, 39-40.

[74] Clausewitz, *Nachrichten*, pp. 420-29. Boyen enumerated the reasons for Prussia's downfall as: 1. the leadership which thought in terms of concessions and prestige values; 2. the overconfidence of the army officers;

In Austria far-reaching military reforms had been carried out before 1805. There the energy and perseverance of the Archduke Charles had made possible the establishment in 1801 of a Ministry of War under a single responsible head. In the same year what amounted to a General Staff was created, and universal service for men between the ages of eighteen and forty was decreed in the hereditary Hapsburg lands. A reform of the army's organization, supply, and justice was also carried out. Although interrupted by the campaign of 1805 the work of the Archduke Charles by 1809 had not only incorporated many of the advantages of French practice in the Austrian army, but had introduced principles of training and organization that anticipated those of a half-century later.[75]

The solution to the military problems that faced the absolute monarchies fighting Napoleon depended upon the discovery of men who could instill the spirit of the new methods of war in their armies without shaking the state by revolution. No one man played this role in Prussia but Scharnhorst was the outstanding figure after 1806.[76] By emphasizing the use of the whole nation in war at a time when nationalism was drawing rulers and subjects together, Scharnhorst and the later reformers were able to build on the foundations of the old army.

3. the unwillingness of the civil officials to grant more money to the army; 4. the neglect of all that had to do with real preparation for war. *Erinnerungen*, I, 184-86.

75 Criste, *op. cit.*, II, 10-14, 171-78, 199-227, 391-412. The Austrian military reforms were known to Scharnhorst. See his letter of Mar. 18, 1809 to Count Götzen, thanking him for information on the organization of the Austrian army. *Scharnhorsts Briefe*, I, 362-63.

76 Eberhard Kessel, "Die Wandlung der Kriegskunst im Zeitalter der französischen Revolution," *Historische Zeitschrift*, CXLVIII (1933), 265-66.

CHAPTER IV
THE BATTLE OF JENA AND THE FIRST REFORMS

At Basel in 1795 when Prussia had withdrawn from the First Coalition, an uneasy peace had been secured between revolutionary France and autocratic Prussia. From that date until the outbreak of war in 1806 the Prussian policy of neutrality had not only assisted Napoleon in obtaining control of German politics, but had cost the Prussians the support of their former ally, Austria, not to mention the loss of whatever moral prestige Prussia had possessed. Neither Austria nor Prussia as the leading Germanic powers showed any real concern for the ancient forms of German public life, and when the secularization of ecclesiastical lands began in 1801 both had shamelessly entered the traffic for abbeys and whole dioceses. Prussia's gains were minor, some Westphalian bishoprics and monastic properties, and several former free towns, but they could be included among the so-called dividends of neutrality. The real territorial prize with which Prussia hoped to be rewarded for dangling between Napoleon and his enemies was Hanover.

Origins of the War of 1806

Some restraint was imposed on Prussian eagerness to annex Hanover by the circumstance that its elector was also the King of England. As a member of the Armed Neutrality, Prussia was emboldened in 1801 to occupy Hanover for a few months; this occupation of a state nominally under Prussian protection together with the secularization of church lands had serious repercussions throughout Germany. Despite the strain between England and France in the spring of 1803 Prussian diplomacy moved too ponderously to keep pace with events, and Frederick William III was loath to accept his ministers' advice and again seize Hanover. When French troops became established in the electorate, Prussia was reduced to an ignominious bargaining that further injured its prestige abroad and disgusted patriotic elements at home. Very shortly thereafter the patriots reached a new level of despair because of the fumbling diplomacy that lost the opportunity in 1805 to stand with Austria and Russia against Napoleon.[1]

A new course had been forecast in that year when Frederick William became enraged by French troops trespassing upon Prussian territory. Since Russian troops were threatening the same violation in the east, Frederick William's faith in his policy of neutrality was shaken to the extent of admitting an agreement (the Treaty of Potsdam, November 3, 1805) with Tsar Alexander. The Prussian army was mobilized and Napoleon was threatened with armed intervention if he did not comply with Prussian demands for a new European settlement. All the force of this proposal was lost by the procrastination of Haugwitz, the Prussian envoy. He was adroitly handled by the Emperor, who succeeded in impressing him with the advantage of an alliance even before the French army had settled the issue at Austerlitz. This reversal of Austro-Russian fortunes brought the nation, which in the previous month had boldly proposed a new map of Europe, once again under French tutelage.

The humiliation of Prussia's diplomatic defeat in 1805 was softened only by the promise contained in the treaty of alliance with France: when a general European peace had been arranged Prussia was to obtain Hanover. Throughout the spring of 1806 Prussian diplomacy followed a tortuous path in order to attain that goal. Both the king and his ministers deliberately closed their eyes to the danger of Napoleon's troops concentrating in Germany and even made haste to comply with his requests in domestic affairs. Every illusion that these sacrifices would bring the promised reward was swept away by the news, which reached Berlin on August 6, that Napoleon had offered Hanover to England. Frederick William III's reaction was

[1] For the background of Prussian diplomacy, consult G. S. Ford, *Hanover and Prussia, 1795-1803: A Study in Neutrality* (New York, 1903); and Albert Sorel, *L'Europe et la Révolution Française* (Paris, 1885-1904), VII, 87-101.

swift but rash. This new proposal which came so soon after the establishment of the Confederation of the Rhine convinced him that Prussia was in great peril. On August 9 the army was mobilized and a free rein was given in both army and court circles to the anti-French war party. Prussia now demanded that Napoleon remove all his troops from Germany. For such a bold demand Prussia had neither the diplomatic nor the military resources. Except for some 21,000 Saxon troops of dubious military value, Prussia was unable to obtain immediate aid from any other nation. Austria remained neutral, and Russia, delayed by a war with Turkey, intervened too late to prevent the disasters that overwhelmed the Prussian army.

THE BATTLE OF JENA

On the Prussian side the supreme command was entrusted to the Duke of Brunswick, whose age and whose sympathy for the French combined to deprive the army of vigorous leadership. And the Duke's authority was impaired from the start by the king's decision to accompany the army into the field. Frederick William's presence reduced the commander in chief to the role of presiding over innumerable and interminable councils of war. No military plans had been laid in advance and valuable time was consumed in debates about Brunswick's insistence on a cautious defensive and Hohenlohe's proposal for an advance to the Main. Because the king wished to wait for the French reply to his ultimatum, insufficient attention was paid Scharnhorst's advice that the army must press forward as a unit and seek battle. Scharnhorst urged that the army move through the Thuringian forest to the plains beyond where the Prussian cavalry could be employed effectively.[2]

The actual march routes selected for the ponderous movements of the Prussian army led nowhere; Napoleon on the other

[2] The best accounts of the battle of Jena are in Oscar von Lettow-Vorbeck, *Der Krieg von 1806 und 1807* (Berlin, 1892-1899, 4 v.); and P. Foucart, *Campagne de Prusse 1806* (Paris, 1890). In English both F. L. Petre, *Napoleon's Conquest of Prussia — 1806* (London, 1907), and F. N. Maude, *1806, the Jena Campaign* (London, 1909), can be recommended.

BATTLE OF JENA AND THE FIRST REFORMS 91

hand marched straight on Prussia and Saxony. Despite the urgent necessity of concentration, for the Prussians had been able to mobilize only 147,720 men to oppose a *bataillon quarré* of 160,000 French, the council of war deferred to the princes each of whom insisted on a separate command. Some unity of action might still have been obtained had the army not been scattered over such a great area. But a faulty disposition contributed to the defeat by exposing the separated corps to crushing attacks.

In the campaign that followed French leadership was immeasurably superior to the Prussian, although at first the conflicting orders of the marshals hampered the French preparation for war. The confusion ended when Napoleon took personal command on September 28. His foresight in placing the army in cantonments on the Danube after the campaign of 1805 enabled the French to concentrate rapidly behind the screen of the Thuringian forest. All the French forces were on the march by October 8 and since the Prussian leaders had not resolved their plan, the initiative rested with Napoleon. Political considerations helped to determine his strategy: the menace of the alliance between Prussia and Russia could be eliminated at a stroke by a crushing defeat of the Prussians, who had been rash enough to take the field without waiting for their ally.

With confidence both in the quality of his army and in its numerical superiority, Napoleon plunged boldly through the Thuringian forest intent on battle. The first clash between the rival armies occurred on October 10 at Saalfeld. Here a detached force under Prince Louis Ferdinand was overwhelmed by Lannes' attack, which cost the Prussian nobleman his life and thereby increased the gloom that was beginning to settle over Brunswick's headquarters. As late as October 12 his scattered forces might have been concentrated, but time was wasted in idle movements and discussions. Meanwhile, the French by the extraordinary tempo of their marches had turned the left flank of the Prussian army, whose leaders now completely aroused to the dangers facing them, determined upon a retreat to protect their communications toward Berlin.

This decision was unknown to Napoleon when he reached Jena on October 13 and set out with Lannes to reconnoiter the plateau above the town on which Hohenlohe's corps was arrayed. Since the French cavalry had been held back in order to achieve a complete surprise, Napoleon had not been fully informed of the Prussian dispositions. He concluded therefore that the main strength of the enemy lay before him at Jena. Actually it was only an advance guard of 48,000 men posted there to protect Brunswick's withdrawal of the principal army to what the Prussian command referred to as "better positions." While this movement was being carried out, Davout's corps advancing westward upon the Prussian flank collided with Brunswick's army at Auerstädt. The stage was then set for the twin battles of Auerstädt and Jena fought virtually within sight of one another on October 14, 1806.

A dense fog during the night of October 13-14 concealed the tremendous efforts of Napoleon's troops to bring cannon and wagons up the commanding height of the battlefield of Jena, the Landgrafenberg. Hohenlohe's feeble attempts to interfere with this coup and his stubborn belief that the French would try to reach the plateau by the wagon road instead of the almost trackless and choked ravines led to his undoing. All his preparations proved futile, even his appeal to Rüchel who commanded another isolated advance guard. When the sun broke through the fog in the morning the Prussians were faced by a French army of 55,600 men. By noon French reenforcements swelled this strength to 95,900 men, drawn up with Soult and Ney on the right, Lannes and the Guards holding the high ground in the center, while Augereau was on the left.

Lannes' advance opened the battle and though Hohenlohe's troops offered furious resistance their strength was overcome when the French wings joined the assault. Early in the afternoon Napoleon sensed that a decision was near and ordered the Guards and the cavalry reserve into action. Their vigorous attack swept into retreat not only the remnants of Hohenlohe's corps but all of Rüchel's troops, who had arrived too late to be

BATTLE OF JENA AND THE FIRST REFORMS 93

of any assistance. All these fugitives, pressed northward by the French cavalry, began to mingle with the Prussian troops falling back from Auerstädt in order to join Hohenlohe for support! When the fate of his corps became generally known the Prussian officers lost all control and what had been a retreat became a rout.

Auerstädt and its Aftermath

A generous historian could point to Napoleon's numerical superiority as the cause of the Prussian defeat at Jena, but no real explanation for Auerstädt other than Davout's superior leadership and the superb fighting qualities of his troops can be offered. Brunswick commanding 48,000 Prussians of whom 12,000 were in reserve under Kalckreuth, was defeated by 26,000 men led by the Marshal. The battle was a triumph for French mobility; Davout by rapid movements succeeded in reenforcing his lines wherever they were threatened, and made his small force count for more than his opponent's cumbersome army. The Prussian reserve was thrown in only during the last moments because Kalckreuth was reluctant to act without explicit orders from Brunswick. That ill-fated commander had been mortally wounded during the battle and it was Frederick William III who made the decision to withdraw toward Jena. No news had reached him of the disaster that had occurred there and he expected to join the fresh troops of Hohenlohe and Rüchel.

Prussian survivors from both battles immediately began a flight toward the fortress of Magdeburg and then to the Baltic coast for a last stand. Yet the Prussian army was powerless to offer battle again; the disorderly retreat threw the army into extraordinary confusion; the baggage and most of the artillery were abandoned. Great hardships befell the troops because the officers, true to their code of war, refused to requisition food from Prussian subjects. They were not so considerate of their honor in other respects. Scarcely two days after the battles there began a disgraceful series of capitulations; the eighty-four year old Marshal von Möllendorf led off by yielding 10,000 men in Erfurt to Murat and Ney. Berlin was occupied by the French on October 25 and three days later, at Prenzlau near Stettin, Hohenlohe surrendered to Murat. Only Blücher remained in the field and he bowed to overwhelming forces at Lübeck on November 7. One by one the Prussian fortresses, Spandau, Stettin, Magdeburg, Hameln, and Cüstrin, hauled down their colors, often without even so much as the firing of a shot. The French did not bother to pursue those weak forces that made their escape across the Vistula. Amid this wreckage of his armed forces the king and his ministers painfully made their way to East Prussia to await the advancing Russians.[3]

ROYAL REFORM DECREES

For once in a lifetime of indecision the king rose to the occasion and issued a series of decrees recommending immediate changes in the tactics, discipline, and organization of his remaining armed forces. These proclamations were models of clarity, when compared for example, with his somewhat muddled account of the battle of Auerstädt.[4] For about a year the monarch's interest in reform remained at fever heat; and his own proposals were followed by naming a commission which began the task of overhauling the army.

Four decrees issued by the king toward the end of the year 1806 formed a program for this task. In his memoir from Osterode, dated November 18, 1806, and in his *Instruction for the Generals with the Army in East Prussia* issued somewhat later, Frederick William described the operations to be carried out in

[3] There is abundant contemporary literature describing and analyzing the military events of 1806. Consult H. D. von Bülow, *Kritik des Feldzuges in Deutschland im Jahre 1806* (Berlin and Leipzig, 1808); *Die wahrscheinlichen Hauptursachen der Unglücksfälle bei den deutschen Waffen im Jahre 1806* (Jena, 1807); J. J. Rühle von Lilienstern, *Bericht eines Augenzeugen von dem Feldzuge ... 1806* (Tübingen, 1807); Julius von Voss, *Was war nach der Schlacht bei Jena zur Rettung des preussischen Staates zu tun?* (Berlin, 1807).

[4] Cf. Paul Bailleu, "Die Schlacht von Auerstedt. Eigenhändige Relation König Friedrich Wilhelm's III.," *Deutsche Rundschau*, CI (1899), 382-99.

the war with France which was still in dismal progress.⁵ Prussia's military weakness and the enemy's great experience made artful maneuvers useless. Every effort was to be made, however, to carry on vigorous warfare; operations and tactics were to be energetic and bold. By making a complete reconnaissance—a new element of warfare for that generation of Prussian officers—the attack could be made at the most favorable moment. There was some evidence of the painful lesson learned at Auerstädt and Jena in the king's italicized sentence that scattered dispositions were to be avoided!⁶

A third memorandum dated December 1, 1806 was issued from Ortelsburg in East Prussia. This document began a summary reform of the officers' corps by cashiering the commanding officers of every fortress which had surrendered without offering any real resistance. The luckless commandant of Cüstrin was sentenced to be shot. All the officers involved in the capitulation of Hohenlohe's corps at Prenzlau were dismissed from the service. The same fate befell every other officer and civil servant who had neglected his duty, or violated his oath to the crown, or brought shame on his station. None of these was mentioned by name since the royal announcement was intended only as an introduction to a thorough investigation of the officers' corps. Still, the king's action was unprecedented in Prussian history.⁷

For the future the *Ortelsburger Publicandum* laid down the rule that capitulations would be punishable by death, that offic-

---

5 General instructions of this kind had occasionally been issued by Frederick the Great to his officers. *Cf.* David G. von Scharnhorst, *Unterricht des Königs von Preussen an die Generale seiner Armee* (Hanover, 1794). That part of the *Osterode Publicandum* dealing with tactics may be found in *Reorganisation der Preuss. Armee*, I, 13-15.

6 *Ibid.*, I, 14-15.

7 The *Ortelsburger Publicandum* is given in *1806 Das Preussische Offizierkorps und die Untersuchung der Kriegsereignisse* (Berlin, 1906), pp. 7-10. This work will be cited hereafter as *1806 Das Preuss. Offizierkorps. Cf.* Count Henckel von Donnersmarck, *Erinnerungen aus meinem Leben* (Zerbst, 1846), pp. 52 ff., for the reaction of the army officers to the king's announcements.

ers who left the field of battle unwounded would be cashiered, and that men who threw away their arms and took flight would be shot. Finally, the king's disgust for the miserable conduct of his aristocratic officers led him to take the revolutionary step of opening the corps to the non-aristocratic elements. He wrote, " As long as the war lasts, the non-commissioned officer and man, when distinguished by cleverness and presence of mind, will make as good an officer as the noble." [8] A fourth memorandum, undated but written about the same time, dealt exclusively with tactics and the conduct of the troops in battle. Here the king made a remarkable departure from the cherished line formations of the Prussian army by recommending columns for the attack. In this and his other writings Frederick William made it clear that Prussia would make greater use of *tirailleur* tactics as well as the other new methods of fighting.[9]

Eylau and Friedland

Though the royal reform proposals were excellently conceived, not even a complete change in tactical methods could compensate for the numerical weakness of the Prussian army. There were available only 29,000 men of L'Estocq's corps consisting of the East Prussian and South Prussian regiments which had not been mobilized with the rest of the army in August, 1806. When it became certain that Tsar Alexander would provide assistance against the French, an order of September 30 placed these troops on a war footing and they were sent eastward to join the Russians. Upon this contingent and the Tsar's army Frederick William now rested all his hopes.[10] By the end of November, 1806 his ally had placed strong forces

---

[8] *1806 Das Preuss. Offizierkorps*, pp. 10, and 8-10; Herrmann, *op. cit.*, pp. 495-96.

[9] *Reorganisation der Preuss. Armee*, I, 11-13; Sautermeister, *op. cit.*, pp. 21-25. Frederick William had even been stirred by the idea of a universal levy. During the fall of 1806 various East Prussian leaders had been consulted about the formation of a *Landsturm*, but it had been generally agreed that Prussia lacked the means for arming and organizing a mass army. Jany, *op. cit.*, III, 599.

[10] *Ibid.*, III, 549, 595.

BATTLE OF JENA AND THE FIRST REFORMS 97

in the field and in the first serious clash with the French, at Eylau on February 7-8, 1807, the Russians aided by L'Estocq's corps fought a bloody but indecisive battle.[11]

Frederick William's conduct during the fall and winter was admirable: he resisted Napoleon's attempts to draw him into negotiations for a separate peace, and with his hopes raised by the valiant fighting at Eylau, he flatly rejected Napoleon's peace offer of February 20. Napoleon did not rely upon diplomacy alone. During the winter the *Grande Armée* had been reinforced by new levies and when the spring campaign began it considerably outnumbered the Russians. Additional French troops were released from siege duty by forcing the surrender of Danzig and Neisse, two fortresses remaining in Prussian hands, before the Russians opened their campaign.

The leadership of Bennigsen, the Russian general, left much to be desired. For vague reasons he occupied the town of Friedland with the river Alle at his back. Early on the morning of June 14, 1807 he attacked a French advance guard posted outside the town which held firm long enough to permit the main French army to assemble. By late afternoon Bennigsen was trapped in an extremely awkward position facing a numerically superior enemy. Napoleon's well-planned counterattack succeeded in driving half the Russian force through the narrow streets of Friedland and over the pontoon bridges amid a holocaust of artillery fire, while holding the other half of the Russian army away from the town. This isolated force fought stubbornly but thousands of Russians perished and many men flung themselves into the river to escape. Though the French victory was more costly than the Emperor's bulletin admitted, the *Grande Armée* was clearly able to continue the campaign to its own advantage.

---

11 For accounts of the campaign in 1807 see Lettow-Vorbeck, *op. cit.*; F. L. Petre, *Napoleon's Campaigns in Poland 1806-1807* (London, 1906); and Colmar von der Goltz, *Von Jena bis Eylau* (Berlin, 1907). There is a short but very clear account of Friedland in Harold T. Parker, *Three Napoleonic Battles* (Durham, 1944).

98   PRUSSIAN MILITARY REFORMS 1786-1813

This circumstance, together with England's refusal to send strong forces to the continent and Austria's unwillingness to abandon its neutrality, made Tsar Alexander willing to listen to Napoleon's overtures. A truce was arranged on June 21 and four days later Alexander and Napoleon met with much solemnity on a raft anchored in the river Niemen. Frederick William, thus abandoned by his erstwhile ally, was not admitted to the conference until the second day and then only as a chagrined spectator. Not even the entreaties of the beautiful Queen Louise of Prussia could obtain better terms from the conqueror. Prussia had no choice but to bow to the hard conditions imposed at Tilsit on July 9, 1807.

The Peace of Tilsit

This settlement provided a breathing space in which the reorganization of the state and the army could begin. By the terms of the Peace of Tilsit Prussia lost approximately half its population and territory. The pre-war Prussian lands of 5,570 square miles with 9,752,731 inhabitants shrank after Tilsit to 2,877 square miles with 4,938,000 inhabitants. Military reform had been made difficult before 1806 by the financial weakness of the state; after Tilsit the loss of rich provinces made the possibility of a complete military reorganization even more remote. A new burden was imposed in the form of heavy contributions to the French, and the support of the victor's garrisons which were dotted over all the provinces west of the Vistula.[12] Prussia was prostrate before the conqueror, with its field armies smashed by successive defeats and driven into the eastern corner of the realm. Except for Graudenz, Pillau, Colberg, Glatz,

---

12 The evacuation was to have been completed by the French on October 1, 1807, but they removed their troops from the right of the Vistula only. Lehmann, *Scharnhorst*, II, 154. *Cf.* Herman Granier, ed., *Berichte aus der Berliner Franzosenzeit 1807-1809* (Publikationen aus den Königlich Preussischen Staatsarchiven, Leipzig, 1913), LXXXVIII, 89-90, 246-51, 278, for documents depicting the burden of French occupation. This volume will be cited hereafter as *Preuss. Archiv*, LXXXVIII.

Silberburg, and Cosel, all fortresses were to be garrisoned by the French. In the space of ten months Prussia had been reduced from the first military power in Germany to a position among the last.[13]

Military matters were considered only in two articles of the Peace of Tilsit, and even these did not relate to the Prussian army. In Article XVI the King of Saxony was given the right to a military road through Prussia, and in Article XXVIII it was stipulated that Prussia and France would promptly make a treaty governing the return of occupied territory and providing for its civil and military administration.[14] Prussia's control over the size of the army and its organization was in no way impaired by the Peace of Tilsit. To what extent the numerous French garrisons might interfere with its military autonomy was another matter, but there were neither legal obligations nor extraordinary diplomatic commitments affecting national defence. For the course of the reforms until the autumn of 1808 this comparative freedom from French restrictions was an important consideration. Only the emptiness of the treasury and the opinion of the king restrained the enthusiasm of the military reformers.[15] Moreover Frederick William was less inclined to oppose a reform if it did not violate the spirit of a Prussian treaty. Not until September 8, 1808 when the Prussians signed the Treaty of Paris was the size of the army limited to 42,000 men.[16] Hence it cannot be argued that immediately after the Peace of Tilsit there was a need for a *Krümper* training program to deceive the French.

[13] Georg F. von Martens, *Recueil des principaux traités* (2nd ed., Göttingen, 1817-1835), VIII, 661-68.

[14] *Ibid.*, VIII, 665 (Article XVI), 667-68 (Article XXVIII). Article XXVIII was put into effect by a treaty signed at Königsberg on July 12, 1807. None of its provisions affected the size of the Prussian army. *Ibid.*, VIII, 668-70.

[15] *Cf.* H. von Beguelin, "Die finanzielle Lage des preussischen Staates nach der Katastrophe," *Franzosenzeit in deutschen Landen*, I, 175-78.

[16] *Recueil des traités de la France* (Paris, 1864-1907, 23 vols. in 24), II, 272-73.

Establishment of the Military Reorganization Commission

It had been customary since 1786 to entrust military reform to a commission and Frederick William III did not depart from this practice. On July 15, 1807 he asked Scharnhorst and Count Lottum to supervise the demobilization of the army and arrange for the release of officers taken prisoner.[17] They were not to consider new troop levies until the financial condition of the nation had been thoroughly examined. Ten days later, on July 25, more members were added to this delegation whose purpose was made evident in its title, the Military Reorganization Commission. In order than this body might obtain information about foreign military developments an advisory membership was considered for Lieutenant Colonel Hieronymus Roedlich, an Austrian officer who entered Prussian service during the summer of 1807. He did not actually become a member, but his nomination was indicative of Prussian interest in the military reforms previously carried out in Austria.[18]

Although the reform commission was an undertaking of the king's own will, he imperiled its work by dividing the membership between reformers and conservatives.[19] Scharnhorst was the most outstanding member of the reform party. To his pres-

---

17 *Preuss. Archiv*, XCIV, 1-2. All officers and officials living in ceded territory were released from their oaths. See *Sammlung der für die Königlichen Preussischen Staaten erschienenen Gesetze und Verordnungen von 1806 bis zum 27ten Oktober 1810* (Berlin, 1822), pp. 168-69. This volume will be cited henceforth as *Gesetzsammlung 1806-1810*.

18 *Preuss. Archiv*, XCIV, 8. Roedlich was an inventor and a writer on technical-military subjects. Scharnhorst had a high respect for him. *Cf. Scharnhorsts Briefe*, I, 442.

19 Jacques M. E. Godefroy Cavaignac, *La formation de la Prusse contemporaine* (2nd ed., Paris, 1897-1898), I, 389. In a letter to Clausewitz of Nov. 27, 1807 Scharnhorst referred to the membership of the commission as "heterogeneous." *Scharnhorsts Briefe*, I, 334. R. Stadelmann, "Das Duell zwischen Scharnhorst und Borstell im Dezember 1807," *Historische Zeitschrift*, CLXI (1940), 263-76, disputes the theory of a struggle between two parties on the commission. His article is an excellent summary of the recent findings with respect to the social and political forces as well as the motives of the leading personalities in the era of reform.

tige as a military writer and scholar he had added a great reputation as a staff officer for his distinguished service in the East Prussian winter battles. His grasp of military operations together with his personal bravery on the battlefield had singled him out as a leader of exceptional force. Yet to many narrow-minded Prussians he remained a "foreigner," a circumstance that explains in part why he never became an intimate associate of the king.[20]

Gneisenau whose liberal outlook was tempered by an equally practical point of view was allied with Scharnhorst. Boyen, who joined the commission early in 1808, also believed in the necessity of a thorough military reorganization. Other reformers were Major von Grolman, a radical who made the most extreme proposals, and Count Götzen, who belonged to the commission for a short time during 1808.[21] Although not a formal member of the commission, Captain Clausewitz, the devoted pupil and adjutant of Major General Scharnhorst, was sufficiently familiar with its work to make suggestions and be entrusted with the drafting of plans.[22] Two civilians sided with the reformers and offered them valuable aid and counsel: Stein, who had the right of participating in the commission's work, and General Auditor Könen, who dealt with the administration of military justice.[23]

Four conservatives completed the membership of the commission on which the equal division of opinion gave rise to much bickering and even to open quarrels. Major General von Massenbach was a dull cavalry officer who opposed change but was

[20] Boyen, *Erinnerungen*, I, 218, 289, 294. Frederick William's attitude toward the commission is interpreted in Schmidt-Bückeburg, *op. cit.*, p. 13; and Herrmann, *op. cit.*, pp. 497-98.

[21] Grolman's appointment was deliberately secured in order to offset the influence of the commission's conservative members. Cavaignac, *op. cit.*, I, 389-90.

[22] See Scharnhorst's letter to Clausewitz of Nov. 27, 1807 in *Scharnhorsts Briefe*, I, 333-36, a fine summary of Scharnhorst's reform ideals.

[23] Lehmann, *Scharnhorst*, II, 105-06. *Cf. Reorganisation der Preuss. Armee*, I, 24-52.

not inclined to defend his opinions vigorously. The Lieutenant Colonels von Lottum and von Bronikowsky were resolute champions of the old Prussian military system. Lieutenant Colonel von Borstell, who joined the commission in October, 1807, was an enlightened conservative who admitted the need for certain changes in the army's organization and methods. However, Borstell took every objection to his opinions as a personal affront and by December his dislike for Scharnhorst became so intense that the work of the reformers was imperiled.[24]

This crisis made evident the need of a leader in the reform movement and the king wisely chose Scharnhorst. Borstell and Bronikowsky withdrew and their places were taken by Count Götzen and Major von Boyen. Lottum remained a member of the commission and since he had succeeded Kleist as General Adjutant on August 18, he had access to the king's private councils. There can be little doubt that he used this advantage to speak against some of the reform proposals. Stein eventually obtained the right of direct audience for Scharnhorst, but his work as the reform leader was made less effective because Frederick William continued to rely upon his private military advisers. From the membership of the commission alone it was apparent that the reformers faced powerful adversaries. Changes that did meet with the commission's approval had still to overcome the entrenched opposition of army officers trained in the school of Frederick the Great; these officers regarded the reforms of Scharnhorst and his associates as the impractical suggestions of military theorists.[25]

[24] Stadelmann, *op. cit.*, pp. 267-75, sheds new light on this difference of opinion. Also consult Cavaignac, *op. cit.*, I, 390-91. Major General von Massenbach is not to be confused with Colonel Christian von Massenbach, who had been a reformer before 1806 but was made a scapegoat for the disasters of that year because he advised Hohenlohe to capitulate at Prenzlau.

[25] *Preuss. Archiv*, XCIV, 41. See Scharnhorst's letter to the king of Dec. 4, 1808 protesting the criticism and denunciation of York, Kalckreuth, and Köckeritz, *Scharnhorsts Briefe*, I, 352-54. Also consult Boyen, *Erinnerungen*, I, 294. According to Boyen the king still wanted a well-drilled and well-disciplined line army. *Ibid.*, I, 295. *Cf.* Justus Ide, *Die Entwicklung der preussischen Armee als Verfassungsbestandteil* (Kiel, 1936), pp. 24-25.

Reform Programs

At the outset the king did not disappoint the reformers. He prepared an agenda of nineteen points, the *Guiding Principles for the Reorganization of the Army,* in which his recommendations rather than his commands were set forth.[26] In the first instance the king stressed the necessity of cashiering and punishing those officers whose conduct in the last campaign had not reflected honor on their uniform or their oath to the crown. The remaining paragraphs briefly outlined the changes that he desired: the end of foreign recruiting, the admission of non-aristocratic officers, a new method of educating officers, organization in divisions, better uniforms, reform of the supply system, reduction of baggage, prohibition of *Freiwächter,* a new organization for the cavalry, revised Articles of War, and new regulations for each branch of the service. In the space of nineteen paragraphs the king pointed out most of the shortcomings of the old army and concluded with a blessing for the work of the Military Reorganization Commission.[27]

September of 1807 brought forth strong reform proposals from two important ministers, Hardenberg and Altenstein, who dealt with military affairs at great length.[28] Both men agreed that without a formidable army Prussian recovery was impossible. Altenstein, in particular, felt that Prussia ought to become a military state, directing all its energies to its military institutions and to preparedness. To this end Altenstein advocated, "A

[26] *Preuss. Archiv,* XCIV, 8-15 (the title derives only from the archivist's summary). Scharnhorst commented favorably on the king's ideas in a letter to Count von der Goltz, Aug. 8, 1807, *Scharnhorsts Briefe,* I, 324.

[27] *Preuss. Archiv,* XCIV, 8-11; also *ibid.,* XCIV, 45-62, for amplification of the king's views presented through his adjutant before Aug. 20, 1807. Boyen considered the immediate needs to be: 1. ending the "company economy;" 2. better organization; and 3. an investigation of the officers. *Erinnerungen,* I, 293-94.

[28] Geh. Oberfinanzrat von Altenstein, *Über die Leitung des Preussischen Staats,* Sept. 11, 1807, in *Preuss. Archiv,* XCIII, 364-566, and Hardenberg, *Über die Reorganisation des Preussischen Staates,* Sept. 12, 1807, *ibid.,* XCIII, 302-63. See also H. Haussherr, "Hardenbergs Reformdenkschrift Riga 1807," *Historische Zeitschrift,* CLVII (1938), 267-308.

wholly new creation, not a renewal of the old, but rather an annihilation of the aged and decrepit forms." [29]

Both ministers favored the reconstruction of the army on a popular basis. " Military conscription should be wholly altered. All previous exemptions, without any exception, should be terminated. Everyone who does not serve the state in some way, should be obliged to perform military service in the regular and reserve troops." [30] This was Hardenberg's suggestion and Altenstein agreed in similar terms.[31] Details of the new army, its organization, armament, and training were worked out in both manuscripts, which were significant forecasts of what the reformers were to accomplish. A weakness of the pre-1806 system was sounded by Altenstein in his recommendation that military and civil administration be coordinated.[32] Altenstein's grasp of military costs was more realistic than Hardenberg's, since he recognized that finances would limit the army to 75,000 men.[33] Hardenberg's view that the pre-war strength could be maintained by the use of volunteers and conscripts was visionary.[34] On the whole, however, both memoirs presented practical views and encouragement to the reformers from men high in the affairs of state.[35]

INVESTIGATION OF THE OFFICERS' CORPS

Not until November 14, 1807 did the Military Reorganization Commission reply to the first point of the king's program

29 *Preuss. Archiv*, XCIII, 420.
30 *Ibid.*, XCIII, 323.
31 *Ibid.*, XCIII, 423-25.
32 *Ibid.*, XCIII, 430.
33 *Ibid.*, XCIII, 475.
34 *Ibid.*, XCIII, 345.

35 Note also Oberfinanzrat von Klewitz' *Grundidee zur Organisation des Preussischen Staats*, July 9, 1807, which urged unification of the army and the nation after the French example. *Ibid.*, XCIII, 568-69. Blücher also struck out in his blunt way for universal service in a report of Aug. 11, 1807. *Ibid.*, XCIV, 38.

BATTLE OF JENA AND THE FIRST REFORMS 105

which called for a purge of the officers' corps. The commission's slowness was evident but their outline of instructions for the investigating commission that was to deal with the disgraced officers recommended vigorous action against them.[36] By November 27 a new investigating body suggested by the king and vested by him with authority had come into being. This first offshoot of the Military Reorganization Commission was entitled the Superior Investigating Commission and a royal instruction fixed its membership, agenda, and procedure.[37]

Frederick William's irresolution was evident in his appointments which balanced adherents of the old order against the new. Indeed, the investigations of this commission provided fewer results than the reformers had hoped for, although its tedious sessions at Königsberg dragged out until 1814. At first public attention was focused on the officers' trials because they promised to be spectacular. Less notice was taken by the public of the Military Reorganization Commission which worked quietly upon more serious but less publicized matters.[38]

Instructions to the Superior Investigating Commission were specific: it was to investigate the capitulations of the fortresses and the field armies and determine in each case the strength of the enemy, the capacity for defence, and the preparations of the commanding officer. Battle orders were also to be examined in order to determine whether the officers' conduct had been completely honorable. Sentences for the guilty officers had to be approved by the king whose mood at first promised little clemency.[39]

Such sweeping powers to probe the conduct of the officers were undoubtedly made necessary by the public outcry against them in 1806. The debacle called forth widespread criticism which flayed all officers, even those of the highest rank, for their pedantry and incompetence. In its search for a scapegoat the

36 *Ibid.*, XCIV, 148-50. *Cf. 1806 Das Preuss. Offizierkorps*, pp. 12-13.
37 *Preuss. Archiv*, XCIV, 171-73; *Reorganisation der Preuss. Armee*, I, 55-57.
38 Herrmann, *op. cit.*, pp. 498-99; Ide, *op. cit.*, pp. 25-26.
39 *Preuss. Archiv*, XCIV, 171-73; *1806 Das Preuss. Offizierkorps*, pp. 13-15.

public singled out the officers and poured forth its wrath upon them. Even the press joined in the hue and cry. Archenholz, the famous editor who had been confident of victory before Jena, scoffed at the discomfited aristocrats.[40]

On December 10, 1807 at Königsberg the Superior Investigating Commission began its laborious inquiry. Because the dissolution of the army had scattered military personnel so widely, it proved impossible to locate all the officers and witnesses that were called. For this reason the inquiry was decentralized by forming tribunals in every regiment. Though the public showed great interest in these proceedings the king was at first opposed to newspaper reports.[41] Secrecy proved impossible because public advertisements were needed to find those officers who had left the service, and because journalists did not hesitate to attack the officers' corps in sensational articles. These accounts deepened the impression that the officers alone had been responsible for the military disasters of 1806.[42]

Most of the junior officers accused of dishonorable conduct during the campaign were tried in the regimental tribunals. Supervising these trials became the real business of the Superior Investigating Commission, although it did try commanding officers, the commandants of fortresses, and officers involved in the field capitulations. The commission worked ponderously after the fashion of the military bureaucrats: the papers accumulated for the archives amounted to not less than 606 volumes each containing more than 700 pages![43] At the outbreak of war

[40] See *Galerie preussische Charaktere, Vertraute Briefe, Feuerbrände*, and other publications and periodicals of 1806-1807 for accounts hostile to the Prussian officers. Cf. *Franzosenzeit in deutschen Landen*, I, 179-80.

[41] See the text and documents in *1806 Das Preuss. Offizierkorps*, pp. 15-17; also Vidal de la Blache, *op. cit.*, pp. 89-90.

[42] *1806 Das Preuss. Offizierkorps*, p. 18. Scharnhorst was very critical of such contemporary histories of the campaign as Lilienstern, *op. cit.*, but he praised Freiherr von Müffling, *Operationsplan der preussisch-sächsischen Armee im Jahre 1806* (Weimar, 1807). Cf. *Scharnhorsts Briefe*, I, 335, 340.

[43] *1806 Das Preuss. Offizierkorps*, pp. 20, 22. By 1808 the commission was acting as a bureau for the rehabilitation and employment of officers for

BATTLE OF JENA AND THE FIRST REFORMS 107

in 1813 the commission was still investigating the causes of the failure in 1806. Since the new campaign demanded the services of every officer, it was decided informally not to consider the military events in 1807 at all.[44]

FATE OF THE OFFICERS

Lack of documents and the contradictory nature of the testimony complicated the investigation of the twelve cases of surrender in the field during 1806. Every commanding officer, except Blücher who had surrendered at Lübeck for want of food and munitions, was held guilty. It proved very difficult to establish the guilt of officers who had surrendered their fortresses after a small show of force. Wherever a fortress had been located in a town, the civil population had urged the commandant to yield in order that they might be spared the hardship of a bombardment. But the king recommended vigorous prosecution because the fortress capitulations, curiously enough, had brought the loudest outcry from the public.[45] In the regimental tribunals the procedure was equally complicated. However, the regimental officers who sat on these tribunals tended to be lenient toward their comrades in arms. If an immediate acquittal could not be obtained, the matter was usually referred to the king or to the *Generalauditoriat*. By 1809 the regimental investigations had been concluded.[46]

The results of the disciplinary proceedings against the officers fell far short of the desired purge. There had been approximately 7,000 officers in the army before 1806, at least 6,500 of whom had participated in the campaign of 1806-1807, and 4,600 had been directly associated with the dissolution of the

whom the reduction of the army had brought actual hardship. *Ibid.*, pp. 30-31. Poverty among the officers is commented on in *Preuss. Archiv*, LXXXVIII, 278.

44 The entire inquiry had been made difficult by the loss during the retreat of almost all the army's plans and papers.

45 Boyen, *Erinnerungen*, I, 221-23; *1806 Das Preuss. Offizierkorps*, pp. 40-50.

46 *Ibid.*, pp. 50-64, 64-85.

army; nevertheless, only 208 officers were found guilty.[47] The attempt to remove all the incompetent and cowardly members from the corps amounted to little more than a bureaucratic exercise.[48]

The folly of condemning the entire officers' corps for the collapse of 1806-1807 is apparent from the fact that many officers who had been scapegoats at Jena and Auerstädt became heroes at Leipzig. More than half of the officers serving in 1813-1814 had been in the army in 1806-1807. And this half included almost all the officers of the field armies and most of the officers in responsible posts. Between 1807 and 1813 the total number of officers who left the service, including those who were furloughed or cashiered, amounted to 4,933. There remained in active service some 1,791 officers who had participated in the campaign of 1806-1807. Only ninety-eight of these men died before the war of 1813.[49]

At that time the expansion of the army and the creation of special units, such as the *Landwehr, Landsturm,* and volunteers, gave rise to a need for the old officers. Thousands of experienced officers had waited as inactives, living on half pay, and receiving quarters, bread, and charcoal from the government until the outbreak of war brought them back to active duty.[50] Not less than 3,898 officers of 1806-1807 served in the War of Liberation. In this war the total number of Prussian officers was not much greater than it had been in 1806, for there were approximately 7,350 officers in August, 1813. Amid the enthusiasm aroused by a victorious war the public forgot

[47] *Ibid.,* pp. 50, 65, 86.

[48] *Ibid.,* p. 86, and Anlage I, pp. 104-07. Schmidt, *op. cit.,* p. 432, cites a total of 7,166 officers in 1806.

[49] *1806 Das Preuss. Offizierkorps,* pp. 95-99, 105-07. These data are given in Schmidt, *op. cit.,* pp. 452-53: between 1807 and 1813, 2,911 officers left the army, or a total of 3,253 if the casualties of 1806-1807 are included. Jany, *op. cit.,* IV, 17, provides data for the year 1808: a total of 5,085 officers pensioned, dismissed, or on the inactive list; in active service were 1,638 officers.

[50] Scharnhorst, *Auszug,* pp. 34-35, 46-49.

that the officers had once been ridiculed for their failure at Jena and Auerstädt.[51]

REORGANIZATION OF THE ARMY

Since the end of July, 1807 the Military Reorganization Commission had been at work planning a reorganization of the armed forces. Reorganization rather than reform describes its work, and for the first six months the main task was the reconstruction, on paper, of the Prussian army. At first the estimates of the proper strength of regiments and battalions were too great and complements more suited to the financial resources of the state had to be assigned. For about a year after the formation of the Military Reorganization Commission it considered the reduction rather than the expansion of the army, and this necessity arose from Prussia's financial plight. New tables of organization had hardly been published when limits imposed on the size of the army by the Treaty of Paris (September 8, 1808) obliged the reformers to begin their tasks anew.[52]

Scharnhorst's first reform memoir of July 31, 1807 dealt with the capacity of the nation to restore its army. From the Prussian population of five millions an army of 120,000-150,000 men could be drawn, but revenues did not permit training more than 65,000 to 70,000 men. Consequently he considered the maximum strength to be sixteen infantry regiments and eighty cavalry squadrons. Seventeen battalions of garrison

---

51 All the authorities agree that about 3,900 officers of the old army served through the later wars against Napoleon, but there are great discrepancies in the compilations. See the table in Schmidt, *op. cit.*, p. 458. Non-commissioned officers in 1813-1814 were the same as those of 1806-1807. *Cf.* Scharnhorst, *Auszug*, p. 35.

52 Scharnhorst wrote graphically of the problem of limiting the army in letters dated Mar. 4 and 27, 1808, *Scharnhorsts Briefe*, I, 339-41. Writing to Müffling, he said, "Our reorganization of the army consists thus far in the organization of reductions." *Ibid.*, I, 340. It is noteworthy that this was written six months before the Treaty of Paris. Contrast Scharnhorst's remark with the customary interpretation of the reformers rebuilding the army, training *Krümper*, and eliminating abuses from the very inception of the Military Reorganization Commission.

troops would be required for the fortresses, but with the *Garde du Corps* and the artillery, 55,000 out of a total of 70,000 men would be free for field service.[53]

In addition to these proposals Scharnhorst considered the method of raising troops, and from his suggestion has arisen the mistaken notion that the building of *Krümper* dates from the summer of 1807. His recommendation read: "It is extremely important in these arrangements, to give them such form, that the army, and in particular the infantry, can be increased quickly. This can be done most easily in the following way: 1. in every company one more officer than is necessary is to be enrolled. 2. from every company for the first three years, twenty serviceable men are to be released annually into the canton ... replacing the retired men with others."[54] It should be evident that this recommendation was merely a restatement of the customary type of training and furloughing that was used in the Prussian army, and that a rapid expansion of the army based on an increase in the tempo of training had been canvassed thoroughly by the reformers before the war.[55]

STRUCTURE OF THE ARMY

By September 25, 1807 the Military Reorganization Commission had prepared an answer to at least four points on the king's agenda and had proposed to organize the army in three corps, the Silesian, Prussian, and Brandenburg-Pomeranian. Each corps area was to have a population of 1,600,000 persons and was to provide two divisions, totalling eight infantry regiments, four cavalry regiments, four batteries of six-pound unmounted artillery, two batteries of six-pound mounted artillery, and as reserves a battery of twelve-pounders and another of

---

[53] *Preuss. Archiv*, XCIV, 21; *cf.* Osten-Sacken, *op. cit.*, II, 8-9.

[54] *Preuss. Archiv*, XCIV, 21.

[55] *Denkschrift des Generalmajors von Scharnhorst*, July 31, 1807, *ibid.*, XCIV, 19-23. Also in *Reorganisation der Preuss. Armee*, I, 76-81. The use of trained reservists that Scharnhorst described was not original with him but had been suggested by Colonel von Below, Commander of the Prince Henry Infantry Regiment. *Preuss. Archiv*, XCIV, 21.

BATTLE OF JENA AND THE FIRST REFORMS 111

mounted artillery. Each infantry regiment was to consist of two companies of grenadiers, two battalions of infantry, a battalion of light infantry, and a depot company, four companies to a battalion. Cavalry regiments were to consist of eight squadrons, but the king reduced this strength to four, and announced that each corps would have a cavalry contingent of one cuirassier, three dragoon, and two hussar regiments.[56]

Training and furloughing followed the normal practice of the army: "Every company during the first few years takes in annually thirty of the youngest men, over eighteen years of age, and releases as many of the oldest soldiers, in order that, first, an adequate reserve for garrisoning fortresses, replacements in war, etc. may be maintained. Every squadron releases twenty of the oldest riders and hussars and takes in an equal number of men, eighteen years or older. The length of service is determined according to the population." [57] Paragraph 10 stipulated: "Every infantry company has fifty men definitely in service, and of these twenty are old soldiers and thirty newly installed men. Every cavalry company has sixty-two men in service, including twenty recruits and forty-two old riders." [58]

The extra men trained in this way were intended for use in fortress garrisons as well as for the normal replacement of casualties. This was not considered an extraordinary measure; in fact, so far as the king was concerned it was less important than fixing the number of squadrons per regiment, or the number of companies per battalion.[59] Before these recommendations could become law the declining revenues made further reductions necessary, and a memoir from the Military Reorganization

---

56 *Reorganisation der Preuss. Armee*, I, 63-64. Grolman's notes for the period from Aug. 20 to Sept. 7, 1807 indicate a great range of topics discussed by the commission. *Preuss. Archiv*, XCIV, 62-66, and 66-71.

57 *Reorganisation der Preuss. Armee*, I, 65.

58 *Loc. cit.*

59 Of all the proposed military measures, Frederick William took the keenest personal interest in the design of new Prussian uniforms. He was strongly influenced in this work by his admiration for the Russian army.

Commission of September 25, 1807 proposed the elimination of one battalion in every infantry regiment, and one regiment of infantry in each division. For each cavalry regiment there would be five to six squadrons instead of eight, and in an army corps, only three regiments of cavalry instead of four.[60] Even these changes proved temporary for the loss of territory, the heavy contributions, and diminishing commerce and industry made drastic economies necessary. Accordingly, it was proposed that the active list of a company be set at fifty men and all others be furloughed, with unconditional release for all soldiers born in the provinces west of the Elbe. For the entire army in Pomerania, Prussia (*sic*), and Silesia, immediate demobilization to a peacetime basis was believed advisable. Cavalry was the most expensive arm to maintain and its effectives were reduced by a third, leaving only 10,000 horsemen in the army.[61]

On this basis the army was reorganized in the demobilization of the fall of 1807.[62] By a Cabinet Order of November 20, 1807 the strength of the infantry units was established. Every regiment was set at two grenadier companies, two musketeer battalions, and a light battalion, called after December 1, 1807, garrison companies. A Cabinet Order of October 10, 1807 fixed the complement of companies at five officers, fifteen non-commissioned officers, three to four musicians, and 170 men, of

60 *Reorganisation der Preuss. Armee*, I, 102-04. Lieutenant General Friedrich Karl von Schmidt wrote in 1807: "Every courier coming from Prussia brought new reductions to the corps, and the desired reorganisation of our army, and my hopes for a definite assignment dwindled and finally seemed to disappear altogether." *Erinnerungen aus dem Leben des Generalleutnants Friedrich Karl von Schmidt* (Berlin, 1909), part II, p. 92.

61 *Reorganisation der Preuss. Armee*, I, 106-08, economy proposals of Oct. 9, 1807. A letter of Scharnhorst to Ludwig von Ompteda of Oct. 25, 1807 indicated that the train and artillery horses had been turned out on the land and that 5,000 cavalry horses had been sold. *Scharnhorsts Briefe*, I, 331.

62 The combination of the existing regiments with the parts of the dispersed and disbanded regiments is described in Scharnhorst, *Auszug*, pp. 22-26 for the infantry, p. 27 the *Jäger*, pp. 27-28 the artillery, and pp. 28-34 the cavalry. Personal experiences in the time of the reductions are related in Schmidt, *Erinnerungen*, part II, pp. 97-105.

BATTLE OF JENA AND THE FIRST REFORMS 113

whom fifty were to remain with the colors and 120 were to be furloughed in the cantons after the customary fashion. An important new practice for the infantry was stipulated by the regulation that the entire third rank be trained as sharpshooters, and for their replacements, twenty to thirty men from each company were to be given the same instruction.[63]

A Cabinet Order of October 16, 1807 reduced all cavalry regiments, except the *Garde du Corps*, from five to four squadrons, and the Uhlans, previously called the Towarczys, from fifteen to eight squadrons. Complements were set at six officers, fifteen non-commissioned officers, three trumpeters, and 132 men, of whom seventy-two were furloughed and sixty remained with the colors. The cavalry formed eighty-six squadrons (about one-third of the pre-war strength) of which seventy-seven were in Pomerania.[64] By March 29, 1808 the remnants of the field artillery scattered over East Prussia and Pomerania had been given a provisional organization. Only a few batteries and companies of artillery survived the catastrophe of 1806 and not until 1809 was this arm reconstituted as an effective branch of the army.[65] Fortress artillery was based at Graudenz, Pillau, and Colberg; the company of miners was garrisoned in Graudenz and the pontoon company in Königsberg.[66] An important consequence of the reorganization of 1807 was the regrouping of the old Prussian regiments. All regiments with cantons in the territory ceded under the terms of peace had no means of obtaining cantonists and were dissolved. Regimental names as a symbol of the colonel's proprietary interest were discarded in favor of numbers. Thus perished some of the historic regiments

63 *Kabinettsorder an das Oberkriegskollegium*, Nov. 20, 1807, *Preuss. Archiv*, XCIV, 160-62; also in *Reorganisation der Preuss. Armee*, I, 132-37.

64 *Ibid.*, I, 127-31. Superfluous men were released on passes into the cantons after the manner common before 1806. Scharnhorst, *Auszug*, pp. 36-37.

65 Cf. *Die Preussische Artillerie von ihrer Neuformation 1809 bis zum Jahre 1816* (Berlin, 1909), pp. 3-5, and two documents in *Reorganisation der Preuss. Armee*, I, 104-06, dealing with the organization of the artillery.

66 Cf. Scharnhorst, *Auszug*, pp. 13-15, and Jany, *op. cit.*, IV, 7-8.

of the Prussian army, such as those of Wied, Manteuffel, Seydlitz, and Zieten.[67]

THE STRENGTH OF THE PRUSSIAN ARMY IN NOVEMBER, 1807 [68]

INFANTRY

Officers	1,076
Non-commissioned officers	3,137
Surgeons	173
Musicians	731
Men	32,637
Total	37,754

CAVALRY

Officers	487
Non-commissioned officers	1,079
Surgeons	72
Trumpeters	222
Men	10,128
Farrier-sergeants	72
Total	12,060

ARTILLERY

	Field Artillery	Fortress Artillery	Pontoons
Officers	107	23	3
Non-commissioned officers	444	65	6
Surgeons	22	6	—
Musicians	49	—	—
Bombardiers	367	75	—
Men	2,439	507	48
Train personnel	17	—	—
Knechte	188	—	—
Total	3,633	676	57

Total strength of the Prussian army in November, 1807: 54,180 officers and men.

---

[67] Herrmann, *op. cit.*, p. 499. Details of the Prussian regiments may be found in Alt, *Das Königliche Preussische stehende Heer* (Berlin, 1869-1870, 2 v.).

[68] *Preuss. Archiv*, XCIV, 164-69. These figures compare with 1,696 officers and 52,142 men given in Jany, *op. cit.*, IV, 8. For June, 1808 the army numbered, without the Royal Guard, 49,817 officers and men. Of this number 23,683 men were furloughed. *Ibid.*, IV, 9. The furloughing followed the pre-1806 practice of keeping a reserve in the cantons in expectation of mobilization.

BATTLE OF JENA AND THE FIRST REFORMS 115

BUILDING A RESERVE

The army declined steadily in number throughout 1807 and 1808, and at the time the Treaty of Paris was signed, September 8, 1808, it had reached its lowest point, some 50,000 men, of whom almost half were furloughed. By fixing the number of troops at 42,000 the treaty provisions corresponded approximately to Prussia's capacity to support an army at that time, which bore witness to the accuracy of the estimates that the commanders of the French army of occupation made for the guidance of French diplomacy.[69] The steady shrinkage of the army throughout the year 1808 had been due to the reduction of effectives with the colors, as provided for in the Cabinet Order of February 27, 1808 which allowed only twenty-five to thirty-two men in an infantry company. In October, 1807 it had been set at fifty and the original complement of a company had been more than a hundred men. In the cavalry the reduction was equally great, for only fifty men remained in each squadron and the number of horses was reduced from 125 to 100.[70]

Because the standing army was so small it appeared especially necessary to prepare a reserve army for the contingency of war. Accordingly, the possibility of organizing a reserve was examined thoroughly by the reformers in the summer and fall of 1807. This investigation was nothing more than a discussion of the militia problem which had been considered by Knesebeck, Rüchel, and Courbière. Their recommendations in this respect actually contributed more to the eventual form of the German army than those of Scharnhorst. He always thought of the militia in its eighteenth century sense, that is, simply as an adjunct to the standing army without any connection, either for training or augmentation, with the troops of the line.[71]

The plans of the reformers, 1807-1813, were distinguished by the absolute separation of the permanent army completed by

[69] Cf. Preuss. Archiv, LXXXVIII, 295-97.
[70] Jany, op. cit., IV, 8.
[71] See Lehmann, Scharnhorst, II, 87-92.

reserves, from the popular levy, called at various times the militia, *Landwehr,* provincial troops, or national guard. On the form, structure, and purpose of the latter part of the nation's armed forces the reformers were in no agreement whatever.[72] It was evident, however, that a revolutionary army putting everyone under arms was unthinkable in 1807; the single mention of conscription was enough to bring a virtual wave of protests on the king from the provincial estates. To combine Frederick the Great's assumption of the "peaceful burgher," undisturbed by war, with the military and financial obligations of the state, a militia for the wealthy and the standing army for the poor seemed the only solution.[73]

Throughout the year 1807 the Military Reorganization Commission rested its hopes for the expansion of the army on a militia. The normal war reserve, or *Kriegs-Augmentation,* was to be developed by means of the old furloughing procedure.[74] This practice was in no way expected to enlarge the army, and it was not the beginning of the *Krümper* system. During the fall of 1807 many plans were developed for *Ersatz* battalions,[75] that is, second line units or war reserves used to form infantry depots, or to replace losses of battle, sickness, and desertion.[76] The purpose of these measures was clearly stated in the report of the Military Reorganization Commission of November 28, 1807: " In order to have the troops in the field at full strength, in the event of the outbreak of war, and in order to obtain the necessary garrisons for the fortresses, it is necessary to have forces to fulfill this double purpose without significant increases in peacetime costs." [77] Nothing could be clearer than this statement, and

[72] Cavaignac, *op. cit.,* II, 319.

[73] *Cf.* Max Lehmann, *Knesebeck und Schön* (Leipzig, 1875), pp. 252-54.

[74] *Cf.* Scharnhorst's memoir of July 31, 1807 in *Preuss. Archiv,* XCIV, 19-23.

[75] *Ibid.,* XCIV, 181-84.

[76] *Ibid.,* XCIV, 176-79.

[77] *Ibid.,* XCIV, 176.

BATTLE OF JENA AND THE FIRST REFORMS 117

it was well that the commission closed on a note of economy, for the bureaucrats were even then carrying on a feud with the military over the cost of the army, and the need for keeping its size in some relation to the income of the state.[78]

SCHARNHORST'S MILITIA PROJECTS

The increase of the army was the main problem after 1806 and Scharnhorst, in his memoir of July 31, 1807, first proposed the militia as a solution.[79] All military thinkers, he began, had favored such troops; this was a large assumption in view of the miserable showing made by untrained troops in the past. Nevertheless, Scharnhorst's militia was to be entrusted with the twofold task of maintaining internal order, and defending the land together with the regular troops. He went on to suggest that the classes exempted by the canton regulation of 1792, particularly the sons of property owners and civil servants, should be drawn upon for the militia. What Scharnhorst sought was a change in the canton law, and his proposals were the opening shot in a battle for reform that was to last six years.[80]

Scharnhorst intended to use the militia for the garrison duty which had drawn so many effectives from the regular army. The militia would also serve as police in the larger cities and as light troops. As a means of obtaining militiamen Scharnhorst considered the canton system adequate if only the provisions of exemption could be modified. Other matters dealt with in the memoir of July 31, 1807 included: furloughing, the size of the army, arms and equipment, and fortresses. Apparently the king

[78] Cf. ibid., XCIV, 238-39. In 1807 Scharnhorst added: "The financial condition of the state did not permit the army to be brought to the size warranted by the population." Cited in Emil Knorr, *Von 1807 bis 1893. Zur Entwicklungsgeschichte unserer Heeresverfassung* (Berlin, 1893), p. 43.

[79] Cf. Courbière, *Heeresverfassung*, p. 165, for recognition that the Military Reorganization Commission revived the work of Knesebeck which had been rejected before the war. Knesebeck's work is also mentioned by Osten-Sacken, *op. cit.*, II, 8.

[80] Ide, *op. cit.*, pp. 28-29.

received it favorably, for Scharnhorst was encouraged to write other memoranda dealing with the militia.[81]

The next document, dated August 31, 1807, came from the Military Reorganization Commission, though it is probable that the main ideas in it were Scharnhorst's. Whereas the first paragraph declared every citizen liable for service, the second proceeded to make exceptions in the spirit of the canton regulations: "All able-bodied men in the state, who cannot arm, clothe, and train themselves in the use of arms, will be clothed, armed, and trained at the expense of the state. They will form the standing army."[82] As in the past those who could not afford weapons, the uneducated and unpropertied classes, would contribute recruits for the line. Still, universal service was proclaimed, even if exemptions were to be applied in practice. Some military obligations were imposed on the higher strata of society, for, "All able-bodied men between eighteen and thirty years, who do not belong to the second class, shall arm, clothe, and train themselves at their own expense in peacetime. They shall constitute the Reserve Army."[83] It was also entrusted with the maintenance of internal order as well as the defence of the land. No artillery was proposed for the Reserve Army, which was to consist simply of infantry and cavalry under the command of its own officers. The organization was comparable to the line but was distinct from it.[84]

The Compromise on Universal Service

From these proposals it is evident that the reformers did not intend at first to base the regular army on universal service. Military reform lagged behind the ideals of the Baron vom Stein, who was ready to issue his proclamation emancipating the serfs. Stein's hope of making citizens of the Prussian sub-

81 *Preuss. Archiv*, XCIV, 22-23; *Reorganisation der Preuss. Armee*, I, 78-81.
82 *Preuss. Archiv*, XCIV, 82.
83 *Loc. cit.*
84 *Ibid.*, XCIV, 83-85. *Cf.* Lehmann, *Knesebeck und Schön*, pp. 249-50.

BATTLE OF JENA AND THE FIRST REFORMS

jects found no counterpart in the suggested changes for the army, which deferred to the class interests of an absolute state. Instead of striking boldly for the reconstruction of the armed forces on a national basis, the reformers contented themselves with a revision of the eighteenth century military system. The subsequent course of the reforms showed even more respect for the military organization which had been inherited from Frederick William I and Frederick the Great.[85]

Though the reformers cherished the traditions of the army more than their opponents were willing to admit, their militia proposals departed sufficiently from the customary methods of obtaining recruits to arouse the ire of conservatives in military and court circles. The reform projects of 1807 were destined to lag because Frederick William was not prepared to sanction the modest alteration of the canton method of conscription that the reformers believed necessary for adequate defence.[86] In spite of repeated discouragements the Military Reorganization Commission in December of 1807 began to revise its memorandum dealing with the Provincial Troops, as the proposed militia was now called.[87] Apparently the king wished to consult with the civil authorities about the militia because the military reformers began to prepare a new draft that would meet Stein's approval.

[85] German historians are perhaps inclined to minimize the dislocation of the state and army after 1806 and to exaggerate the ease whereby a new structure was built upon the old. Herrmann's judgment is typical of this point of view: " The rebirth of the Prussian state through the reforms named for Stein, Hardenberg, and Scharnhorst, appears hardly less brilliant to us by the proof that this did not replace the decayed past with something wholly and organically new, instead by widespread grafting on the bases of the old Prussian military and bureaucratic state, preserved the continuity of our political evolution, and further, by the proof that before 1806, in the army and administration, reforms were considered zealously, and also, that much was accomplished." Herrmann, *op. cit.*, p. 489. *Cf.* Otto Hintze, " Preussische Reformbestrebungen vor 1806," *Historische Zeitschrift*, LXXVI (1896), 413-43.

[86] Consult Boyen, *Erinnerungen*, I, 294-95.

[87] The first draft is given in *Reorganisation der Preuss. Armee*, I, 88-93, though there are some significant omissions in the text.

On March 15, 1808 the plan for the Provincial Troops was once more brought to the king's attention.[88]

Once again the native Prussian's obligation to defend the state was asserted: "Without the plain law of the Prussian military constitution 'that every subject of the state is its born defender,' the state would not have grown to its present size in so short a time. Through the imitation of this constitution, the Austrian army after the Seven Years' War, and the French army after the first campaigns of the revolutionary wars, became what the Prussians had always been, a true standing army, that is, an army not only brought to a proportionate and measured size in relation to the population, but also maintained by it." [89]

Large mercenary armies were admitted in the argument to be best for prosperous states with ambitious policies. But when small states were threatened with conquest they had a resource which could oppose the superior discipline and great experience of veteran troops: this was the voluntary sacrifice of popular rights and personal property for the safety of the state. In case of attack a popular army might for a short time prove the equal of mercenaries, but foreign war and national prestige required a standing army. Prussia's armed forces should thus consist f two elements, a small standing army, and a militia in which the people could be trained to resist aggression. Because the militia would be drawn from members of the propertied classes it would also add to the internal security of the state. The commission also remarked that only a militia which consisted of lower class elements could arouse apprehension! In Prussia the militia to be known as the Provincial Troops would be made up of responsible persons; their arms and uniforms would be similar to the line but their organization would be separate. Officers would be drawn from the ranks. On the issue, "Whether it is better to let the men selected for the Provincial Troops pass through the standing army, or to form them without this prep-

[88] This revised plan is found in *Preuss. Archiv*, XCIV, 320-32.
[89] *Ibid.*, XCIV, 321.

BATTLE OF JENA AND THE FIRST REFORMS 121

aration," the Military Reorganization Commission chose the latter alternative.[90]

RELATION OF THE MILITIA TO THE STANDING ARMY

Scharnhorst opposed the training of the militia with the standing army because the experience would endanger the national patriotism of the militiamen. Their spirit would be depressed by enforced association with mercenaries; only a militia organized on a separate footing would retain that ardor and patriotism which Scharnhorst believed indispensable for the overthrow of Napoleonic tyranny. Hence the organization of the militia and the reserve army suggested by Scharnhorst and the Military Reorganization Commission differed from the proposals that had been made before 1806.[91]

Another shortcoming of a militia trained in the standing army would be the slow creation of a reserve. The standing army could not devote its full energy to training a militia because it was busy completing its own cadres, and training the cantonists who were required for garrison and replacement troops. Militiamen would receive indifferent instruction from officers preoccupied with these matters and five or six years might elapse before the militia would be ready for service. The Military Reorganization Commission thus tacitly recognized that building a reserve was a slow process, which at best could supply the regular army only with its own replacements and garrison troops. It was unthinkable that the training period could be shortened and the furloughing speeded up to the degree which subsequent historians have imagined, whereby a doubling or quadrupling of the army could take place within a few years.[92]

90 *Ibid.*, XCIV, 322-23.
91 *Ibid.*, XCIV, 323. *Cf.* Höhn, *op. cit.*, pp. 8-9.
92 *Reorganisation der Preuss. Armee*, I, 91; *Preuss. Archiv*, XCIV, 323. All military experience pointed to the need for a longer period of training. The army of 70,000 men recommended in Scharnhorst's memoir of July 31, 1807 could train 17,000 men as replacements and reservists in three years, or about enough to cover the casualties of the first battles. *Ibid.*, XCIV, 22.

Still another difficulty was recognized in a militia trained with the line troops: other states would fear that the Prussian standing army was being expanded.[93] On a separate footing a militia might not arouse any suspicion. The commission therefore recommended universal conscription without exemptions, together with a militia which would add to the strength of the national defences without forcing the upper classes to associate with the rough elements in the standing army. Only those subjects who could make a deposit of one hundred thalers, who could arm and clothe themselves, and in the cavalry buy their own mounts, and who could maintain themselves during two months' training the first year and one month in every subsequent year, would be eligible for the proposed militia. Other arrangements for the Provincial Troops resembled those suggested previously for the Reserve Army.[94]

Stein and Schön Consider the Militia

For advice on this militia the king turned to Stein and Schön. Stein criticized exemptions based on wealth and class, and pointed out that under the conditions established by the commission, too few persons would be liable for the reserve and too many for the line. Furthermore, this would be an arbitrary classification. Stein's criticism held a different conception of the state and its defence than that of the reformers, who still deferred to class differences and appealed to the wealthy on the basis of protecting their property.[95] With the national state of citizens in mind, Stein proposed real universal service: "All inhabitants of the state between the ages of eighteen and twenty-five are bound to serve in the line army as determined by lot." [96]

93 *Ibid.*, XCIV, 323-24. *Cf.* Courbière, *Heeresverfassung*, p. 166.

94 *Reorganisation der Preuss. Armee*, I, 91-93. The militia proposals were accompanied by a memorandum written by Gneisenau who urged that the national schools train the youth for military ends and awaken in them an enthusiasm for the nation and its defence. *Ibid.*, I, 93-94; other educational proposals in *Preuss. Archiv*, XCIV, 184-95.

95 *Reorganisation der Preuss. Armee*, I, 94-95.

96 *Preuss. Archiv*, XCIV, 241.

BATTLE OF JENA AND THE FIRST REFORMS 123

All those who were not called in this way would be obliged to serve in the Reserve Army. There would be no loopholes; men were to serve either in the line or the militia.[97]

Schön's comments were even more straightforward; he at once discerned the weakness of the commission's proposal that the armed forces consist of two elements. His objections were explicit: the categories of service were based on wealth, and there would be an inevitable tendency for the militia to look upon the line as an inferior branch of service. If the army were to represent the nation, only the capacity to serve must be considered. It was a curious circumstance that the civilians, Stein and Schön, rather than the military, were demanding the most thorough conscription.[98]

OBSTACLES TO REFORM

None of the projects for the establishment of a militia was carried out. This failure cannot be attributed to the Treaty of Paris, as many writers state, but to the king, who had decided against the militia even before the end of 1807. His motives are not difficult to imagine. While the proposals of the reformers were in no sense revolutionary, all the factors that had combined to thwart the establishment of the militia before 1806 were still operative.[99] And by the end of 1807 the intense desire for reform at any cost—the immediate reaction to Jena and Auerstädt—had begun to wane. There was more praise for the old arrangements. Scharnhorst was blamed as a foreigner, and the Military Reorganization Commission was called a clique of radicals from whose deliberations the throne and the state had the most to fear.[100]

[97] *Reorganisation der Preuss. Armee*, I, 95; Jany, *op. cit.*, IV, 12.

[98] *Reorganisation der Preuss. Armee*, I, 96-99; *Preuss. Archiv*, XCIV, 201-02. Blücher insisted that, "No one in the world must be exempted." *Ibid.*, XCIV, 27.

[99] Ide, *op. cit.*, p. 32, and Gragert, *op. cit.*, pp. 25-26.

[100] Boyen, *Erinnerungen*, I, 294. Perhaps the position of the conservative group on the Military Reorganization Commission has been misinterpreted by historians; certainly the reforms outlined in Borstell's memorandum of

More work was done in 1807 to reorganize the army than to reform it. At least a few of the outstanding abuses were corrected by the Military Reorganization Commission, however. From the public's standpoint the most important of these was the purge of the officers' corps. Another change that was less a reform than a recognition of the French imperium over Europe, was the official prohibition by the Cabinet Order of December 17, 1807 of foreign recruiting.[101] In the future the army was to consist, at least officially, of natives. For some years the Prussian army had been able to enlist only native subjects as the expansion of the French Empire had absorbed the best recruiting grounds. When nationalism had sealed the bond between citizens and the army, soldiers became much easier to obtain. Military expenditures did not decrease, however, because national armies tended to be much larger than those composed entirely of mercenaries.

Five months of work had not brought any other important reforms, if one may except the substitution of grey trousers for white, and the use of shakoes instead of hats.[102] The order

Sept. 20, 1807 differed only slightly from the suggestions of the reforming circle. Borstell submitted ideas ranging from the establishment of general conscription in place of the canton system, the development of a *Landsturm*, the end of foreign recruiting, reform of the punishment system, to the introduction of better tactics. *Preuss. Archiv*, XCIV, 87-90. It is Stadelmann's view that Borstell was not a military reactionary. Cf. Stadelmann, *op. cit.*, pp. 266-70.

[101] This law was a significant addition to the legal structure of the national army of citizens. *Reorganisation der Preuss. Armee*, I, 139. Cf. Lehmann, *Scharnhorst*, II, 99, and Beilage V, pp. 647-49. Elimination of the foreigners was not as complete as it is often represented to be, however. Foreigners were permitted to enlist under certain circumstances: if they came from the former Prussian provinces; if they enlisted for three years without the usual bribe; and, if they were of German origin. Foreigners were treated much as they had been before 1806; natives were furloughed up to the number of foreigners admitted. How many foreigners there were in the army after 1807 remains unknown. Scharnhorst, *Auszug*, pp. 100-01.

[102] Changes in uniforms are summarized in *ibid.*, p. 21. Cf. A. Mila, *Geschichte der Bekleidung und Ausrüstung der Königlich Preussischen Armee in dem Jahren 1808 bis 1878* (Berlin, 1878).

that the third rank was to be trained in sharpshooting and scouting was long overdue. But as long as special instructions were not provided for the average infantry officer this reform remained ineffective. More might well have been accomplished, yet it is difficult to assign all responsibility to the Military Reorganization Commission. Before the year had elapsed all the points raised by the king in his memorandum of nineteen paragraphs had been answered.[103]

The reformers were beset by one of the principal weaknesses of an absolute monarchy: the difficulties attending supervision and approval by a single individual. Frederick William could not examine with equal care all the documents that reached him. Papers arrived not only from the Military Reorganization Commission but from Stein and other civil officials, as well as from private individuals who tried to inform the crown of the need either for change, or the preservation of the existing order. This imposed work in addition to the routine administration of the government and the army. The reorganization swamped military bureaucrats with duties, but they also received scores of unsolicited manuscripts on the reform of the army. Some of these contained valuable suggestions, while others paraphrased the theories of Berenhorst and Bülow, or repeated the recommendations that had been made by the Military Reorganization Commission.[104] Although the private interest in military reform hindered the official reform measures, the extent and the seriousness of that interest were a tribute to the effectiveness of the pre-1806 discussion societies, and their books and periodical literature, in disseminating information about the art of war.

Nevertheless, the displeasure of the monarch was directed against the Military Reorganization Commission for the delays,

[103] *Cf. Preuss. Archiv*, XCIV, 8-11, 45-62.

[104] Listed in *Reorganisation der Preuss. Armee*, I, 141-47. Note the memoirs of Prince August, in *ibid.*, I, 147-81, favoring moderate reforms, and that of General von Grawert, Sept. 27, 1807, in *Preuss. Archiv*, XCIV, 108-19, urging the reforms then being considered by the commission.

the bickering among its members, and the lapse of five months with so few accomplishments. In a spirit of dissatisfaction and ill-humor, the king issued a Cabinet Order on December 21, 1807 which once again outlined the measures that were to be considered, and commanded a systematic presentation of the commission's reports. Only in this way, the king's instructions ran, could the great task of rebuilding Prussia's civil and military institutions be completed within reasonable time.[105] This reminder hardly need have been made: in the year 1808 a number of exceedingly important military reforms were to be enacted.

[105] *Ibid.*, XCIV, 231-35. An excellent analysis of Frederick William III as a statesman is found in Eugene Anderson, *Nationalism and the Cultural Crisis in Prussia, 1806-1815* (New York, 1939), pp. 260-61, 281-82, 286-87. Conditions of the French occupation which contributed to the delay in rebuilding the army are set forth in a confidential memoir of October 10, 1807 found in Karl August, Prince von Hardenberg, *Denkwürdigkeiten des Staatskanzlers Fürsten von Hardenberg* (Leopold von Ranke, ed., Leipzig, 1877), V, 544-51.

CHAPTER V
THE WORK OF THE REFORMERS IN 1808

AT the end of the year 1807 the work of the military reformers had seemingly reached an impasse. The conservative opposition both in the civil government and in the army insisted on a return to Prussian military traditions rather than on reform. In the Military Reorganization Commission a series of personal quarrels threatened the very existence of the body that had been constituted to rebuild the Prussian army. December of 1807 had witnessed the outbreak of a bitter dispute between Scharnhorst, the leader of the reform party, and Borstell, who was identified with the conservative opposition. Their quarrel was as much a personal clash as it was disagreement about military matters, but as the friction increased it became clear that Scharnhorst's prestige as well as his leadership of the military reform movement was at stake.[1]

In this crisis Frederick William III did not desert Scharnhorst. To the king's great credit, steps were taken to silence Scharnhorst's opponents on the commission. Means were then found for the convenient withdrawal of the conservative members, who were replaced by men in full sympathy with the reform program. The Borstell incident was the turning point not only for Scharnhorst's career but for the course of the military reforms as well. Without the king's steadfastness, which contrasted with his customary vacillation, the work of rebuilding the army might have been curtailed. But with the unanimous

---

[1] *Preuss. Archiv*, XCIV, 235-36; Stadelmann, "Das Duell zwischen Scharnhorst und Borstell im Dezember 1807," *op. cit.*, pp. 270-73. Stadelmann believes that Borstell was originally selected for the commission because of his expressed interest in military reforms. The quarrel between him and Scharnhorst was over leadership, with Scharnhorst, a Hanoverian and a "new man," disputing with an "old Prussian." That Scharnhorst's position was not secure at first is shown in his letter to General Heinrich von Zeschau of Nov. 12, 1810. *Scharnhorsts Briefe*, I, 408.

support of the Military Reorganization Commission, Scharnhorst recaptured the original enthusiasm and early in 1808 the military reforms were begun in earnest.[2]

Scharnhorst and Stein worked in complete accord, exchanging opinions freely on both domestic and foreign issues. The course of the military reforms followed to a very great extent the rise and fall of Stein's prestige. As long as Stein remained in power Scharnhorst's proposals had an earnest advocate in the inner councils of the government.[3] Throughout the winter and spring of 1808 the Military Reorganization Commission drafted the suggestions that were to rid the army of its worst abuses. The enactment of these reforms between July 13 and August 6, 1808 culminated the first phase of the reorganization of the Prussian army.[4]

Foremost among the achievements was the unification of military administration in a Ministry of War. However, a universal service law was not secured by the reform program of 1808. Not until the second phase of reorganization that took place in the winter and spring of 1813 were any substantial changes made in the canton system. This delay did not diminish the importance of the other reform measures, all of which, it is important to note, were enacted before Prussia agreed to the Treaty of Paris of September 8, 1808. The limitations that were then imposed on the size of the Prussian army necessitated a recasting of the army's framework, but the basic principles of the military reforms were in no way impaired.

THE NEW FRAMEWORK OF THE ARMY

Under the terms of the Treaty of Paris the size of the Prussian army was limited to 36,000 men: 22,000 infantry, and 8,000 cavalry, with 6,000 artillery and technical troops, to

[2] Stadelmann, *op. cit.*, pp. 274-75.

[3] See Erich Botzenhart, ed., *Freiherr vom Stein. Briefwechsel, Denkschriften und Aufzeichnungen* (Berlin, 1931-1937), II, 474-75, 494-95, 504-07. This seven volume source collection will be cited hereafter as *Stein Denkschriften*. Consult Herrmann, *op. cit.*, pp. 502-03.

[4] Osten-Sacken, *op. cit.*, II, 16.

THE WORK OF THE REFORMERS IN 1808 129

which might be added 6,000 men of the Royal Guard, making a total of 42,000 effectives. No extraordinary levy, militia, or civil guard, or other measure intended to augment this force was permitted.[5]

The Military Reorganization Commission had planned to form the army into six divisions corresponding to the provinces of the land. This plan proved unworkable when the Peace of Paris forced the disbandment of some regiments and the lowering once again of the established strength of every unit. It was proposed instead to form six brigades and draw the surplus troops remaining in Silesia into this framework. A Cabinet Order of November 16, 1808 established six brigades retaining the provincial names that had been designated on September 7 and 14, 1808. Each brigade consisted of seven to eight battalions of infantry and twelve squadrons of cavalry. In wartime two brigades would form an army corps.[6]

ORGANIZATION OF THE PRUSSIAN INFANTRY AND CAVALRY AFTER
NOVEMBER 16, 1808 [7]

East Prussian Brigade
One Grenadier Battalion
Two Infantry Regiments
One Cuirassier Regiment
One Dragoon Regiment
One Life Hussar Regiment

Brandenburg Brigade
One Regiment Royal Guard Infantry
One Guard *Jäger* Battalion
One Life Grenadier Battalion
One Life Infantry Regiment
One Regiment *Garde du Corps*
One Life Uhlan Squadron
One Cuirassier Regiment
Two Hussar Regiments

West Prussian Brigade
One Grenadier Battalion
Two Infantry Regiments
One Dragoon Regiment
One Life Hussar Regiment
One Uhlan Regiment

Lower Silesian Brigade
One Grenadier Battalion
Two Infantry Regiments
One *Jäger* Battalion
Two Dragoon Regiments
One Uhlan Regiment

---

5 *Recueil des traités de la France*, II, 272-73. This specification was made as a result of the heavy withdrawal of French troops from Prussia to cover losses in Spain. Despite these reductions a large French garrison force was retained in Prussia. The limitation of the Prussian army is often, but erroneously, ascribed to the Peace of Tilsit, July 9, 1807.

6 Osten-Sacken, *op. cit.*, II, 33-34; Preuss. *Archiv*, XCIV, 262-66, 678-84, 713-15, 736-41.

7 Jany, *op. cit.*, IV, 27-28.

Pomeranian Brigade
One Grenadier Battalion
Two Infantry Regiments
Two Dragoon Regiments
One Hussar Regiment

Upper Silesian Brigade
One Grenadier Battalion
Two Infantry Regiments
One Sharpshooter Battalion
One Cuirassier Regiment
Two Hussar Regiments

Artillery was organized in three brigades by an order of November 24, 1808. Each of these consisted of twelve unmounted companies and three mounted companies. For war each company was made up of a single battery, with six cannon and two howitzers. On mobilization each brigade was to receive one mounted and one unmounted six-pound battery, while each army corps had three batteries in reserve. The remainder of the artillery was distributed among the fortresses. Engineers and pioneers did not receive an organization until November 4, 1809. And not until that year were complements of the various units in the army finally established.[8]

STRENGTH OF THE UNITS OF THE PRUSSIAN ARMY IN 1809

Unit	Peace Strength	War Strength
Infantry Company	50 men	135 men
Infantry Battalion	541	801
Infantry Garrison Company	120	200
Cavalry Squadron	60	110
Cavalry Regiment	481	601
Unmounted Artillery Company	133	200
Mounted Artillery Company	148	167
Pioneer Company	123	123

Only by 1809 were the troops billeted in their garrisons. The army (without the Royal Guard) then consisted of forty-five battalions, eleven garrison companies, seventy-seven squadrons, forty-five artillery companies, and three pioneer companies. With the reduced complements the regular army together with the Royal Guard should not have exceeded 42,000 men, with approximately 10,000 horses and 100 guns. But the Upper Si-

---

[8] Preuss. Archiv, XCIV, 722-25. Consult Osten-Sacken, op. cit., II, 34-38; and Die Preussische Artillerie von ihrer Neuformation 1809, pp. 4-8.

THE WORK OF THE REFORMERS IN 1808   131

lesian Brigade had not adopted the new organization and the army thus actually totaled 45,897 men in the spring of 1809.[9]

The adoption of the brigade organization was a significant reform. It not only enabled the infantry and cavalry to train together, but the units in a brigade were expected to fight together in battle. This it was hoped would overcome that previous tendency of the battalions to fight alone and without regard for the other units in the army, or for the actions of the other arms.[10]

SELECTION AND ADVANCEMENT OF OFFICERS

One of the reformers' main concerns was the improvement of the officers' corps. The public felt that they had been responsible for the debacle of 1806, and the king had already called for the punishment of guilty members. The reformers were more intent on correcting the loose structure of command and improving the kind of education that officers received. These reforms were achieved in a series of orders issued during 1808. The problem of relations between the military and civil branches of government was partially solved by the creation of *General Kommandos,* or General Governments of the Provinces, one for each brigade in the army. As an intermediary between the king and the army the Governors of the Provinces had duties similar to those of the Inspectors before 1806.[11]

New provisions for selecting officers were enumerated in the law of August 6, 1808 drafted by Grolman: *Regulations for the Appointment of Cornets, and the Choice of Officers in the Infantry, Cavalry, and Artillery.*[12] Henceforth, every subject irrespective of birth or class might become an officer by meeting the educational qualifications that were laid down. Since the average subject could not fulfill these requirements, the new law

9 Osten-Sacken, *op. cit.,* II, 37; Jany, *op. cit.,* IV, 24.
10 *Ibid.,* IV, 26.
11 Scharnhorst, *Auszug,* pp. 155-61, 167-69.
12 *Preuss. Archiv,* XCIV, 533-36; cf. Boyen, *Erinnerungen,* I, 311-16.

did not greatly alter the social composition of the officers' corps. During wartime promotion might be effective immediately. But between 1808 and 1813 there was no need for increasing the officers' corps in view of the reduction of the army, and only an insignificant number of junior officers were commissioned. Furthermore, it has been shown that about half of the officers in 1813-1814 had served in the campaigns of 1806-1807. When a universal levy was applied in 1813 and a larger officers' corps became necessary, special provisions announced at that time qualified the broad principles enumerated in 1808.[13]

After that date the candidate for a commission was to enter service at seventeen years and serve three months as a common soldier. No longer were *Junker* sons of twelve or thirteen permitted to serve as corporals until old enough to be commissioned. Nor was promotion entrusted entirely to the commanding officer. The cornets (*Portpeefähnriche*), the lowest rank of commissioned officer, were selected by a regimental examination commission. Non-commissioned officers and men, as well as cadets, were allowed to take these examinations. Fourteen cornets might be chosen in an infantry regiment and eight in a cavalry regiment. For lieutenant's commissions a special examination committee in Berlin selected the most qualified cornets. All officers of higher rank were required to take an examination for promotion. It is noteworthy that these examinations dealt with general education as well as the technical aspects of the military profession.[14]

Between 1808 and 1812 no fixed complement of staff officers was provided so that the number changed constantly. It was planned that six brigades would form three main armies with an

13 See Cavaignac, *op. cit.,* II, 388 and footnote 4.

14 Vidal de la Blache, *op. cit.,* pp. 94-99; Scharnhorst, *Auszug,* pp. 117-23; *Preuss. Archiv,* XCIV, 535-36, 547-48. An important reservation was announced in a Cabinet Order of Mar. 10, 1809, whereby the king could appoint commanding officers without regard for seniority, thus assuring the direct allegiance of the officers' corps that had characterized previous armies of the Hohenzollerns.

THE WORK OF THE REFORMERS IN 1808   133

organized staff for each. But during peacetime only one staff officer was attached to each brigade (Cabinet Order of December 26, 1808), and though he was no longer considered merely a personal aide to the brigadier general, little could be done to make the army's staff work more effective. In 1808 the number of staff officers reached thirty-four, but in 1812 there were only twenty-one. Only the most brilliant graduates of the military schools were selected for the special instruction in staff work under Scharnhorst's personal direction. After January 29, 1810 they received training in all branches of service. Staff officers had little to do with military reform and the mobilization instructions of 1809 were their sole achievement of any consequence between 1807 and 1813.[15]

MILITARY SCHOOLS

Without schools the new opportunities for promotion would have been meaningless. Therefore the reformers strove to improve the quality of education received by cadets and officer-candidates, and to increase the number of schools giving instruction in military subjects. It was natural that Scharnhorst should be interested in this work; he had been head of the Academy for Officers before the war and his temperament remained academic. One of Scharnhorst's greatest services to the Prussian army was his insistence upon higher standards of military education and improved military schools.[16]

Before 1806 Prussian military education had been haphazard and disorganized. The schools were not coordinated with one another; the curriculum was not standardized; and the quality of instruction was poor. Four Cadet Institutes trained boys aged ten to eighteen for a few years before they entered the army as junior officers. In addition, cadets of the Military Orphans' Home in Potsdam were regarded as potential officer

[15] Scharnhorst, *Auszug*, pp. 152-53; Preuss. *Heer 1812*, pp. 20-23. *Cf.* Conrady, *op. cit.*, II, Anlage V, pp. 390-94 for a sketch of a proposed General Staff, October, 1814.

[16] *Preuss. Archiv*, XCIV, 187-95. *Cf.* Vidal de la Blache, *op. cit.*, pp. 63 ff.

material.[17] Higher military education was limited to Inspection Schools where young officers discussed technical matters during the winter months, and three Academies for Artillery and Engineering. Under Scharnhorst's direction the Academy for Officers had become the model institute for military education, but it had facilities for only a small number of officers drawn from the Berlin Inspection. Largely because of the lack of advanced military schools, the reformers before 1806 had concentrated their efforts for instruction in military societies which were able to reach large groups. Instead of narrow technical schools educating specialists, Scharnhorst wanted institutions giving a profound but general military education.[18]

After 1806 Scharnhorst was not slow in taking advantage of the opportunity afforded by the reform of the army. He contributed two proposals in the winter of 1807 which outlined a new military education system, beginning with schools for cadets and ending in an advanced school for selected officers.[19] Not until May 3, 1810, however, was a plan approved which carried out Scharnhorst's program. The Cadet Institutes were entrusted with the work of preparing boys for the cornet examinations. The age of admission was set at twelve years and a five year course was prescribed for all. It was significant that only the sons of officers were to be admitted. Only two Cadet Institutes remained after 1807, for two had been located in ceded territory, and the Military Orphans' Home was abolished.[20]

For the education of commissioned officers a nine months course of instruction was offered at three War Schools newly

17 A. von Crousaz, *Geschichte des Königlich Preussischen Kadetten-Corps* (Berlin, 1857), pp. 243-55, and Beilage C, pp. 35-36; Jany, *op. cit.*, III, 425. *Cf.* B. von Poten, *Geschichte des militärerziehungs und Bildungswesens* (Berlin, 1889-1900, 6 v.).

18 *Cf.* Gottlieb Friedlaender, *Die königliche allgemeine Kriegsschule und das höhere Militär-Bildungswesen 1765-1813* (Berlin, 1854), pp. 188-213.

19 *Preuss. Archiv*, XCIV, 187-95.

20 Crousaz, *op. cit.*, pp. 255-78.

THE WORK OF THE REFORMERS IN 1808   135

established at Berlin, Breslau, and Königsberg. Attached to the Berlin school was a special War School for Officers which provided a three year course in advanced military science for fifty selected officers. Artillery and engineering were particularly stressed.[21] This school was the successor of Scharnhorst's Academy and it met in the celebrated quarters at Number 19 Bergstrasse. All military education was placed under the supervision of a single director who coordinated the studies and established uniform standards.[22]

MILITARY JUSTICE

A reform of military justice was also carried through by the Military Reorganization Commission. For the success of the reform movement among civilians it was necessary to make military punishments consistent with the provisions of the civil code.[23] If universal service were to be obtained, and this might be conceived as the ultimate though not the immediate goal of Scharnhorst and his followers, the conditions of service would have to be made more tolerable to the vast numbers of subjects who had not previously been called into service. As long as the punishment known as the Gassenlaufen (running the gauntlet) remained in effect, the middle classes would strive to keep their sons out of the army. They would not submit to a system of discipline developed for mercenaries and serfs.[24]

The reform of military justice had actually begun just before the Jena-Auerstädt campaign. On September 11, 1806 the king

[21] Friedlaender, op. cit., pp. 258-97; Scharfenort, Die Königlich Preussische Kriegsakademie 1810-1910, pp. 6-24.

[22] Scharnhorst, Auszug, pp. 154, 235-37; Preuss. Heer 1812, pp. 47-55. Scharnhorst's outline of instruction for artillerists is given in a letter of Dec. 4, 1809, Scharnhorsts Briefe, I, 382-85.

[23] Cf. Vidal de la Blache, op. cit., pp. 108 ff.

[24] The question of the harshness of discipline under the Articles of 1797 is mooted. Most of the reformers deplored the brutalities that were permitted, but conservatives, such as Count Lottum, still defended harsh punishments. The Articles of 1797 are found in Reorganisation der Preuss. Armee, I, 554-57. Cf. "Entwickelung der Preussischen Kriegsartikel," op. cit., pp. 383-84; Boyen, Erinnerungen, I, 316-18.

had commissioned High Chancellor von Goldbeck and General Auditor von Könen to revise the Articles of War and bring the administration of military justice into conformity with the times. The war naturally prevented the completion of this project. With the establishment of the Military Reorganization Commission the matter was taken up again and throughout the spring of 1808 the basis of a new code was prepared.[25] A new and complicated issue was injected into the discussions by Frederick William's inquiry whether the scope of military justice might not be limited to the service regulations. This question indicated that the king considered the separation of civil and military justice expedient.[26]

Before any progress on this technical question could be made, the differences of opinion on the Military Reorganization Commission had to be resolved. Gneisenau, Stein, and Scharnhorst were of one mind on the question of eliminating the *Gassenlaufen*, but they disagreed on the type and degree of punishment that was to be substituted. By April, 1808 their outstanding differences had been settled. Both whipping and running the gauntlet were to be eliminated, and instead of capital punishments varying periods of confinement were proposed.[27]

ARTICLES OF WAR AND THE SOLDIERS' OATH

During April and May a series of exchanges among the monarch, Stein, Könen, and the Military Reorganization Commission made possible a rough draft of the new Articles of War. Stein was of course eager to abolish the barbarous punishments

---

[25] *Reorganisation der Preuss. Armee*, I, 557-59; *Preuss. Archiv*, XCIV, 231, 361-66, 368-90.

[26] The civil and military courts had a great deal of overlapping jurisdiction. Civil suits involving soldiers, or mixed parties of civilians and soldiers, could be heard in Prussian military courts. Civilians could be tried in military courts for certain offences. For a discussion of this matter, see *Reorganisation der Preuss. Armee*, I, 590-91, and pp. 591-601. Also see Lehmann, *Scharnhorst*, II, 105-06, 108-10, 204-05. Military jurisdiction in civil matters did not end until July 19, 1809. *Gesetzsammlung 1806-1810*, pp. 579-80.

[27] *Preuss. Archiv*, XCIV, 361-65, 368-69.

THE WORK OF THE REFORMERS IN 1808 137

of the old army.²⁸ Scharnhorst and the Military Reorganization Commission shared Stein's feeling because the brutal punishments permitted in the military code of 1797 made the common man fear military service. According to Scharnhorst: "A universal conscription . . . could not be combined with the existing caning system. Military life must be made more agreeable to the nation by removing its hateful aspects. All regulations must carry out this purpose and enliven anew the soldierly spirit. The elimination of blows of the cane is indispensable to this end." ²⁹

Könen's first draft of the Articles of War was finished on May 20, 1808, but during June and July the work of revision was strongly opposed by conservative army officers. This impasse was overcome by Gneisenau's famous plea, *Freiheit des Rückens* (Freedom of the Back).³⁰ The emotional enthusiasm aroused by Gneisenau's eloquence enabled the reformers to win the king's approval. It was fitting therefore that the new Articles of War should appear on August 3, 1808, the birthday of Frederick William III. On the same day the *Orders on Military Punishments* and the *Orders on the Punishment of Officers* were also announced.³¹ The articles were basically the work of Könen, although reinforced here and there by the opinions of Gneisenau, Scharnhorst, and Stein. The document fulfilled the reformers' wish of making the Articles of War suitable for the citizen army of the future.³² The way was prepared for universal service by the declaration that, "In the future every subject of the state, without regard for birth, will be obliged to do military service under conditions of time and circumstance still to be determined, so that the army hereafter will consist almost entirely of natives." ³³ While this was not less thorough than the intro-

28 *Ibid.*, XCIV, 473-74.
29 Scharnhorst to Stein, July 3, 1808, *ibid.*, XCIV, 500.
30 See Max Lehmann, "Zur Geschichte der preussischen Heeresreform von 1808," *Historische Zeitschrift*, CXXVI (1922), 444-46.
31 *Gesetzsammlung 1806-1810*, pp. 253-75.
32 *Preuss. Archiv*, XCIV, 409-27; cf. *Preuss. Heer 1812*, pp. 353 ff.
33 *Preuss. Archiv*, XCIV, 410.

ductory phrases of the canton regulation of 1792, it was the only legal statement of universal obligation to bear arms promulgated in the era of reforms before 1813. It represented the high point of the king's enthusiasm for the idea of a nation in arms.[34]

During the preceding fifty years Prussian military discipline had tended to become less severe. Punishments in the articles of 1787 and 1797 had not been as rigorous as those in previous codes, and the treatment of the men by the officers had become less arbitrary since Frederick's day.[35] In the articles of 1808 terms of imprisonment instead of canings were specified, nor could a soldier be beaten for errors in drill and minor infractions of the service regulations.[36] All severe punishments, except the death penalty, had to be decreed by military courts subject to the king's confirmation. Death sentences could be ordered by the king alone. Instead of the firing squad a deserter faced ten years of fortress arrest. Yet desertion remained such a common offence that many officers asked that the death penalty be restored.[37]

With the publication of the Articles of War the soldiers customarily took an oath of obedience to the crown and to the military laws. Since Frederick William I's day there had been two oaths, one for the officers and one for the men. In 1808 only the second was considered by the reformers, who objected to the emphasis in the oath upon the soldier's personal loyalty to the crown. Since 1797 soldiers had sworn: " I swear to God, the all-knowing, a mortal oath, that I am resolved to serve His

[34] Helfritz, *op. cit.*, pp. 228-29, considers Aug. 3, 1808 the turning point of the military reforms.

[35] " Entwickelung der Preussischen Kriegsartikel," *op. cit.*, pp. 381-84. The Articles of War of 1797 are also found in *Heerwesen des Absolutismus*, Beilage LXXXX (*sic*), pp. 341-49.

[36] *Reorganisation der Preuss. Armee*, I, 581-83. Physical punishment for some offences was still permitted; at least forty blows with a rod could be struck. Scharnhorst, *Auszug*, p. 224.

[37] The entire articles are found in, *Gesetzsammlung 1806-1810*, pp. 253-64. Also see Scharnhorst, *Auszug*, pp. 222-30, and " Entwickelung der Preussischen Kriegsartikel," *op. cit.*, pp. 384-87.

THE WORK OF THE REFORMERS IN 1808 139

Majesty the King of Prussia, Frederick William III, my most gracious War Lord (*Kriegsherr*), on each and every occasion, in time of war and peace, truly and righteously." [38] This wording ignored the position of the king as a civil ruler and considered him solely as a military leader. Stein believed that this wording and its implication of dual civil and military constitutions was wholly inadequate. If military service were to be a part of the relation of the citizen to the state, then the monarch should be referred to as the chief executive instead of the war leader. In place of the term, *Kriegsherr*, Stein and the reformers wished to substitute *Vaterland*.[39] But their efforts failed and the word *Vaterland* was not used in the oath. Instead, the title *Landesherr* was substituted for *Kriegsherr*.[40]

COURTS-MARTIAL

The second of the proclamations of August 3, 1808 defined the disciplinary procedures for the officers. It was assumed that the aristocratic character of the corps was a sufficient guarantee of good behavior. And this assumption rested on the conviction that despite proclamations admitting commoners to the officers' corps, and advancement irrespective of class or birth, the aristo-

[38] *Heerwesen des Absolutismus*, Beilage LXXXX (*sic*), p. 349. *Cf.* Lehmann, " Zur Geschichte der preussischen Heeresreform von 1808," *op. cit.*, p. 447.

[39] *Ibid.*, CXXVI, 446-49; *cf. Preuss. Archiv*, XCIV, 427, 474. Arndt criticized previous oaths to a *Kriegsherr* because he believed that men who swore it were not free but animals. In place of the *Prince* he would put *Germany*.

[40] *Gesetzsammlung 1806-1810*, p. 264. In the Articles of War of 1844 the words, King and Fatherland, appeared together, but not in the soldiers' oath. From the 1840's until the 1880's there was no emphasis on the expression Fatherland. When the articles were revised in 1872 for the new imperial army they were published in the *Armeeverordnungsblatt*, instead of the *Gesetzsammlung* where all previous articles had appeared. At the same time the word Fatherland disappeared even from the Articles of War. In the entire history of the German army to the Great War of 1914 neither the soldiers' oath nor the oath to the colors contained the word Fatherland. Lehmann, " Zur Geschichte der preussischen Heeresreform von 1808," *op. cit.*, pp. 453-54.

cratic element would predominate.⁴¹ Nevertheless, various degrees of punishment were specified, at the least, arrest in quarters, and for serious crimes, fortress confinement. It was expected that the honor of the corps would make a formal justice administration unnecessary, hence only honor courts were provided. By a three-fourths vote of his fellow officers the accused could be deprived of the right to promotion. This practice had actually begun with the regimental tribunals which had heard the cases of officers accused of dishonorable conduct in the campaign of 1806-1807.⁴²

No significant changes were made in the structure of the main justice authorities of the army. The General Auditoriat remained the principal one, and after 1808 it found a place in the newly organized Ministry of War. In place of the battalion and regimental auditors of the old army, brigade courts were established after 1812. In 1809 the dual system of military and civil courts came to an end; the jurisdiction of courts-martial was limited to matters involving army personnel. All violations of the Articles of War and the service regulations, and all criminal charges against soldiers, remained within the jurisdiction of the military courts. Civil suits involving military personnel had previously been tried in military courts but were now to be referred to the justice administration of the land. Before the War of Liberation in 1813 there was very little system or order in the administration of military justice, consequently a great number of cases being heard when the changes went into effect became hopelessly confused. Yet the state-within-a-state arrangement characteristic of justice administration in the mercenary army was brought to an end. Military interference ceased in all matters of a civil nature such as marriage or legitimacy, and only the purely disciplinary control of the soldiers remained.⁴³

41 *Cf.* Scharnhorst, *Auszug*, pp. 228-30.
42 *Reorganisation der Preuss. Armee*, I, 585-88; *Gesetzsammlung 1806-1810*, pp. 272-74.
43 Bornhak, *op. cit.*, III, 117-18; *Reorganisation der Preuss. Armee*, II, 392-97. Note Schroetter's and Schön's proposals, *Preuss. Archiv*, XCIV, 791-813.

THE WORK OF THE REFORMERS IN 1808 141

THE NEW SUPPLY SERVICES

More important for the prosecution of war was the reform by the Military Reorganization Commission of the supply services. The "housekeeping" of the army presented many problems, especially in view of the limited revenues and the necessity of economy. Throughout 1807-1808 the details were worked out and the new tables of pay and rations were put into effect.[44] The events of the war had demonstrated the shortcomings of the supply system in which the regiment had been the basic unit. Hence the brigades were made the largest administrative units. The issue of clothing and equipment, as well as quartering arrangements, were carried out by the regiments under the general supervision of the brigades. Conscription which had formerly been under regimental control was also transferred to the brigade.[45]

General administration of the supply services was entrusted to a new office, the War Commissariat, which was represented in the brigades by six war commissars.[46] All supplies within the brigade were distributed and the accounts were kept by the war commissar as the representative of the central war ministry. Under his control were the provisioning officers and the magazines in the cantons which contained the supplies for brigades on the march. Accounting in the regiments was done by the *Rechnungsführer* instead of the regimental quartermasters, yet the maintenance costs of the regiments were still excluded from the military budget.[47]

44 *Cf.* Scharnhorst, *Auszug*, tables 10, 11A, 11B, 12, 13, 14, and 16; also see *Preuss. Archiv*, XCIV, 94, 750-53, 852-60.

45 Bornhak, *op. cit.*, III, 114, 116-17. Consult Helfritz, *op. cit.*, pp. 268-90, for details of the economic administration.

46 *Ibid.*, pp. 253-56. *Cf.* F. Ribbentrop, *Sammlung von Vorschriften... über den Dienst der Kriegs-Kommissaire* (n. p., 1814). Ribbentrop did much to establish a permanent staff of civil servants in military administration.

47 Bornhak, *op. cit.*, III, 116; *Reorganisation der Preuss. Armee*, II, 216-29. During the War of Liberation the new supply system seems to have worked fairly well; requisitions were handled by brigade commanders and supplies delivered through normal channels were supervised by the brigade commissars. Jany, *op. cit.*, IV, 89.

When the new supply administration was put into effect on August 1, 1808, the captains' personal profit derived from the management of the company and squadron "housekeeping" came to an end. No longer were captains permitted to sell small stores to their men; a regimental commission attended to their distribution. Muskets that had been owned by the captains were purchased by the state with a special fund set up for that purpose. At the same time the old custom of furloughing the professional soldiers that they might work as artisans was prohibited. The pay of all men on legitimate furloughs was to go into the royal treasury instead of the pockets of the company commanders. By these arrangements national control terminated what had been for centuries a private business enterprise of the officers' corps.[48]

Supply services for mobilization were also under the authority of the War Commissariat. With the establishment of war commissars in the brigades the old confusion and duplication of mobilization officials was partially corrected. To replace the regimental bread wagons used formerly, every brigade obtained thirty-two bread wagons on mobilization. Yet the personnel of the trains did not receive any training in peacetime, and except for four train depots at Königsberg, Breslau, Berlin, and Colberg, there was no permanent organization for the transport of the army. The amount of baggage was reduced and each company of infantry was permitted to retain only a single pack horse for the officers' requirements. Only three pack wagons were allowed in a battalion. Cavalry moved with much less baggage; two wagons were permitted for the regiment, while squadrons might have only two extra pack horses for carrying tools and

[48] Lehmann, *Scharnhorst*, II, 144-45; Boyen, *Erinnerungen*, I, 309-11. In order to compensate somewhat for the soldiers' loss of their artisans' income the bread ration was increased to a pound and a half daily. City officials were enjoined to sell food at low prices and small plots of land were cleared around the garrisons where the men could grow their own vegetables. Scharnhorst, *Auszug*, pp. 55-56.

THE WORK OF THE REFORMERS IN 1808   143

equipment. Supply trains remained heavy, however, since the army still depended upon magazines.[49]

THE MINISTRY OF WAR

The elimination of the worst features of the old military administration, and in particular, the establishment of a Ministry of War, was an outstanding accomplishment of the reformers in 1808. Before that date military administration had been very confused. No ministry of war guided the two principal bureaus which handled the business of the army. The adjutants and inspectors were equally free to discharge their offices as they saw fit. Both Stein and Scharnhorst had long been aware of the need for a single office handling military affairs and in 1807 they opened their attack on the old system.[50]

Late in 1807 Stein presented a draft plan of the new government (November 23, 1807) in which the fifth great division formed a War Ministry.[51] It consisted of two offices, one dealing with organization and command, and the other with administration and supply. Stein's proposed changes were not immediately accepted as they concerned an important element in the Prussian constitution: the direct relationship of the king to the army. Frederick William III would not abandon the tradition of royal command and was loath to see control over the armed forces pass into the hands of one of his servants. His attitude prevented the complete unification of military administration under a single responsible head, although the War Min-

[49] *Ibid.*, pp. 61-65; Jany, *op. cit.*, IV, 34, 47; *Reorganisation der Preuss. Armee*, II, 86-87, 221-22.

[50] In April, 1806 Stein had written his *Darstellung der fehlerhaften Organisation des Kabinetts* (in *Preuss. Archiv*, XCIII, 4-13) which pointed the way toward eventual political reform. Schmidt-Bückeburg, *op. cit.*, pp. 10-11. Whether Hardenberg was as enthusiastic about establishing a central authority for the army has long been questioned. His document on the reorganization of the Prussian state, written in Riga, Sept. 12, 1807, does not make clear whether he agreed with Stein's aims. See *Preuss. Archiv*, XCIII, 302-63, particularly pp. 320-31.

[51] Max Lehmann, *Freiherr vom Stein* (new edition in one volume, Leipzig, 1921), pp. 250 ff.

istry of 1808 was a vast improvement over the previous bureaus and agencies.[52]

Stein's insistence secured temporary approval for a coordinated military administration; the Cabinet Order of July 15, 1808 decreed that all army affairs would be handled by a War Ministry with two principal departments. The first, called the War Department (*Allgemeine Kriegs Department*), was to be headed by Scharnhorst, and the second, or Military Economy Department (*Militär Ökonomie Department*), was to be headed by Count Lottum. Both men had the right of direct audience with the king, and their authority was equal; hence neither one enjoyed enough power to be called a war minister.[53] Yet from the first Scharnhorst tended to dominate the ministry, although his personal relations with Count Lottum were far from satisfactory. Lottum's appointment was evidence of the king's desire to safeguard existing traditions, for on the Military Reorganization Commission he was a leader of the conservative element.[54]

A definite order creating the Ministry of War came forth on December 25, 1808. It continued the organization first outlined in Stein's recommendation of the previous year, and confirmed Scharnhorst and Lottum as chiefs of their respective departments. Neither was made Minister of War.[55] In this way the king escaped the responsibility of naming a single minister.

[52] This question and the unity of military authority is discussed in Huber, *op. cit.*, pp. 113-20.

[53] *Das Königlich Preussische Kriegsministerium* (Berlin, 1909), pp. 5-10; *Preuss. Archiv*, XCIV, 518-19.

[54] As late as February, 1812 Scharnhorst was the real director, from behind the scenes, of the Prussian army. Boyen, *Erinnerungen*, II, 117-18. The significance of the Chief of the War Department lay in the fact that he executed all the orders and decisions, and communicated the information about the condition and size of the army to the king. Such complete control over the army by a servant of the crown was unique in Prussian history. Schmidt-Bückeburg, *op. cit.*, p. 15; *Preuss. Heer 1812*, pp. 15-16.

[55] *Preuss. Archiv*, XCIV, 833-45; see Helfritz, *op. cit.*, pp. 244 ff., for a comprehensive discussion of the reform of military administration.

THE WORK OF THE REFORMERS IN 1808 145

Scharnhorst as Chief of the War Department also bore the title, Chief of the General Staff; although the army had staff officers it did not have a General Staff. The title was therefore honorary and did not carry the prestige or authority that was to be associated with it much later. When French diplomatic pressure forced Scharnhorst from public office in 1810, the loss of his personal leadership made the ministry more or less the clerical bureau that the High Council of War had been.[56] Both heads of the War Ministry retained their right to confer directly with the king, and they were permitted to communicate with other departments and ministries as circumstances required. All military matters bearing on the policy of the state were to be related in detail to the ministers and department heads, while financial details of the army were to be worked out with the Ministry of Finance.[57]

Three divisions made up the War Department, or first section of the War Ministry. Each had a director and a staff of officers who were permitted to return to the line if they wished. The first division dealt with army personnel: promotion, dismissal, pay, pensions, medals, discipline, justice, and police. Under it was placed the Secret War Chancellory, where reports on individuals and the lists of officers (*Rangliste*) were prepared.[58]

The second division of the War Department dealt with the training of the army and also with cantons, conscription, the training of the reservists, military education, mobilization, marches, maps and plans, uniforms, and the supply of fortresses. A staff officer was put at the head of this division. Finally, the third division of the War Department handled artillery, engi-

---

[56] *Cf.* Boyen, *Erinnerungen*, II, 118.

[57] *Preuss. Archiv*, XCIV, 836-37; *Kriegsministerium*, pp. 8-9. When the term War Ministry is used here, it refers to both departments as they form a single unit. War Department refers specifically to the *Allgemeine Kriegs Department*, or first part of the War Ministry.

[58] The troubled history of the first division is summarized in Schmidt-Bückeburg, *op. cit.*, pp. 19-24. Also see *Preuss. Archiv*, XCIV, 838.

neers, miners, pontoons, the construction and repair of fortifications, the manufacture and store of arms and ammunition, and testing inventions.[59]

The second great department of the War Ministry, or Military Economy Department, was made up of four divisions dealing with supply and finance. The first division was the Military Treasury, with supervision of bookkeeping, pay, and all financial matters. Supply of bread and flour, forage for the cavalry, and food were entrusted to the second division. Inspection and supply of uniforms comprised the work of the third division, while the fourth managed the *Invaliden* and their pensions.[60]

Finance administration was centralized by combining the General War Treasury with the General State Treasury to form the General Military Treasury. All funds that had accumulated in the numerous independent treasuries of the old system were surrendered, and in the provinces the local revenues and separate accounts of the War Treasuries and Chambers of War and Domains were added to the central finance accounting.[61] Naturally, the War Commissariat, or the bureau which dealt with supply and finance for the brigades, was included in the second department of the War Ministry.[62]

CONSERVATIVE OPPOSITION TO REFORM

The heads of the two departments of the War Ministry were in no sense General Adjutants, but military officials whose responsibility had been defined in law. By the establishment of a War Ministry some of the secret influence of the king's adju-

[59] *Ibid.*, XCIV, 838-40.

[60] *Ibid.*, XCIV, 840-42; Ribbentrop, *Dienst der Kriegs-Kommissaire*, pp. 5-6.

[61] Jany, *op. cit.*, IV, footnote on p. 33. *Cf.* Ribbentrop, *Sammlung von Vorschriften ... auf den Dienst der Militair-Ökonomie Beamten* (Berlin, 1814).

[62] *Preuss. Archiv*, XCIV, 842-44. An even greater unity of military administration was achieved in 1814 when the two departments were combined to form the *Kriegsministerium* under Boyen. The General Staff which had some administrative independence in 1808-1809 was made the second department of the new War Ministry. *Cf.* Schmidt-Bückeburg, *op. cit.*, p. 28, and *Kriegsministerium*, pp. 19-21.

THE WORK OF THE REFORMERS IN 1808 147

tants was eliminated. Nevertheless, the spirit of cabal was not wholly removed from Prussian military administration;[63] many of the king's advisers were simply appointed to important positions in the new ministry. And the king might still handle army affairs independently of the new administrative machinery. Every innovation had to be approved by the king, and the conservatives still found it possible to block reform proposals by helping to shape the king's opinions about the necessity of reform.[64]

In this respect nothing obstructed the work of the reformers more than the control by the opposition of what was called the " secret military cabinet." This was the body of officers and officials whose personal relations to the king enabled them to influence his military decisions. It was only an ill-defined body of courtiers and courtier-soldiers who were close enough to the monarch to bring pressure on him at decisive moments. On December 8, 1807 Stein had complained to Hardenberg that the spirit of plotting and intrigue had become evident again, and that he feared the return of all the old evils which had caused the state to collapse.[65] Scharnhorst's struggle with Borstell was one aspect of this intrigue, and another was the balancing of conservatives and reformers in the investigating commissions and in the new departments and bureaus. Boyen commented that when Scharnhorst found it difficult to get royal approval for his plans he allowed Clausewitz, Rauch, Oppen, and others to present the most important of the proposed changes.[66] Fred-

[63] *Cf.* Scharnhorst's letters of Dec. 4 and 5, 1808 to Frederick William III, *Scharnhorsts Briefe*, I, 352-55, and a letter to Count Götzen, Febr. 9, 1809, *ibid.*, I, 361. Also see a letter from Gneisenau to Count Götzen, June, 1809, in *Gneisenau; Ein Leben in Briefen* (Karl Griewank, ed., Leipzig, 1939), p. 113.

[64] Schmidt-Bückeburg, *op. cit.*, p. 16; Herrmann, *op. cit.*, p. 504.

[65] *Ibid.*, XI, 502-03. Letters in *Scharnhorsts Briefe*, I, 352-54, 361, 406-10, portray graphically the circumstances in which Scharnhorst labored, with spite, mistrust, and antagonism on every side. See also Scharnhorst's answer of May 10, 1812 to Kalckreuth's charge that he had plotted secretly against the crown. *Ibid.*, I, 430-31.

[66] Boyen, *Erinnerungen*, I, 320. It is hard to substantiate Friedrich Thimme's assertion that Frederick William approved all the recommenda-

erick William III's attitude toward the new military administration was not friendly; his unwillingness to make Scharnhorst a Minister of War responsible for rebuilding the Prussian army was evidence of his lack of sympathy. Inside the War Ministry there were many frictions, which were exploited by Scharnhorst's enemies in order to diminish the prestige of the new officials.[67] Thus, the creation of a Ministry of War did not prevent the opponents of change from exerting their influence, and more important, it did not hinder the development of the monarch's " secret military cabinet." [68]

The cause of the military reformers was weakened by Stein's dismissal on November 24, 1808. On numerous occasions his strong personal influence had overcome the opposition to the work of reform. There were domestic issues and opponents that had undermined Stein's position, but his eventual downfall was mainly the consequence of his attitude toward Napoleon and his plans for the regeneration of Germany. Stein's work in the reorganization of the Prussian government had early attracted Napoleon's attention, and when the French intercepted an indiscreet letter to Prince Wittgenstein, Napoleon's vengeance came down upon his head. In a famous order of the day, on December 16, 1808, the Emperor declared Stein an outlaw, but a warning

tions of the Military Reorganization Commission without delay. *Cf.* Friedrich Thimme, " König Friedrich Wilhelm III., sein Anteil an der Konvention von Tauroggen und an der Reform von 1807-1812," *Forschungen zur Brandenburgischen und Preussischen Geschichte*, XVIII (1905), 42-43.

67 Lehmann, *Scharnhorst*, II, 211.

68 The problem of Frederick William's influence on the military reforms remains unsettled. One of the best analyses is that in Anderson, *op. cit.*, pp. 257-97, emphasizing the king's indecision, fear of responsibility, and preference for commonplace talent. Herrmann is inclined to be more favorable but admits his weak and procrastinating nature. Lehmann is not uncritical but assumes that, on the whole, the king was friendly to reform suggestions. Hintze, the official historian of the Hohenzollern dynasty, glosses over the shortcomings of Frederick William III while stressing his virtues. Stadelmann is inclined to feel that Frederick William III had a larger share in the military reforms than the older historians attributed to him. Thimme in a purely nationalist vein praises Frederick William III as the leader of the reform movement.

THE WORK OF THE REFORMERS IN 1808 149

came in time and he was able to flee Prussia and seek refuge on Austrian soil. Life in a provincial town proved too boring for a man of Stein's energy, and in the spring of 1812 he left Austria to resume his public career in Russia under Tsar Alexander I. When Russian armies following in the wake of Napoleon's shattered troops occupied East Prussia in 1813, Stein was appointed political commissar for the province. In this capacity he was once again to influence the course of the military reforms in Prussia.[69]

When the Ministry of War began to function in March, 1809, the Military Reorganization Commission came to an end. While the officers' corps and military administration had been reorganized, nothing had been done for the training of the troops. The canton law of 1792 stood intact. Only one of the six brigades that had been planned, the East Prussian, had its full complement in 1808; neither of the Silesian Brigades had been created. Artillery was still in the throes of a complete reorganization and it existed mainly on paper. Numerous regulations had been approved but none touched the practical training of the army for war. And throughout 1807-1808 the Military Reorganization Commission had only partially solved the basic problem of rebuilding the Prussian army: providing trained man power.[70]

69 *Cf.* Guy Stanton Ford, *Stein and the Era of Reform in Prussia, 1807-1815* (Princeton, 1922), pp. 265-96. After the fall of Stein the slanders of a particular group of courtiers were turned against Scharnhorst. Boyen describes these petty attacks in *Erinnerungen*, I, 343-45. As early as July 17, 1807 Count von der Goltz had written to Hardenberg about the intrigue and the tendency to restore the "old state of affairs." Hardenberg, *Denkwürdigkeiten*, III, 522-24.

70 *Cf.* Jany, *op. cit.*, IV, 19-20. Scharnhorst and Gneisenau admitted their disillusionment with the course of events. Consult Cavaignac, *op. cit.*, I, 397-99. Boyen pictures the Military Reorganization Commission fading away as its members took up other duties and the king neglected its proposals for ever longer periods. *Erinnerungen*, I, 320.

CHAPTER VI
CONSCRIPTION AND THE *KRÜMPER*

FOR the recovery of Prussian military strength after the disasters of 1806 the most pressing need was trained man power. Until 1813 the attempts of the reformers to meet this need met with very little success. Notwithstanding, the legend has persisted that under the compelling circumstances of the Treaty of Paris (September 8, 1808) the Prussian army was at least tripled by the secret training of *Krümper*. This program, which is usually attributed to Scharnhorst, has been made the keynote of the historical treatment of the military reforms after the battle of Jena.

From the standpoint of the reformers, the decision to retain the eighteenth century training and furloughing program was a compromise measure after their militia and conscription proposals had failed. They considered the laws which made the canton system only a means for conscripting serfs as the most formidable barrier to the establishment of equal universal service. As long as the law of 1792 was enforced a nation in arms was impossible. Throughout 1809 and 1810, therefore, the reformers waged a hard campaign to modify or to eliminate the canton system based on liberal exemptions, and to make conscription of every class the basis of man power.[1]

MODIFYING THE CANTON LAWS

Despite all the pleas and arguments of the reformers no substantial modification of the canton system was made before 1813. From 1807 until 1813 the canton regulations of 1792 remained in force. The method of conscription, the administration of the war reserve of trained men, and the exemption of all but

[1] See Lehmann, " Scharnhorst's Kampf für die stehenden Heere," *op. cit.*, pp. 276-99. The meaning and the implication of a universal service army for the reformers is treated in Huber, *op. cit.*, pp. 120-29.

CONSCRIPTION AND THE KRÜMPER 151

the lowest classes followed the practice that had been established during the 'eighteenth century.²

Frederick William remained opposed to such a far-reaching change as that from a professional to a national army,³ and he was not alone in his opposition. Hardenberg had favored exemptions for those in the service of the state and he now proposed substitutes for various other classes. Niebuhr was emphatically opposed to the principle of universal service because he felt that conscription was barbarous. Gentz pilloried the revolutionary sentiment implicit in the idea of a national army. Vincke, the admirer of England, implored Stein to spare the land the burden of universal military service.⁴ While Staegemann sympathized with the reformers he urged them not to make public any preliminary announcements about changes in military service until the reorganization of the army had been completed. His well-meaning advice was interpreted by the reformers, including Stein, as a rebuff.⁵

Stein's attitude toward conscription had been determined when Napoleon conquered south Germany. Although Stein had begun his career as a civil servant in the westernmost provinces of Prussia, which had preserved their freedom from military service, he was quick to declare that the independence and integrity of the state depended upon the army, and that no sacrifice was too great to maintain it. Jena and Auerstädt made it doubly clear that the army must come first. Stein added, "Safety is more important than prosperity," and, " I maintain it is a deep descent into egoism if military life is not considered the most honorable period of one's life." ⁶

2 Reinhold Nord, *Die Deutsche Heeresverfassung nach den Gewaltfrieden von Tilsit und Versailles 1806-1935* (Berlin, 1936), p. 9.

3 *Cf.* Herrmann, *op. cit.*, p. 508.

4 Vincke to Stein, Sept. 30, 1808, *Preuss. Archiv*, XCIV, 598-601.

5 Lehmann, " Zur Geschichte der preussischen Heeresreform von 1808," *op. cit.*, pp. 437-39.

6 *Ibid.*, CXXVI, 442-43.

MILITIA PROPOSALS

In 1807 the reformers had attacked the canton system by proposing a militia in which every subject would have to serve, but none of their suggestions for broader military service had been accepted. As late as March 15, 1808 the Military Reorganization Commission had advocated the establishment of a militia to be known as the Provincial Troops.[7] Stein approved the plan and the opinion of the commission was overwhelmingly favorable. Frederick William was not yet prepared to abrogate the canton regulation, however, and the project was dropped. After September 8, 1808 the conditions of the Treaty of Paris made the creation of a militia or a national guard even more unlikely.

Article III (of the secret clauses) of the Treaty of Paris forbade extraordinary measures for national defence, or the formation of a civil guard.[8] Nothing was said, however, about abandoning existing bodies of special or police troops. At Napoleon's own order a *Bürgergarde* (civil guard) consisting of about 1,680 men had been formed in Berlin to police the city. In Königsberg and Breslau similar bodies of military police were formed, and after the evacuation of Silesia, Frederick William ordered a *Bürgergarde* wherever one seemed necessary to maintain order.[9]

For the reformers the various forms of civil guards offered a means of circumventing the Treaty of Paris, as well as a method of continuing their campaign for a militia and a modification of the canton law. Scharnhorst's *Denkschrift* of December 21, 1808 proposed that such city militia be developed in

[7] *Preuss. Archiv*, XCIV, 320-32. Article one of the earlier draft was retained without change: "All inhabitants of the state are its born defenders." *Ibid.*, XCIV, 324.

[8] *Recueil des traités de la France*, II, 273.

[9] *Preuss. Heer 1812*, pp. 82-83; *Preuss. Archiv*, XCIV, 236-38, 765-66, 789-90. The *Bürgergarde* proved more bother than worth. See *Preuss. Archiv*, LXXXVIII, 328, 348, 354, 364-66, for indications of the disputes that followed the establishment of these units.

CONSCRIPTION AND THE KRÜMPER 153

every town that lacked a garrison.[10] From Grolman's pen, but in the name of the Military Reorganization Commission, came the *Recommendations for the Establishment of a National Watch.*[11]

This program went far beyond the auxiliary police force that the king had in mind, for it would have given the National Watch equal status with the army; and its proposed constitution declared: " Every male inhabitant is the born defender of the state, all previous exemptions and class distinctions with reference to the military are eliminated." [12] The intention of breaking down the canton laws was thus made clear; the National Watch would be simply the Reserve Army, or the Provincial Troops under a new name. Arms and uniforms were to be purchased by the individual, who was also obliged to post a one hundred thaler bond. There were even to be trained reservists for the National Watch.[13]

THE DEMAND FOR CONSCRIPTION

When the king failed to endorse Grolman's plan for a National Watch, formal efforts to create an armed militia ceased. Then the Military Reorganization Commission attacked the problem of universal conscription directly in its report of December 20, 1808 which urged a thorough reform of the canton system.[14] The memoir presented new proposals for a conscrip-

10 *Reorganisation der Preuss. Armee*, I, 318-19. Even Scharnhorst thought of such troops as police. Not once would he trust the garrisoning of the fortresses to the provincials.

11 *Ibid.*, I, 319-24; Conrady, *op. cit.*, I, Anlage I, pp. 289-95.

12 *Reorganisation der Preuss. Armee*, I, 321.

13 Details in *ibid.*, I, 323-24.

14 *Preuss. Archiv*, XCIV, 817-22. Whether the demand for universal service resulted from the French Revolution or the working of Prussian legal and military forces has been earnestly debated; the latter point of view is presented dogmatically in E. von Meier, *Französische Einflüsse auf die Staats und Rechtsentwicklung Preussens in XIX. Jahrhundert* (Leipzig, 1908), II, 389-96. The Military Reorganization Commission suggested: " Since the recently established conditions in the army make the canton division unserviceable, and since there is at hand a basic universal conscription constitution, in which every citizen of the state is pledged to the defence of the

tion system and advanced reasons for its immediate adoption. Conscription was intended for all men between the ages of twenty and thirty-five, but their selection was to be by lot. Although the conscription proposal was rejected by the monarch, two features of the memoir were eventually adopted: the shorter period of service, and the organization of the army in six brigades.[15]

In the winter of 1808-1809 the practical work of administering the army's affairs was taken over by the new Ministry of War. No further duties remained for the Military Reorganization Commission and it came to an end without having secured a conscription law. New hope was raised by the outbreak of war in 1809 between France and Austria. Napoleon's defeat at Aspern (May 21, 1809) together with the revolt in the Tyrol moved the king on June 6, 1809 to establish a new commission to study universal service. On this commission were included the boldest and most reform-minded persons in Prussia: Scharnhorst, Boyen, Ribbentrop, and Schön. None of these reformers believed that a great alteration, either in the civil or military administration, was necessary to attain universal service. They assumed that Prussia had had universal service since 1733, and that only a modification to suit the immediate crisis was necessary.[16]

Unfortunately, many of the documents of the conscription commission have been lost, but among the extant papers is an important one of July 1, 1809. Though the style suggests that Schön might be the author, the document cannot be ascribed definitely to him.[17] For a half year the king left this proposal

Fatherland, the undersigned commission respectfully lays before Your Royal Majesty a provisional draft of a conscription regulation." *Preuss. Archiv*, XCIV, 817.

15 *Ibid.*, XCIV, 819, 822; *Preuss. Heer 1812*, p. 84.

16 Max Lehmann, "Preussen und die allgemeine Wehrpflicht im Jahre 1809," *Historische Zeitschrift*, LXI (1889), 97-98, 101; Herrmann, *op. cit.*, pp. 511-12.

17 Lehmann, "Preussen und die allgemeine Wehrpflicht im Jahre 1809," *op. cit.*, pp. 98-104. Lottum and Boguslawski dissented from the commission's views and sent the king their own memoranda, which concluded that the

CONSCRIPTION AND THE KRÜMPER 155

unanswered, although his self-imposed exile in Königsberg was not a sufficient excuse for delay. The memoir was eventually returned to Scharnhorst in December of 1809 with marginal notations indicating that the king was not in full agreement with the suggestions for a more popular army.[18] Frederick William's previous dislike for universal service, except in case of extreme emergency, remained as strong as ever. Indeed it had been strengthened by the strenuous objections that had been raised on March 2, 1809 by the provincial diets of Pomerania. Their characterization of conscription as a French swindle comparable to "equality and freedom," settled the matter in Frederick William's mind.[19] Moreover, his use of this public remonstrance against conscription obscured a more significant obstacle: the critical financial situation. Also, the military fortune of Napoleon had returned at Wagram (July 5-6, 1809); and the Treaty of Schönbrunn, signed on October 14, 1809, renewed the threat of invasion and kept Frederick William under French domination.[20]

THE FINAL APPEAL FOR CONSCRIPTION

The work of the conscription commission went on through the winter of 1810 and culminated on February 5 in a last appeal in which Boyen urged the immediate establishment of universal service. His proposal was significant for its adaptation of the old Prussian military constitution to the immediate need. This problem was so well met by Boyen that his appeal of February 5, 1810 became the foundation of the law of September

peasants alone were fit for military service, since exposure, poor food, hard marches, and the rigors of army life would prove too much for the upper classes. *Ibid.*, LXI, 104-09.

18 *Preuss. Heer 1812*, pp. 85-86.

19 It is generally agreed that provincial disapproval was decisive for the monarch's opinion about conscription. *Preuss. Heer 1812*, p. 87; Lehmann, "Zur Geschichte der preussischen Heeresreform von 1808," *op. cit.*, pp. 438-39.

20 *Cf.* Thimme, "König Friedrich Wilhelm III., sein Anteil an der Konvention von Tauroggen und an der Reform von 1807-1812," *op. cit.*, pp. 46-48.

3, 1814 (the Boyen Law) on obligatory military service.[21] Boyen's argument pointed out the inconsistencies in the existing canton regulations and their unfairness to the lower classes. The change, he argued, would only revive the traditional Prussian military constitution which other states had copied, and would include the conscription that was the basis of the canton system.[22]

To the members of the government the conscription proposal seemed unrealistic for a state already harassed by a grave financial crisis and renewed French demands. In a separate memoir Finance Minister Altenstein, who had proved unequal to the task of fiscal reform imposed on him after Stein's dismissal, challenged the assumptions of the reformers and spoke out sharply against proposed changes in the law. To force educated men into ranks with manual laborers would be the grave of culture. He admitted that in time of war conscription might be very useful, but in peacetime it was dangerous, contrary to the tendency of the age, and likely to provoke large-scale emigration. In Altenstein the voice of the servant of an eighteenth century enlightened monarch could be heard.[23]

Minister Count Dohna agreed that conscription was dangerous, disadvantageous, and inadmissible. He maintained that substitution was indispensable in time of peace, because the freedom and culture of the nation had to be nurtured as well as training in arms.[24] Among the civil authorities only High Chancellor Beyme approved the proposal for universal conscription,

[21] *Preuss. Heer 1812*, p. 88. The *Entwurf zur Ausführung der Konskription in den preussischen Staaten*, in *Reorganisation der Preuss. Armee*, II, 107-10, declared at the outset that the basis of service was the same as that announced in the Articles of War, that every subject was obliged to do military service. Cf. *Gesetzsammlung 1806-1810*, p. 253. Substitutes were forbidden, but students of the arts and sciences might be furloughed.

[22] Also see Max Lehmann, " Preussen und die allgemeine Wehrpflicht im Jahre 1810," *Historische Zeitschrift*, LXIX (1892), 432-37.

[23] *Denkschrift des Ministers Altenstein*, Febr. 12, 1810, *ibid.*, LXIX, 437-40. In 1807 Altenstein had proposed, with Hardenberg's approval, the most thorough military reforms including the rigorous use of general conscription.

[24] *Denkschrift des Ministers Dohna*, Febr. 14, 1810, *ibid.*, LXIX, 440.

CONSCRIPTION AND THE KRÜMPER 157

although he did not praise the institution directly. He contented himself with the statement that everything ought to be subordinated to the task of strengthening the state. As for culture, "Both ancient and modern history prove that culture may be combined very satisfactorily with military service, for culture without military service has as its consequence the weakening of the body and the spirit."[25]

No immediate action was taken, however, and in the spring of 1810 some members of the now dissolved commission presented another memoir to the Ministers Altenstein, Goltz, Dohna, and Beyme in which they again argued the case for conscription.[26] Yet financial limitations presented an almost insuperable obstacle to its adoption, since the Prussian revenues were almost entirely consumed by the payment of the war indemnity to France. After peace had been concluded between France and Austria (October 14, 1809), Frederick William had tried to obtain a postponement of the indemnity payments. Napoleon replied tersely on January 8, 1810 that greater economies could be effected if Prussia dissolved the army except for the Royal Guard. If payments were not continued he threatened to annex part of the province of Silesia. When the king decided to meet the French terms the last hope of expanding the army vanished.[27] Nevertheless, when Hardenberg assumed office in the spring of 1810 Scharnhorst persisted in an attempt to gain approval for universal conscription. An eloquent memoir attacked the privilege allowed the canton conscripts of providing substitutes.[28]

[25] *Denkschrift des Grosskanzlers Beyme*, Mar. 8, 1810, *ibid.*, LXIX, 441.

[26] *Denkschrift* of Scharnhorst, Hake, Rauch, and Boyen, April 5, 1810, *ibid.*, LXIX, 441-51.

[27] Vidal de la Blache, *op. cit.*, pp. 161-64; Lehmann, *Scharnhorst*, II, 308-09, 311-12.

[28] Max Lehmann, ed., "Vier Denkschriften Scharnhorst's aus dem Jahre 1810," *Historische Zeitschrift*, LVIII (1887), 102-05. See also two other *Denkschriften* arguing the case for conscription, in Lehmann, "Preussen und die allgemeine Wehrpflicht im Jahre 1810," *op. cit.*, pp. 451-57.

SCHARNHORST'S DISMISSAL

This was Scharnhorst's last attempt before the outbreak of war with France in 1813 to gain a conscription law, for at Napoleon's insistence he was removed on June 6, 1810 from his post in the Ministry of War.

As a leader of the war party in Prussia, Scharnhorst's efforts for military reform had been viewed with the greatest suspicion by the French. His energetic opposition to Napoleon's demand of January 8, 1810 that the Prussian army be dissolved made it perfectly clear that he was a menace to the French Empire. Scharnhorst retired publicly but he remained secretly in communication with government officials, and in particular with the War Ministry, which was entrusted with the execution of the reforms approved in 1808. Yet the loss of his leadership brought an end to the agitation for conscription.[29]

Under Hardenberg, who was named Chancellor on the same day that Scharnhorst resigned, there was strict economy and heavier taxation. These conditions made the leaders of the government think increasingly in terms of the reductions of 1807-1808 rather than new levies or the augmentation of the army.[30] By 1811, however, Hardenberg had been converted to Scharnhorst's view that a mass rising of the Prussian people might save the nation. From the king's standpoint immediate universal service was still not practicable, and to the suggestion of a new defence law he gave the laconic reply: " You are quite correct, the introduction of a universal system of conscription would lead to a useful increase in the defenders of the Fatherland; nevertheless, it must be carried out with reference to the other

---

[29] Lehmann, *Scharnhorst*, II, 316-22. See Scharnhorst's letters of Mar. 18, 1810 and June 4, 1810 to Frederick William III, *Scharnhorsts Briefe*, I, 387-89, 394-95, and Scharnhorst's letter of resignation to Hardenberg, June 4, 1810, *ibid.*, I, 391-94.

[30] Vidal de la Blache, *op. cit.*, pp. 289-95, 350-55. The king was fearful that the French might discover that the Prussian army exceeded 42,000 men and his reports concealed its true size by omitting certain troops. Boyen, *Erinnerungen*, II, 79, and the king's report of June 24, 1810, *ibid.*, II, Beilage I, pp. 345-48.

institutions of the state, and I will order universal conscription as soon as the circumstances warrant."[31]

The opportunity that Frederick William spoke of did not come before 1813. Until then Prussia lacked an effective conscription law. The defeat of universal conscription was virtually assured by the unhappy circumstance that the proposals were made at the time of the financial crisis of 1809-1810. The army budget for that period (1809-1810) was reduced from 7,038,-976 thalers to 6,402,500 thalers, the saving being effected by furloughing, and in spite of Scharnhorst's demand for more money.[32] So it was that the canton system defined in 1792 remained in force, and beyond administrative changes of a purely mechanical nature, conscription remained exactly as it had developed in the previous century.[33]

THE *Krümper* SYSTEM

What is commonly called the *Krümper* system was taken up between 1809 and 1812 only because the larger program of the reformers had failed.

Under these circumstances the normal type of reserve training was carried out as it had been since the time of the first Prussian king. The reformers recognized in the canton system the basis for a conscript army resting on short term service. But maintaining the canton system made impossible either a genuine reform of the army or a phenomenal rise in its numbers.

The term *Krümper* has come to designate the means whereby the Prussian army sought after 1807 to increase its numbers. The military use of the word began as early as the War of the

31 *Reorganisation der Preuss. Armee*, II, 112. Nevertheless, Friedrich Thimme praises Frederick William's "realism" in the political crisis of 1811. See F. Thimme, "Zur Geschichte Friedrich Wilhelms III. und der Krisis von 1811," *Historische Zeitschrift*, IXC (1903), 65-80.

32 Lehmann, *Scharnhorst*, II, 309; *cf*. Vidal de la Blache, *op. cit*., pp. 166-67.

33 In 1814 the king was still not in sympathy with universal service. Max Lehmann, ed., "Boyen's Darstellung der preussischen Kriegsverfassung," *Historische Zeitschrift*, LXVII (1891), 55-56.

Spanish Succession. From the term for folding or shrinking cloth, *schrumpfen* or *zusammenschrumpfen,* the military usage derived *krümpen* or *krempen,* a colloquial expression describing the manner of "shrinking" new recruits into the army.[34] Another theory connects the origin of the word with the term, *Krümper,* meaning a surplus of cavalry horses. Variations in spelling throughout the eighteenth century gave rise to *krempen,* describing the process, and *Kremper,* applying to the men.[35]

By 1807 the word had long been in common use in the army. Yet in Cabinet Orders and in legal phraseology these terms were preferred: *Überkompletten, Überüberkompletten, Kriegsaugmentation,* or *Beurlaubten,* each meaning available trained man power held in the cantons on furlough. Of these, *Beurlaubten* was employed most frequently in official documents and instructions. In the official usage Prussia had a *Beurlaubungs-System;* state papers, memoranda, and Cabinet Orders invariably referred to the training and furloughing practiced in the army as *Beurlaubung.* To the last *Krümper* remained an unofficial usage. It has become established in the historical vocabulary principally because the older accounts of the military reforms were based to a very great extent on memoirs of army officers who were familiar only with the military term.[36]

THE FIRST *Krümper* TRAINING MEASURES

The origin of the system is generally ascribed to Scharnhorst's memoir of July 31, 1807, which suggested that every company and squadron set aside annually a reserve of twenty trained men whose places were to be taken by raw recruits.[37] This suggestion led to the Cabinet Order of August 6, 1808

---

34 Cf. Jany, "Die Kantonverfassung Friedrich Wilhelms I.," *op. cit.,* p. 251, footnote 3.

35 Cf. *Reorganisation der Preuss. Armee,* I, 354, II, 112 ff.; *Preuss. Heer 1812,* Anlage II, pp. 490-91. For some time after 1813 historians used the spelling *Kremper.*

36 Cf. Jany, *op. cit.,* III, 466.

37 *Preuss. Archiv,* XCIV, 19-23. See Lehmann, *Scharnhorst,* II, 157 ff.

CONSCRIPTION AND THE KRÜMPER

ordering the infantry and unmounted artillery companies to send three to five men on furlough each month.[38] As explained in Chapter IV it is clear that the *Beurlaubung* was intended to follow the old established course of training replacements for war. In no sense can the order be interpreted as a means for rapidly increasing the army. Nor was any subterfuge intended, because the Treaty of Paris which limited the army to 42,000 men came a month after the order. Furthermore, the unwillingness of the king to jeopardize Prussian neutrality or to violate formal diplomatic obligations precluded anything so daring as the plan which historians have attributed to Scharnhorst.[39]

It is not possible to assert that from the summer of 1808 important reserves of trained men were developed in Prussia, because the order of August 6 did not affect the entire army. Only the infantry and artillery regiments of the Prussian brigades were ordered to develop their complements, while the entire cavalry was excluded from the order.[40] On November 21, 1808 an additional order was issued that gave *Krümper* training the direction it was to take during the period before the War of Liberation: the use of old soldiers from the regiments that had been dissolved in 1806-1807. In the Prussian lands there were thousands of well-trained soldiers, most of whom were reluctant to abandon the security of military life. It

---

[38] *Kabinettsorder an das Oberkriegskollegium,* Aug. 6, 1808, *ibid.,* XCIV, 542.

[39] Curt Jany, one of the first historians to recognize the small scale of *Krümper* training, as well as to perceive the roots of the plan in the military practice of eighteenth century Prussia, nevertheless places special emphasis on the program of 1805. In his discussion of the Land Reserve Troops, he concludes that the Cabinet Order of July 5, 1806, commanding the development of ten men per company as a war reserve, was the immediate beginning of the plan relied on after 1807. Jany feels that it might have been possible for the later system to have emerged from the pre-1806 reforms without the pressure of a great defeat. In this opinion he is, of course, paraphrasing Goltz. *Cf.* Jany, *op. cit.,* III, 464-65.

[40] Nord, *op. cit.,* p. 51; *Preuss. Heer 1812,* p. 94. After 1809 the cavalry began building a reserve.

was natural for the regimental commanders to make use of them in filling the ranks.[41] The Land Councillors of each circle were ordered to confer with the regiments and establish the number and the names of the old soldiers. When lists had been prepared the regiments might make use of this reserve, but they were to recruit only among soldiers that had served less than ten years.[42]

From the beginning there was friction and discontent among the regimental commanders over the method of recruiting that had been ordered. But the civil bureaucrats, it may be suspected, approved the use of old soldiers because the agricultural work of the peasants would not be interrupted by military service.[43] Other problems arose in the old Prussian provinces where the regiments had never been able to regain their established strength. And experienced officers objected to the order of August 6 for its provision of but a single month of training. They could not forget the recent campaigns in which the inadequate training of the cantonists had been revealed.[44]

The *Beurlaubung* program of the summer of 1808 proved unsatisfactory and an additional order of December 24, 1808 corrected certain errors. The first order of August 6 had specified a month of active training, but it had not been made clear that only trained men were to be furloughed. On December 24, therefore, the regiments were instructed to release the oldest native subjects in service into the cantons, while new conscripts were to be held in ranks for additional training.[45]

[41] The Cabinet Order of Nov. 21, 1808 legitimized the practice. *Reorganisation der Preuss. Armee*, I, 356-59. Detailed instructions for the use of old soldiers are given in Scharnhorst, *Auszug*, pp. 96-97.

[42] *Reorganisation der Preuss. Armee*, I, 357; see *Preuss. Heer 1812*, p. 95.

[43] *Cf.* Schmidt, *Erinnerungen*, part II, p. 113. Opposition of the regiments to *Krümper* training is discussed in Cavaignac, *op. cit.*, II, 407-08.

[44] *Preuss. Heer 1812*, p. 95; Hermann von Boyen, *Darstellung der Grundsätze der alten und der gegenwärtigen Preussischen Kriegsverfassung* (Berlin, 1817), p. 32.

[45] Jany, *op. cit.*, III, 466, IV, 13.

The Extent of Reserve Training

These were the important orders upon which the *Krümper* system rested, but neither the wording of the instructions, nor the intention of Scharnhorst in drafting them, warrants the interpretation of later historians. It cannot be overlooked that the first objective of these measures was to fill units to their proper strength, and to form a war reserve. It is the more surprising that the commonplace interpretation has endured so long, because the editor of the first edition of the documents published in the eighteen sixties, summarized the contents as follows: " The erroneous conception has arisen that the mass of the men, called in the speech of the army by the unofficial name, ' Krümper,' became trained recruits in the shortest time on the basis of the Scharnhorst plan, and in consequence of the above Cabinet Order (August 6, 1808), which was eventually extended in principle to the whole army. Not until 1813 was the Scharnhorst plan given the force of law, and only the slightest use of the authorization of the Cabinet Order was made because the need was not at hand." [46]

Not until April 3, 1809 did the new *Beurlaubung* measures affect the entire army, when in advance of an anticipated mobilization the regiments were ordered to prepare an adequate *Ersatz*, or war reserve.[47] Henceforth, every cavalry regiment was to increase its squadrons from 60 to 125 horses, taking 65 riders out of the cantons. Similarly, each infantry company was to prepare a war reserve of thirty-five men, and on April 14 an order for the field artillery directed the training of enough cantonists to equip an additional twelve-pound battery in each

---

[46] *Reorganisation der Preuss. Armee*, II, 112.

[47] *Preuss. Heer 1812*, p. 94. Cf. *Preuss. Archiv*, LXXXVIII, 420, a report of April 29, 1809 indicating that these preparations were not unknown to the French. And *ibid.*, LXXXVIII, 470, an indication that the Prussian public was stirred by what seemed to be preparation for war (June 13, 1809). Actually, the army was only getting ready to mobilize, which did not have the ominous meaning that it acquired in the twentieth century.

brigade.[48] Whether every unit of the army was able to achieve these increases is open to doubt.

Supplementary training for the *Beurlaubten* who had been returned to their cantons was arranged as early as July 25, 1808. This was not done in order to hasten the development of the reserve, but to satisfy the complaints of the officers that the reservists were being badly trained. As many officers and non-commissioned officers as the regiments could spare from duty were sent into the cantons where the *Beurlaubten* were drilled on Sundays; though the king added to the order with his own hand, " However, without disturbing religious service."[49] Since each canton was divided into circles, the regiments were expected to send arms and equipment to the principal towns for distribution to the reservists. By 1812 there were loud protests that the system was wearing out the army's weapons. In the squares and open places of the small towns the men were to be assembled and given the rudiments of drill as well as instruction in loading and shooting. The effectiveness of this training remains unknown.[50]

The Element of Secrecy

All measures were carried out in the strictest secrecy to avoid alarming the strong French garrisons in the land. Yet there was small reason for mystery since the number of men involved was not very great. While Cabinet Orders forbade unnecessary

48 *Reorganisation der Preuss. Armee*, II, 113-14. The official history indicates that many units, particularly in the Prussian brigade, actually offered passive resistance to the new orders because they were below their effective strength. *Preuss. Heer 1812*, p. 95.

49 *Preuss. Archiv*, XCIV, 524-27, particularly p. 525. It is evident from one of Scharnhorst's letters to Count Götzen, Nov. 27, 1809, that the king was satisfied with the rate of training and wished it to continue until the companies had reached their established strength. In Frederick William's mind the purpose of the measure seems to have been only the achievement of the full complements for peace and war. *Scharnhorsts Briefe*, I, 381-82.

50 *Reorganisation der Preuss. Armee*, II, 125; *Preuss. Archiv*, XCIV, 525-27, 544-46.

discussion, in the popular press there were many reports of Prussia's preparation for hostilities.[51]

Stein also took occasion on September 24, 1808 to inform the Prussian peace commission of the false rumors concerning Prussian war measures that were disturbing French officers and diplomats. " From time to time many rumors of an alleged increase of troops, mobilization, and armament in our state have spread, these have aroused considerable sensation and great distrust among the French officials and have induced them to take the most strenuous measures ... but personal observation shows that neither troop increases nor mobilization nor armament of any sort has occurred among our military forces. The majority of our regiments are by and large incomplete, many have only a small personnel and some have only officers and non-commissioned officers. Nowhere has a mustering of cantonists taken place, instead, a very considerable number of soldiers has been released, and where those dismissed could not, without hardship, be denied support, travel money has even been granted, in order that the strength of the troops might be reduced. No horses for the artillery trains have been provided, indeed, even the customary recording of horses has not been undertaken. There has been little strengthening of the corps in Pomerania. It is really an injustice to give this command the title of a corps. . . . There has been no thought of the creation of a land militia. We make this disclosure to you, in order that the above-mentioned incongruous rumors may be corrected and denied and accurate views thereon be brought into circulation."[52]

Restrictions on the Growth of a Reserve

In spite of Prussia's destitute condition the armed forces remained slightly in excess of the strength stipulated in the Treaty of Paris. A limited number of reservists were being trained, but

51 *Ibid.*, XCIV, 572-73; *Reorganisation der Preuss. Armee*, II, 114. In the *Schwäbischer Merkur* of August 11, 1808 an article suggested that the recruiting of the Prussian army presaged an early renewal of the war. *Preuss. Archiv*, XCIV, 573. See *ibid.*, LXXXVIII, 470, for a report of public tension.

52 *Ibid.*, XCIV, 587-88.

on December 4, 1809 the army's slow growth was curtailed by a new instruction ordering only three *Beurlaubten* instead of five to each company.[53] Impoverishment of the nation, internal confusion, and the difficulties of supply all affected the growth of a reserve. The dislocation of the army was also a factor. Although the order for furloughing dated from the summer of 1808, the army was not established in its garrisons until the beginning of 1809. Further, the furloughing according to Scharnhorst's plan was not applied to the entire army until the spring of 1809. In that year the return of thousands of prisoners of war gave commanding officers a reserve of recruits to draw upon. Previous orders for the use of the old soldiers were reinforced by another of May 11, 1809, which repeated the procedure for the drafting of lists by civil officials and the exchange of surplus men among the brigades.[54]

Because a thoroughly trained contingent was used to build up the strength of the regiments, the number of actual reservists, that is men without previous military experience who were trained briefly in the ranks and then were held in readiness in their cantons, diminished to a handful. From the Peace of Tilsit (1807) until the middle of 1809 the army had only 863 reservists in this sense.[55] Compared with the pre-war period when Prussia could mobilize almost a quarter million men in two weeks, the immediate post-Tilsit era must be regarded as the nadir of Prussian military power. In this crisis the monarch was willing to assist only by loosening the strict regulation of the canton boundaries, so that the regiments could supply one another with men.[56]

To the general difficulties facing the reformers might be added the great confusion that attended the training and furloughing of men from 1808 to 1811. Not until August 28, 1810

53 Nord, *op. cit.*, pp. 52-53.
54 *Reorganisation der Preuss. Armee*, II, 114; see Scharnhorst, *Auszug*, p. 96, for the Cabinet Order of July 8, 1809 outlining the procedure for equalizing man power among the cantons.
55 Lehmann, *Scharnhorst*, II, 287.
56 Herrmann, *op. cit.*, p. 511.

were commanding officers instructed to send correct lists of the furloughed men to the higher military authorities. Until that time strict secrecy had been preserved, so strict indeed that the administrative personnel did not know what was occurring among the troops! Without centralized control each commander was free to interpret the orders and carry out his own conception of training. And for certain regiments such as the *Garde du Corps,* which had neither a canton nor a means of developing a reserve, there were special regulations.[57]

When the reports arrived in the Second Division of the War Department, there appeared to be so many variations in the handling and training of *Beurlaubten* that a new series of orders was made necessary. The War Department had only a vague idea of the number and location of the units of the army! This was particularly true of the artillery.[58] There was confusion over the distinction between *Beurlaubten* intended for a war footing and those marked for the extraordinary reserve. Officially, these categories were supposed to be reckoned together, but the preference of the regiments for old soldiers, and often for men of unusual size and height, made a uniform system impossible. Another difficulty arose from the reluctance of commanding officers to release into the cantons the men who knew the manual of arms, drilled smartly, and presented a soldierly appearance. Veterans were an asset to the regiment, and it was easy to comply with the regulations by giving the peasants only a perfunctory training and keeping the old soldiers in ranks. Order after order had to be issued specifying that old soldiers rather than recruits were to be furloughed.[59]

A not inconsiderable amount of desertion continually restrained the growth of the army. In some districts the cantonists took up arms against the regimental officers. In West Prussia and Silesia, the principal centers of resistance to the army,

[57] *Preuss. Heer 1812,* pp. 97-98. The lists did not arrive in headquarters until the fall of 1810.
[58] *Die Preussische Artillerie von ihrer Neuformation 1809,* pp. 23-24.
[59] *Preuss. Heer 1812,* pp. 96-99, 114; *Reorganisation der Preuss. Armee,* II, 113, 116-17.

the countermeasures of the populace were little less than open revolt. Between February, 1809 and December, 1811 the deserters from the Upper Silesian brigade numbered 1,241. In less than a week in December, 1811 fifty-four men deserted from the Fortress of Silberberg, and twenty men from the Fortress of Cosel.[60] Since the rate of furloughing trained men was far less than this, it is small wonder that the augmentation of the Prussian army between the Peace of Tilsit and the resumption of warfare in 1813 proceeded slowly.

Administration of the Canton System

Despite the reorganization of the army and the widespread misunderstanding of furloughing, the canton system functioned in the manner of the previous century. For the guidance of officials a Cabinet Order of November 20, 1807 had declared the validity of the canton law of 1792. Changes in the administration of the law were made, however, to suit the new organization of the army. Thus, the brigadier generals replaced the regimental colonels in handling canton matters for the army. It was significant that civilian bureaucrats retained preponderant control, and that their decision still governed the actual selection of men to be conscripted. The War Department was the final authority in all matters involving the canton law, however.[61]

The canton revision, that is, the preparation of lists of persons liable to the claim of the regiments, was carried out by the land authorities in cooperation with the War Department. Although a yearly revision was required, apparently only one was made between 1807 and 1812. This was the General Canton

[60] *Preuss. Heer 1812*, pp. 366-68. *Cf.* "Entwickelung der Preussischen Kriegsartikel," *op. cit.*, pp. 382, 386.

[61] Scharnhorst, *Auszug*, pp. 37, 95, 159. Four of the brigade cantons averaged 700,000 persons, while two were over 900,000 persons. *Preuss. Archiv*, XCIV, 822. There were many disputes over the boundaries of the cantons; apparently the regiments were loath to abandon their old cantons and accept the new areas. *Preuss. Heer 1813*, p. 349. After the establishment of the Military Governments in 1813, the new recruiting territories overlapped the brigade cantons. A keen competition for recruits ensued which necessitated a new series of administrative orders. *Ibid.*, pp. 349-50.

CONSCRIPTION AND THE KRÜMPER

Extract of 1811, which was not in the hands of the officials until the winter of 1812-1813. It resembled the extracts for the guidance of the Land Councillors that had been drawn up before 1806.⁶²

There was less order in the administration of the canton system after 1806 owing to the constant change of garrisons. This practice was decreed in order to prevent the stultifying effect of long cantonment in one place. When garrisons were transferred, cantonists might refuse to accompany their unit to its new quarter if they elected service in the incoming regiment. The rigidity of the canton boundaries was broken in other circumstances, for cantonists might report voluntarily to any cavalry, artillery, or pioneer regiment. However, officers were forbidden to recruit for volunteers or to prevent men from volunteering in other regiments. There is no evidence that the number of volunteers without previous military experience gave rise to any grave problems.⁶³

THE USE OF OLD SOLDIERS

It had become evident by the fall of 1810 that the original training measures conceived by Scharnhorst were not capable of creating a reserve force equal to the need of the state. From the reports of commanding officers in the summer of 1810 it is apparent that only 13,371 *Beurlaubten* had been released into the cantons, and of these, 9,883 were intended for the war reserve of the regiments.⁶⁴ Since Tilsit, therefore, only 3,488 recruits had been passed through the army, given a minimum of training, and released to their homes. In addition to the *Beurlaubten* there were available 11,218 soldiers from disbanded regiments, while an additional 11,162 men from the same source were considered unfit for military duty. In the cantons the men

---

62 Scharnhorst, *Auszug*, pp. 34, 102; Preuss. *Heer 1813*, p. 335.

63 *Cf.* Scharnhorst, *Auszug*, pp. 38-39, 67, 96-97, 99-100. A domestic atmosphere still prevailed in the army since there was little change in the number of wives and children in the garrisons. Their transportation and care ceased to be the concern of the state, and after 1810 no more participants in the widows' and children's fund were admitted. *Ibid.*, pp. 67-68.

64 *Reorganisation der Preuss. Armee*, I, 117; Jany, *op. cit.*, IV, 40.

between the ages of eighteen and thirty who were liable for service numbered 98,752. For reasons of economy, lack of equipment, and administrative confusion this great reserve was not tapped.[65]

Without question the soldiers of the old army were the greatest single source of *Beurlaubten*. As early as November 21, 1808 a Cabinet Order provided for the distribution of men from disbanded units among the cantons of the standing regiments. Veterans were preferred by officers not only for the ease of training, but also because they met the requirements of the army in experience and discipline. Not every veteran could be reemployed and it seems clear that the army, especially the infantry units, made a careful selection from among those who were available. York in 1811 for example, called the *Beurlaubten* the oldest and best soldiers. Typical of the infantry regiments were the reports of the number and the experience of the *Beurlaubten* in the spring of 1811 and 1812.[66]

THE NUMBER OF *Beurlaubten* IN THE SPRING OF 1811 AND 1812

Unit	Period	Beurlaubten	Soldiers of 1806-1807
First East Prussian Infantry Regiment...	May 1812	2,000	?
Second East Prussian Infantry Regiment..	May 1811	1,354	608
Second East Prussian Grenadier Battalion	May 1812	755	376
Third East Prussian Infantry Regiment..	May 1812	2,000	?
Fourth East Prussian Infantry Regiment..	May 1811	1,475	601
Life Guard Regiment	May 1812	2,550	1,100
Grenadier Battalion of Life Guards	May 1812	224	143
Second West Prussian Infantry Regiment..	May 1812	776	242
First Silesian Infantry Regiment........	May 1811	3,025	2,210
Second Silesian Infantry Regiment......	May 1811	2,501	2,118

Approximately half of the *Beurlaubten* were old soldiers who had participated in the campaign of 1806-1807. When an auxiliary corps was mobilized in 1812 to assist the French, many of these veterans were sent to Russia and more of the younger men were drawn into the army. Before that date the proportion

---
[65] *Loc. cit.*
[66] *Preuss. Heer 1812*, p. 108; Jany, *op. cit.*, IV, 21, 40, 41.

CONSCRIPTION AND THE KRÜMPER

of younger men was greatest in the musketeers; only a third of the furloughed men had previous military experience. Most of the fusilier reservists were veterans, however. The highest percentage of old soldiers was to be found in the grenadiers.[67]

Although the orders of 1809 had prescribed the training of general war reserves, in the cavalry the question was of less importance because numerous veterans were available. But the rebuilding of the artillery required many new gunners, hence both training and furloughing were actively followed. Yet the reports for August, 1811 listed only 2,078 artillery *Krümper*. By December, 1812, however, 4,354 trained artillerists were held in the cantons, but a serious shortage of officers and noncommissioned officers could not easily be overcome.[68]

ADDITIONAL *Krümper* TRAINING MEASURES

The infantry was actually the only arm to follow the spirit of the various orders. Even here there was such a variety of procedures with respect to enrollment and furloughing that to catalog them would be impossible. Throughout the army the selection of the men and the duration of their training varied so considerably that to characterize the process as a system would be misleading.[69]

Nevertheless, on February 7, 1811 the tempo of training was increased. Every company was ordered to enroll eight extra recruits a month, and every squadron three, for the four months

---

[67] *Ibid.*, IV, 40-41; *Preuss. Heer 1812*, pp. 108-109. See the lists in *ibid.*, pp. 106-07, 110-114.

[68] *Die Preussische Artillerie von ihrer Neuformation 1809*, p. 8. Men were easy to obtain for the artillery but their training, owing to the lack of instructors and materiel, was haphazard. Consult H. von Decker, *Geschichtliche Rückblick auf die Formation der preussischen Artillerie seit dem Jahre 1809* (Berlin, 1866), pp. 8-10, and Paul Rummel, *Ueber die Organisation und Mobilmachung der preussischen Artillerie im Jahre 1813* (Berlin, 1863), p. 10.

[69] *Preuss. Heer 1812*, pp. 98-99, 109. A very great weakness of the *Krümper* system after 1807 was the reservist's uncertainty about the length of his service. See *ibid.*, pp. 113, 115. Examples of the variation in training are given in Cavaignac, *op. cit.*, II, 410-11.

beginning March first. By June at the end of this period an infantry company would have gained thirty-two trained reservists, whereas in the entire previous year only thirty-six had been trained over its established strength. Once again the new order specified that the oldest men were to be released. In the same manner certain artillery companies raised the number of furloughs to twenty men in each company per month.[70] But by the summer of 1811 despite the most strenuous efforts and the creation of special training units, the army was able to train only 14,384 additional *Beurlaubten,* and this figure included the normal war replacements.[71] On September 11, 1811 the brigadier generals at last received orders for establishing these training measures uniformly. The order also marked the official acknowledgment that the strength of a reserve army, composed either of militiamen or cantonists, could not be equal to that of the line.[72]

Political events in 1811 bore directly on the training program of the army. Lest the English land on the Baltic coast, Napoleon ordered Prussia to raise a coast defence force. This opportunity was gladly seized because Prussian leaders believed that it would provide a means of increasing the trained reserve while complying with the Emperor's wish. On April 7, 1811 an order for the occupation of the coast was sent to the East and West Prussian, Pomeranian, Brandenburg, and part of the Lower Silesian brigades, as well as the Prussian and Brandenburg Artillery brigades and their *Krümper.* At many places along the coast and in the interior the reserves of these troops were concentrated, so that in addition to the regulars 11,740 *Beurlaubten* of all arms were assembled. Many reservists were organized as labor brigades in special camps; no arms were distributed and they were required to work on the fortresses under the super-

---

70 Jany, *op. cit.,* IV, 53; *Reorganisation der Preuss. Armee,* II, 117-118.
71 *Preuss. Armee 1812,* p. 100.
72 *Ibid.,* pp. 102-03; *Reorganisation der Preuss. Armee,* II, 121-22.

CONSCRIPTION AND THE KRÜMPER 173

vision of retired officers. In view of this fact the effectiveness of *Krümper* training during the year 1811 may be questioned.[73]

An important result of the concentration of reservists on the coast was the formation of training depots (June 25, 1811) for the rapid increase of the army and the training of the war replacements.[74] The training depots were created when it became apparent that the regiments mobilized along the Baltic coast were in no better position to train additional *Beurlaubten* than the unmobilized regiments that remained in the interior. In these units the training of reservists had to be curtailed because of the continuous observation needed along the frontiers, and the active use of the garrisons in certain provinces as a police force. Whether or not the formation of training depots offset the decline in the rate and effectiveness of *Krümper* training among the line regiments is debatable. Certainly the army lists do not show any remarkable increase after the summer of 1811 when the training depots were formed.[75]

INTERRUPTION OF TRAINING IN 1812

Demobilization of the regiments engaged in the work along the coast began in the fall of 1811 and lasted until the winter of 1812. In that year Napoleon's pressing demands for assistance in his preparations against Russia virtually eliminated the training of additional men. After February 24, 1812 France and Prussia were formally allied and an army of 20,842 men had to be equipped to serve as a contingent in the *Grande Armée*. Troops for the expeditionary force were drawn from the six brigades of the army, but the Prussian brigade contributed the

[73] *Ibid.*, II, 118-20. During the summer of 1811 some of the reservists were sent home to assist with the harvest. *Ibid.*, II, 104. Also see Jany, *op. cit.*, IV, 53-54.

[74] See *Reorganisation der Preuss. Armee*, II, 120.

[75] In effect the establishment of Depot Companies, simply called Depots after 1812, of seasoned men and a generous allotment of recruits, increased the number of units that were drawing in peasants, training them briefly, and releasing them into the cantons. Jany, *op. cit.*, III, 467, IV, 55; *Preuss. Heer 1812*, pp. 117-19.

174   PRUSSIAN MILITARY REFORMS 1786-1813

most men as it was nearest the concentration areas of the French army.[76] So much effort was expended in mobilizing and equipping this force that little training could be given the troops remaining in Prussia. With approximately 20,000 men drawn into Napoleon's army, the stipulations of the Treaty of Paris allowed Prussia only 22,000 additional troops. The reports presented to Napoleon's adjutant in Berlin, Count Narbonne, did not exceed that figure. However, the immobile part of the army was officially reckoned at 38,301 effectives; even this figure was inaccurate but it calmed Hardenberg's fears that the French would learn the real strength of the army.[77]

During the summer of 1812 Colonel von Hake, the head of the military administration after Scharnhorst's forced retirement, proposed a revision of the reserve training program. He objected to the constant troop movements that made control of the army difficult, oppressed the peasants, and ruined the equipment. Hake's suggestions were approved by the king, and an order of August 4, 1812 stipulated that the conscription of cantonists should occur only in the spring and the fall, and fixed the number of cantonists at twelve for each infantry company (twenty-four annually), six for each cavalry squadron, and six to eight for each artillery company. A great improvement might have been effected thereby if the outbreak of war in 1813 had not intervened so soon.[78]

ANNUAL GROWTH OF THE ARMY

The slow expansion of the armed forces during this period is made evident by a yearly tabulation of strength. For the year 1808 several authoritative reports on the number of men in the army may be cited. Scharnhorst, writing to Stein in August, placed the number of standing troops and *Beurlaubten* in East

76 See *Die Preussische Artillerie von ihrer Neuformation 1809*, p. 9, and Schmidt, *Erinnerungen*, part II, pp. 123 ff.

77 Jany, *op. cit.*, IV, 61-62. Cf. *Reorganisation der Preuss. Armee*, II, 77-86. On the expeditionary corps sent to Russia in 1812, see Paul Holzhausen, *Die Deutschen in Russland* (Berlin, 1912), pp. xxi, 3-4, 63-70.

78 *Reorganisation der Preuss. Armee*, II, 125-26.

CONSCRIPTION AND THE KRÜMPER 175

and West Prussia at 25,000, of whom 6,800 were in the cavalry. In Pomerania there were 8,000 men, including 1,200 cavalry and some artillery. All the Silesian troops were being used as garrisons in the fortresses. According to Scharnhorst, Prussia's army including reservists amounted to fewer than 50,000 men.[79] His estimate was in general agreement with the list prepared in Königsberg in June, 1808. In all the Prussian lands the following forces were at hand.[80]

STRENGTH OF THE PRUSSIAN ARMY IN JUNE, 1808

	Infantry	Artillery	Cavalry	Total
Officers	1,079	147	535	1,761
Non-comm. Officers	3,264	503	1,766	5,533
Musicians	659	35	199	893
Surgeons	227	27	86	340
Troops	10,025	2,161	5,651	17,837
Men on leave	17,396	1,653	4,634	23,683
Total	32,650	4,526	12,871	50,047

The great number of men on leave manifests the strenuous measures that were taken immediately after 1807 to reduce expenses. Although listed as *Beurlaubten* most of these men were regulars on inactive duty who were eventually called back to the colors in 1808 and 1809. Only from 1809 did the training of peasant conscripts begin.[81] Jany gives the total strength of the army in 1808 as 1,696 officers and 52,142 men (apart from the *Garde du Corps*), but only 1,359 officers and 20,170 men were in service—the others had been furloughed.[82] After the reduc-

---

79 *Stein Denkschriften*, II, 504-05. Also two *Denkschriften* written by Scharnhorst in August, 1808 which lament the smallness of the army, *ibid.*, II, 490-93. See *Preuss. Archiv*, XCIV, 557-60.

80 *Ibid.*, XCIV, 449.

81 Cavaignac believes that *Krümper* training did not begin until 1810, but he does not offer very substantial evidence. *Op. cit.*, II, 408, footnote 1a.

82 Jany, *op. cit.*, IV, 8. See the *Denkschrift des Generalmajors von Scharnhorst*, of Aug., 1808, which is also given in *Preuss. Archiv*, XCIV, 557-59. Additional data is provided by Count Götzen in a communique of Oct. 7, 1808, *ibid.*, XCIV, 605-07.

176   PRUSSIAN MILITARY REFORMS 1786-1813

tions of 1808 the army declined to 49,817 effectives, including officers and 23,683 *Beurlaubten* in the sense of old soldiers on leave. Not less than 3,664 officers were then being maintained on half pay as a reserve; one that proved very useful in the mobilization of 1813. These officers were distributed throughout the cantons in order to have a continuous supervision of the cantonists, and after 1808, to make reports on the strength and movement of French troops.[83]

For 1809 the number of combatants was reported, in the spring, to be 45,897. Although the king insisted that treaty obligations be fulfilled, there were more troops than Prussia was permitted to maintain. The surplus was found primarily in the Upper Silesian brigade which was still being reorganized.[84]

Lists of August, 1810 showed 33,857 men with the colors, 10,781 furloughed, 1,300 garrison troops, and 3,300 *Invaliden* capable of service. In addition there were in Prussia 22,380 soldiers of the disbanded regiments, 11,218 of whom were still capable of bearing arms. For almost a year the regiments had been training their war replacements totalling 9,883 men. Some 3,488 additional trained reservists were *Krümper*, that is extra men not required for the normal replacement needs.[85]

A year later the army had grown to 74,553 officers, men, and reservists on furlough.[86] For May and June, 1811 the number of *Beurlaubten*, including the normal war replacements of the regiments, was 25,261, and an additional 5,250 capable only of garrison duty. For November and December, 1811 these same categories totaled 31,259 and 3,410; and for September and October of 1812, 33,337 and 3,087. The very slight increase between

[83] Jany, *op. cit.*, IV, 9, 17, 58.
[84] *Ibid.*, IV, 24.
[85] *Ibid.*, IV, 40.
[86] Boyen, *Erinnerungen*, II, Beilage XVI, pp. 416-23, for the report of the army's strength in August, 1811, particularly p. 423. Also see the report of Lt. Col. von Rauch on August 30, 1811 citing the total figure of 74,413 men. *Reorganisation der Preuss. Armee*, II, 171.

CONSCRIPTION AND THE KRÜMPER 177

1811 and 1812 showed that the training of reservists had been held in check by the mobilization for coast defence.[87]

Throughout 1812 the size of the army remained approximately the same, since the formation of an expeditionary corps for service under Napoleon disrupted the training program at home. Exact figures are not available but it is probable that the casualties of the Russian campaign more than offset the growth of the army after 1809. About 20,000 of the best troops were mobilized for service in Russia. After a great deal of hard fighting around Riga the total number of Prussian effectives at the end of 1812 was probably slightly less than the number in 1810-1811.[88]

The Legend of *Krümper* Training

From this data it is clear that the training of 150,000 *Krümper* from 1807 to 1813 is an historical legend. Although the *Krümper* or *Beurlaubung* system is generally believed to have been in operation during all the reform years from 1807 to 1813, actually it was used only from 1809 to 1811. Because the army remained on a semi-war footing after Tilsit, the troops could not be established in their garrisons until the spring of 1809. Formal training of reservists was delayed until that time by the reorganization of the army and the reductions imposed by the need for economy. During the remainder of 1809 and throughout 1810 the drafting, training, and furloughing of men for the reserve was carried out on the basis of the canton law of 1792. In 1811 this program was interrupted and the training of surplus men was considerably affected by the coast defence measures undertaken at Napoleon's insistence. The mobilization in 1812 of a considerable part of the Prussian army to assist in the invasion of Russia completely disrupted the training of reser-

[87] Jany, *op. cit.*, III, 467-68, IV, 41. Scharnhorst in conversations at St. Petersburg in October, 1811 used the round figure of 80,000 men. *Ibid.*, IV, 57.

[88] *Cf.* Carl von Clausewitz, *Der Feldzug 1812 in Russland* (3rd ed., Berlin, 1906), pp. 58, 64, 67, 74-75, 81-82. Only fragments of Prussian cavalry returned from Russia in 1812-1813. *Preuss. Heer 1813*, p. 127.

vists. At the beginning of 1813 the withdrawal of the armed forces to Silesia delayed the resumption of the training program until the actual outbreak of war with France.

Though the secret clauses of the Treaty of Paris were ostensibly the means whereby France intended to hold the Prussian army in check, this restraint proved less effective than the war indemnity and Napoleon's demands for military support. A fundamental limit to Prussian military ambitions was set by the poverty of the state, to which the French contributed by insisting upon heavy indemnity payments and the cession of rich provinces. Although the reformers tried to overcome all these handicaps with the *Krümper* system, it should be noted that this was not an invention of the times, but a means established in the Prussian army during the eighteenth century for the training of reservists.[89]

THE SIZE OF THE PRUSSIAN ARMY AND ITS TRAINED RESERVES 1807-1813

1807	53,523
1808	52,142
1809	45,897
1810	62,609
1811	74,553
1812	65,000
1813 (March)	65,675

[89] Jany summarizes his discussion of the *Krümper* system as follows: "The assertion in many popular works based on the old authors that the number of *Krümper* had risen by the year 1813 to 150,000 men rests only on the incorrect assumption that the new formations of 1813 consisted entirely of *Krümper*, whereas actually these made up only the nucleus of trained soldiers to which recruits were added." *Op. cit.*, III, 468. And there is a similar statement in *ibid.*, IV, 41. Boyen, *Erinnerungen*, III, 229-34, lists 61,671 mobile troops at the declaration of war in 1813.

CHAPTER VII
MILITARY TRAINING AND THE *LANDWEHR*

THE supply of arms for the Prussian army was adequate until the first great expansion took place in 1813. Although great stores of arms had been lost to the French in 1806-1807, and the armament factories remained in enemy hands until 1808, there were enough muskets at hand to equip the reduced Prussian army. At Scharnhorst's insistence the Nothardt musket that was being issued to the troops before 1806 was rebored to a larger caliber to permit the use of foreign and captured ammunition. This "New Prussian Model" was officially adopted in 1809, but the muskets that were being used by the troops were actually of many different varieties. Weapons were supplied by Austrian, Prussian, and English manufacturers, as well as by shops that repaired arms found on the battlefields in Prussia.[1] Enough pistols, sabers, and lances were available for arming the limited Prussian cavalry forces. By 1811 both the infantry and cavalry had sufficient small arms of all types.[2]

Most of the Prussian powder reserves had been in those fortresses which had weathered the French siege operations in 1806-1807. No other supplies were available for distribution to the troops, and with the output of the powder mills secured for French use, by 1810 a real shortage had developed. Only

---

[1] Scharnhorst did not favor the purchase of arms abroad because the quality of foreign armaments was unsatisfactory, and because domestic purchases maintained the capacity of the Prussian armament factories. Scharnhorst to Count Götzen, Nov. 27, 1809, *Scharnhorsts Briefe*, I, 381-82. The Nothardt had the carbine caliber of .60 Rhineland *Zoll* (15.69 mm.), while the standard European musket caliber was .72 Rhineland *Zoll*. Jany, *op. cit.*, III, 470. For Scharnhorst's explanation of the advantage of a larger caliber, see *Preuss. Archiv*, XCIV, 42.

[2] See Max Lehmann, ed., "Vier Denkschriften Scharnhorst's aus dem Jahre 1810," *Historische Zeitschrift*, LVIII (1887), 72-81; *Preuss. Archiv*, XCIV, 44, 583, 659-60; Boyen, *Erinnerungen*, II, 109, 178-79, and Beilage XL, pp. 514-15.

by restricting the troop exercises in that year could an adequate powder supply be retained for use in an emergency. For lack of powder the target practice ordered in the royal instructions could not be held. The training of the troops suffered, yet in spite of these instructions quick loading rather than accurate fire remained the training goal of most infantry officers. It was still not uncommon for the men to practice loading and firing with half charges and without bullets.[3]

Most of the artillery had been lost in the battles of Jena and Auerstädt. With the peace came an opportunity to rebuild it, and an Artillery Testing Commission headed by Prince August was appointed in 1808 to suggest technical improvements. Although the commission worked diligently and prepared designs of new cannon, the poverty of the state forbade the increase of the artillery train. Between 1808 and 1812 the total number of artillery pieces, including fortress types, had increased from 1,318 to 1,659, a lamentable strength in comparison with the 7,095 guns available in 1806. In 1808 only 149 cannon out of the total of 1,318 could be used in the field, yet Scharnhorst believed this number sufficient for an army of 60,000 men.[4] Several new foundries for casting cannon were established by the Artillery Testing Commission, but the rate of manufacture was slow since new guns were made only in the years from 1809 to 1811. Carriages and wagons for the artillery were manufactured by work companies set up in each of the three artillery brigades. Notwithstanding these measures there was always a shortage of gun carriages.[5]

Uniforms had always interested the king more than any other aspect of military life and under his influence a uniform similar to that worn by the Russians was adopted. Overcoats were now provided inasmuch as the troops were expected to bivouac and

---

[3] *Preuss. Archiv*, XCIV, 866; "Vier Denkschriften Scharnhorst's," *op. cit.*, pp. 59, 61.

[4] *Preuss. Archiv*, XCIV, 865.

[5] *Ibid.*, XCIV, 787; "Vier Denkschriften Scharnhorst's," *op. cit.*, pp. 59-60, 71, 78-81; *Preuss. Heer 1812*, pp. 206-12.

MILITARY TRAINING AND THE LANDWEHR 181

fight in every season of the year. And the Prussians finally gave up the fashion of powdered hair and elaborate coiffures. Shakos surmounted by generous plumes were adopted by many regiments, and prominent in all uniforms was the traditional blue of Prussia.[6]

INTRODUCING THE NEW TACTICS

Formal regulations for the tactical training of the army were not ready until 1812. Before that date only a few training guides had been published, but the *Instruction for the Use of the Third Rank*, which appeared on March 27, 1809, was forward-looking since it recommended that at least a third of the line troops be trained as sharpshooters and *tirailleurs*.[7] One pamphlet could not bring about a basic alteration in the tactics of the Prussian army, however. Virtually all of the officers had been trained before 1806 and though a small group realized the need for new methods, the majority were satisfied with the existing tactics. From what is known of the variation from unit to unit even the regulations of 1812 were not respected in the army.[8] Notwithstanding, these official instructions emphasized the increased use of light troops, organization in columns as well as in line, and the cooperation of the several arms in battle.[9]

General suggestions for the reform of tactics had been given in the king's *Denkschriften* of 1806 and 1807. The sixth paragraph of the king's agenda for the Military Reorganization

[6] Cf. A. Mila, *Geschichte der Bekleidung und Ausrüstung der Königlich Preussischen Armee in dem Jahren 1808 bis 1878* (Berlin, 1878). There is praise of the old uniforms by a contemporary in Kleist, *op. cit.*, pp. 54-55.

[7] Scharnhorst, *Auszug*, p. 182. Cf. R. Ollech, *Historische Entwickelung der taktischen Uebungen der Preussischen Infanterie* (Berlin, 1848), pp. 65-68.

[8] V. Chareton, *Comment la Prusse a préparé sa revanche 1806-1813* (Paris, 1903), p. 178.

[9] Sautermeister, *op. cit.*, pp. 47-62. All the new orders and instructions for training are in *Reorganisation der Preuss. Armee*, II, 231-307. Scharnhorst's views are summarized in Hermann von Boyen, *Beiträge zur Kenntniss des General von Scharnhorst* (Berlin, 1833), pp. 27-28.

Commission had emphasized the need for additional light infantry, while other paragraphs dealt with tactical changes made necessary by the experience of the war.[10] But the initial suggestions of the crown had been made under the immediate impression of the great defeats, and the appointment of York as Inspector of Light Troops was evidence of Frederick William's return to military conservatism. York's hostile attitude toward the reformers and their ideas had been made clear on numerous occasions.[11]

Winter exercises were held in 1809, a form of training previously unknown in the Prussian army. Throughout 1810 field training was curtailed for reasons of economy, but the men were given hard drills on the parade ground by non-commissioned officers. The formalities of the parade ground were closely regulated but commanding officers were allowed considerable freedom in their tactical exercises. From the accounts of men who did understand the new methods of warfare, it is clear that the average officer was not familiar with combat in depth, or fighting in villages and in broken terrain, or the use of *tirailleurs* and sharpshooters. Though the artificial styles of firing by squad volleys and alternate sections had been condemned before 1806, the continued use of these old methods was an indication that most officers knew very little about the new tactics.[12] In order to provide practical instruction a select group of commissioned and non-commissioned officers was sent to Berlin in 1810 for training as tactical instructors in their own regiments. And after March 27, 1811 both officers and men in what were called Normal Troops were trained according to the ideas of the best tacticians. These model forces were to demonstrate the art of war to regular units of the army. Before either group could

10 Sautermeister, *op. cit.*, pp. 33-35.

11 See the documents in *Preuss. Archiv*, XCIV, 586-87, 742. Consult Boyen, *Erinnerungen*, II, 110, who makes it clear that the king eventually lost his interest in tactical reform and was loath to see all the old maneuvers disappear.

12 There is a good deal of evidence for this. See Boyen, *Erinnerungen*, I, 346-47; Schmidt, *Erinnerungen*, part II, pp. 106-07, 112; and Sautermeister, *op. cit.*, pp. 66-69, 76.

MILITARY TRAINING AND THE LANDWEHR

have any influence upon the training methods the war with Russia had broken out.[13]

The development of the light infantry was entrusted by the king to General York. As Inspector of the Light Brigades he could send instructions directly to the commanding officers of the light troops, who were not bound by the customary chain of command in matters pertaining to training and exercises.[14] But since the Prussian light infantry had been well-trained before 1806, York was not able to contribute many new ideas. He made no innovations but his recommendations were at least equal to the training measures that had been in use among the best Prussian fusilier battalions. York had a practical turn of mind and his instructions described the light troops as the shield of the army and gave excellent combat advice by stressing the necessity of accurate shooting.[15]

OFFICIAL TRAINING REGULATIONS

An official manual of infantry tactics, *The Exercise Regulations for the Infantry,* appeared on January 15, 1812; it had been drafted by a commission that included Scharnhorst, Clausewitz, and York.[16] Though the best methods of waging war were summarized, it appeared too late for the average officer to profit from its contents.[17] The use of columns both for attack and defence was emphasized, although linear formations were also recommended when the troops were expecting an attack. The long thin battle line brought to perfection in Frederick

---

13 *Ibid.*, pp. 69-70. York complained that the officers lacked clear ideas about the conduct of battle. *Cf.* W. von Hülsen, "Yorck als Erzieher unseres Heeres," *Militär-Wochenblatt*, Beiheft 1908, pp. 447-48.

14 *Preuss. Archiv*, XCIV, 863.

15 Hülsen, *op. cit.*, pp. 441, 444; Scharnhorst, *Auszug*, pp. 3, 179-84, 191-92.

16 For excerpts see *Reorganisation der Preuss. Armee*, II, 255 ff.; *Preuss. Heer 1812*, pp. 140 ff.; *Gefechtsausbildung*, p. 107.

17 Sautermeister, *op. cit.*, p. 81. Contrast with Boyen, *Erinnerungen*, II, 111, who describes a complete reform of tactics. But it must be noted that Boyen is contradictory on this point.

the Great's day was far from being antiquated even in 1812. What was needed in the Prussian army was a more flexible tactical system, and the regulations of 1812 deserve praise for insisting upon the use under appropriate circumstances of columns and deployed order.[18]

Less praise can be given the cavalry regulations of 1812, which were written by a commission headed by Scharnhorst. He was especially qualified as an artillerist, but it was unfortunately true that his knowledge of the other arms was thorough only in an academic sense. The *Exercise Regulations for the Cavalry* of January 15, 1812 specified three forms of attack, in columns, in echelon, or in line, but the emphasis was placed upon the first of these. All cavalry movements were to be carried out in cooperation with the infantry, which deprived the cavalry of the decisive role that it had played under Frederick the Great.[19]

The importance that the French attached to artillery made it clear that the Prussians would have to improve their handling of that arm. Although the new regulations of July 8, 1812 simplified the drill, no new methods were described apart from an attempt to gain mobility by using more six-pound batteries. Some improvement was made by eliminating the regimental artillery which had long been the most inefficient in the army.[20]

---

[18] Sautermeister, *op. cit.*, p. 82; *Preuss. Heer 1812*, pp. 143-64, provides a full summary.

[19] Sautermeister, *op. cit.*, pp. 83-84; *Preuss. Heer 1812*, pp. 178-94; Pelet-Narbonne, *op. cit.*, II, 16-20. Technical troops after 1807 became less specialized: pioneers (engineers) were assigned to bridge building, fortification, mining, and sapping. Scharnhorst, *Auszug*, pp. 13-17, 202-03.

[20] Sautermeister, *op. cit.*, pp. 45, 59-61, 84-85; *Preuss. Heer 1812*, pp. 233-44, 257-58, 262-63. The types of guns are described in *Die Preussische Artillerie von ihrer Neuformation 1809*, pp. 6, 9, 15-18. Napoleon believed that for good troops two guns for each thousand men were enough, but it was always necessary to have as many, or more guns than the enemy. He tried therefore to have four for every thousand men. In 1813-1814 the Prussians averaged two to two and two-thirds guns for each thousand men. The Russians had many more guns than this. On the average the army of this period had three to three and a half guns for a thousand men. Too much artillery was a disadvantage as it slowed the army on the march. H. von Müller, *Die Entwickelung der Feldartillerie* (Berlin, 1893-1894), I, 99, 116-17.

MILITARY TRAINING AND THE LANDWEHR 185

Only a few pages of the three regulations of 1812 dealt with the formation of divisions. For all the general remarks about the cooperation of arms, it is hard to understand how the Prussians intended to achieve this goal without practical instructions on the use of divisions in battle. In its brigade organization the Prussian army had a counterpart of the French divisions, but neither the previous experience nor the specialized training of the Prussian officers fitted them for division leadership. There was little opportunity for the older officers to comply with the limited changes that were suggested in the new regulations. After 1808 the lack of money, scarcity of powder supplies, and the shortage of artillery *matériel* limited the training to the simplest elements. The lack of training opportunities and the absence of qualified leaders did not prevent Scharnhorst from championing divisions. That the training regulations dealt so briefly with divisions was yet another indication of the strong conservative opinion that opposed Scharnhorst's measures.[21]

The spirit of the regulations of 1812 maintained the infantry in the dominant position which it had held in the history of the Prussian army. Cavalry had previously been one of the decisive Prussian arms, but the new instructions, together with the meager supply of horses, cast the mounted forces into a subordinate role. Despite the example of Napoleon's artillery there was little change in the use of the guns.

Plans for a National Revolt

In spite of the sincerity and the great zeal of the reformers the practical war training of the army lagged, while the painfully slow growth of the armed forces and the crushing load of the French indemnity bound the state to military impotence. Discouraged by the small size of the regular army, the patriots

---

21 See *Ueber die Schlacht und Fechtordnung der Brigade* in Scharnhorst, *Auszug*, pp. 215-17. To include instructions of this nature in a manual of administrative procedure suggests that Scharnhorst was anxious to present his ideas on divisions to the troops. Boyen, *Erinnerungen*, II, 112 describes the training of brigades and the general conditions in which the exercises were held. See *Preuss. Heer 1812*, pp. 244-63.

began to think that a revolt of the masses might be able to overcome the disciplined French by the fury of their attack and the weight of their numbers. As early as 1806 such opinions had been expressed in army headquarters by officers of the highest rank.[22] At that time Ferdinand von Schill was already thinking of using the army as the spearhead of a general uprising. Gneisenau's participation in Schill's plans made him increasingly sympathetic toward the idea of national revolt.[23] By the summer of 1808 Gneisenau was fully convinced that Prussia's only hope lay in a popular insurrection. His elaborate plan for an uprising of fifteen and a half million persons in north Germany included an idealistic hope that by saving the state the people would thereby win a constitution and other political reforms. Prussia was to lead the German people to independence and protect it by a system of alliances.[24] Stein had begun to think in the same terms, adding his voice to those who were urging the Germans as a nation to imitate the Spaniards and wage guerrilla warfare against the French.[25]

Scharnhorst was aware of most of the plans for armed revolt.[26] Whether independence could be won by an organized militia or a national uprising was not clear to him, but he preferred at first to work with the existing armed forces and with the approval of the king. Nevertheless, many of Scharnhorst's communications with Stein were pessimistic about the recovery of national military prestige. The militia plans which he fostered

[22] Albert Lionnet, *Die Erhebungspläne preussischer Patrioten Ende 1806 und Frühjahr 1807* (Berlin, 1914), pp. 16-19, 92 ff.

[23] *Ibid.*, pp. 40-50, 71-82, 184-86; *Preuss. Archiv*, XCIV, 612-15, 645-46, 694-700. Major von Schill of the Prussian army made a bold attempt in the spring of 1809 to launch a national revolt in Germany. His effort proved abortive and Schill lost his life in the fighting at Stralsund on May 31, 1809.

[24] Friedrich Thimme, " Zu den Erhebungsplänen der preussischen Patrioten im Sommer 1808. Ungedruckte Denkschriften Gneisenau's und Scharnhorst's," *Historische Zeitschrift*, LXXXVI (1901), 78-80, 83, 95-97, 100-09.

[25] *Stein Denkschriften*, II, 485-86, 511-13.

[26] See Scharnhorst's letter to Schill early in 1809, *Scharnhorsts Briefe*, I, 360.

throughout 1808 indicated his eagerness to combine the patriotic enthusiasm of a popular army with the strength of a regular army under the guidance of line officers. At the end of summer, 1808, Scharnhorst could still write Stein that in two to three weeks 80,000 recruits could be raised and organized in a militia.[27] This implied that even line officers with faith in disciplined troops were beginning to look favorably on an insurrection.[28]

Stein continued to be absorbed with his ideas for a revolt that would include the German people as well as the armed forces of their rulers. In 1809 his plans dealt mainly with an uprising of north Germany which was to be supported by England.[29] Schill's failure in that year tended to dampen the ardor of the plotters, yet in 1811 the patriots gave more thought to a national insurrection than to the regular Prussian army. Boyen believed that with assistance from Russia the Prussians were strong enough in 1811 to challenge Napoleon. A vast popular uprising would harass the French army and stubborn fighting around the fortresses would protract the war until other nations joined Prussia.[30] Despite the capitulations of 1806 Scharnhorst also professed confidence in Prussian fortresses. Another source of strength resided in the unbridled fury of the people. Scharnhorst expected that the Prussian masses would arm and organize themselves for guerrilla warfare and that against such an expenditure of national energy the French army would be pow-

27 *Stein Denkschriften*, II, 506-07. Consult Scharnhorst's plan for a popular insurrection, in Thimme, "Zu den Erhebungsplänen der preussischen Patrioten," *op. cit.*, pp. 97-99. Even in 1807 both Scharnhorst and Gneisenau had asserted emphatically that: " In case of a ... surprise attack by France, a universal army must fight to maintain the king and his family, and in extremity go down honorably with weapons in hand." Boyen, *Beiträge zur Kenntniss des General von Scharnhorst*, p. 31.

28 See *Stein Denkschriften*, II, 490-93. The reform leaders were the first in Prussia to recognize that war had ceased to be a form of duel between the heads of states and now concerned whole peoples. Gragert, *op. cit.*, p. 6.

29 *Stein Denkschriften*, III, 147-49, 157-60.

30 Boyen, *Erinnerungen*, II, 102-03, 179-80.

erless. These plans were evidence that the professional Prussian soldiers despaired of creating a great field army. Much time was required to assemble and train a regular army, and it remained doubtful whether Napoleon's numerous and battle-hardened troops could be overthrown by Prussia alone. Guerrilla warfare backed by existing regular forces fighting in the fortresses might inflame northern Europe and attract the powerful aid of Russia. Plans for warfare of this nature were submitted to the king in 1811, but his timidity and the strength of the pro-French party combined to prevent war against Napoleon, either with weakened regular forces or by a national revolt.[31]

A very great effort would have been required to overthrow the massive French armies that occupied Prussia and northern Europe. Armed forces totaling 165,000 men stood in Warsaw, along the Oder, in Danzig, Magdeburg, Saxony, Westphalia, and along the Elbe. All three of the fortresses on the Oder River were garrisoned by French troops, and around each fortress was a zone barred to members of the Prussian armed forces. Communications within Prussia were imperiled by the numerous French garrison places, and by the military roads that were held open for the use of Napoleon and his allies. By clever calculations the map of Prussia had been redrawn by the conquerors so that the kingdom consisted of two elongated parts. A short advance by the French troops stationed in the Duchy of Warsaw would cut the Prussian state in half. After 1811 in preparation for the assault upon Russia, increasing concentrations of French troops were made in East Prussia. Under these circumstances it was fortunate that the plans for a national uprising were never carried out.[32]

31 *Ibid.*, II, 102, and 103-04; Cavaignac, *op. cit.*, II, 143-51.

32 Boyen, *Erinnerungen*, II, 101-02, 115-16, Beilage VIII, pp. 374-79, Beilage XXXIII, pp. 480-83; Preuss. *Heer 1812*, pp. 5-7. Consult Liebert, "Die Rüstungen Napoleons für den Feldzug 1812," *Militär-Wochenblatt*, Beiheft 1888, pp. 358-67.

MILITARY TRAINING AND THE LANDWEHR 189

RUSSIA UPSETS THE BALANCE OF POWER

France's preponderant military power was substantially reduced by the disasters suffered in the Russian campaign of 1812. It was ironical that the first attempt by a Prussian to exploit the shift in the balance of power should be made by the conservative opponent of the military reformers, General York. He was in command of the Prussian expeditionary forces in Russia and was fully aware that Napoleon had suffered reverses of the first magnitude. Without orders and upon his own responsibility York negotiated the Convention of Tauroggen of December 30, 1812 with the Tsar's government, an action which took the Prussian troops out of the war and declared Prussia to be neutral. A great French historian has commented on the importance of this step by contrasting it with Brunswick's confused and hesitant order in 1792 to retreat from Valmy. One decision had as its eventual consequence the defection of Prussia from the alliance of kings fighting the French Revolution; the other brought Prussia into the revolt of the nations against Napoleonic imperialism.[33]

Government circles in Berlin were startled by York's bold step, but for the moment the crown neither denied nor affirmed the Convention of Tauroggen. Frederick William still hesitated at the thought of placing Prussia openly on the side of Napoleon's enemies. Though the *Grande Armée* had been shattered Frederick William remained content with the method of secret diplomacy in order to checkmate the French. Even Scharnhorst hesitated to throw the Prussian forces on the fragments of the French army streaming out of Russia. His irresolution is all the more surprising inasmuch as reliable information about the extent of the French losses was not slow in reaching the Prussian authorities.[34]

[33] Albert Sorel, *L'Europe et la Révolution Française* (Paris, 1885-1904), VIII, 25. J. G. Droysen, *Das Leben des Feldmarschalls Grafen Yorck von Wartenburg* (11th ed., Leipzig, 1913), II, Beilage I, pp. 467-74. See Huber, *op. cit.*, pp. 141-42.

[34] Colonel von dem Knesebeck's report to Frederick William of Dec. 23, 1812 spoke of the complete annihilation of the French, but not until mid-

The timidity prevailing in the capital was revealed by the orders issued on December 20, 1812 to the governors of East and West Prussia. All cantonists, as well as the military stores in those provinces that might be in danger of Russian capture, were to be removed in order to form the "Reserve on the Vistula." In the same orders General York, who was even then contemplating Tauroggen, was named military governor of East Prussia. This appointment served later to justify his role in the action of the East Prussian *Landtag*.[35]

EVENTS IN EAST PRUSSIA

There was both a military and a patriotic basis for the revolution in East Prussia. The province had been one of the principal concentration areas for the *Grande Armée* and the constant movement of troops, as well as the requisition of horses, forage, and foodstuffs had brought untold misery to the population. Although the land had been stripped of its resources, the French had not hesitated to collect a heavy monetary indemnity which goaded the people into a fury.[36] The restless mood of many East Prussians in 1812 was encouraged by the activities of the nationalist agitator, Arndt, and the distribution of his inflammatory pamphlets such as *Was bedeutet Landwehr und Landsturm*.[37]

When York arrived in Königsberg on January 8, 1813 there was an immediate and pressing need for a militia. Both Russian and French armies were dipping into the military stores remain-

January was the king's mind at ease on this point. Preuss. *Heer 1813*, pp. 11-12. On Dec. 26, 1812 the Berlin press reported that the French army had been decimated. Schmidt, *Erinnerungen*, part II, p. 128. Scharnhorst knew what was occurring in Russia and expected that the French would be driven back to the Vistula during the winter. *Scharnhorsts Briefe*, letters of Dec. 18 and 27, 1812, I, 443-45.

35 Boyen, *Erinnerungen*, II, 330; Preuss. *Heer 1813*, pp. 2-3, 9-10.

36 A. Bezzenberger, *Ostpreussen in der Franzosenzeit seine Verluste und Opfer an Gut und Blut* (Königsberg, 1913), pp. 2-9.

37 See Alfred G. Pundt, *Arndt and the Nationalist Awakening in Germany* (New York, 1935), pp. 106-09.

ing in the East Prussian fortresses. The province was in need of defence but York's troops were badly depleted. Many of the older residents recalled a similar circumstance in 1757 when the province had raised its own militia for defence against Russian troops.[38] Yet in December, 1812 virtually all of the man power liable to military service under the existing laws had been carried off to the " Reserve on the Vistula." Although York succeeded in raising more than 1,200 untrained cantonists in East Prussia, he required additional men. This circumstance and the province's urgent need for defence made imperative the development of a militia from classes hitherto exempt from service.[39]

York's status became clear on January 10, when it became known that his armistice had been repudiated by the king. Prussia remained, therefore, a nominal ally of France. This discouraging news was offset on January 20 by the arrival of Stein. He had gone to Russia in June, 1812 and had joined Alexander I in order to participate in the reconstruction of Germany after the collapse of the Napoleonic system. When Russian troops occupied East Prussia, Stein was promptly named commissar for the province.[40] His appearance in Königsberg aroused some apprehension among conservative East Prussians lest the province be annexed to Russia. Enthusiasm among merchants and businessmen over the prospective end of the continental system was tempered by their misgivings over the forced circulation of paper money that inevitably accompanied the advance of the Tsar's armies. Most royal officials were uncertain about their relation to Stein. Prussia was still at war and it seemed prudent not to cooperate too wholeheart-

[38] Cf. Schwarz, op. cit., pp. 160 ff.

[39] Ide, op. cit., pp. 36-37; Jany, op. cit., IV, 72. York had previously spoken against the reformers' proposals for popular war. Preuss. Archiv, XCIV, 586-87.

[40] Stein Denkschriften, IV, 202, 222-23. Stein's role in East Prussia is treated comprehensively in G. H. Pertz, Das Leben des Ministers Freiherrn vom Stein (Berlin, 1849-1855), III, 267-97.

edly with an enemy agent who proposed to take measures of very dubious legality. Yet none of these groups expressed the real feeling of the province. Every sincere patriot welcomed Stein unreservedly without suspicion about his new role.[41]

Stein was confident of popular support and he immediately announced his intention of raising troops. He demanded that the arming of the nation be considered before any other measure. York also had a practical interest in East Prussian man power but did not hasten to confer with Stein. Neither one embarked, however, on any military projects that were not in accordance with Prussian law. It was apparent to Stein that a levy could be raised more easily if the province had a voice in the matter. There was a widespread feeling that a *Landtag* should be called to consider armaments. Even before Stein's arrival a few patriots had attempted to persuade the bureaucrats to call a general convocation of the circle representatives. Nothing had been accomplished, however. For practical assistance in preparing a military law Stein leaned upon Count Dohna, the President of the Committee for the Estates of East Prussia and Lithuania. Their cooperation was fortunate inasmuch as Dohna had been a Prussian minister from 1808 until 1810 and was familiar with the plans for a reserve army and a national militia. Clausewitz and Dörnberg, who were then serving as officers in the Russian army, were directed by Stein to advise Dohna on technical matters.[42]

A few days before the *Landtag* convened Clausewitz prepared a document which outlined the organization and training of a popular levy.[43] Whether this service entitled Clausewitz to be

[41] Gerhard Ritter, *Stein. Eine politische Biographie* (Berlin, 1931), II, 161, 168-70; A. Wohlauer, *Stein und Schön in der Provinz Preussen zu Anfang des Jahres 1813* (Breslau, 1882), pp. 55-56, treats Schön and other officials more favorably than does Lehmann.

[42] Lehmann, *Freiherr vom Stein*, pp. 441-43, 452-53.

[43] Clausewitz' document, *Das wesentlichste in der Organisation eines Landsturms und einer Miliz*, is found in *Das Jahr 1813 bis zur Schlacht von Gross Görschen* (Bruno von Treuenfeld, ed., Leipzig, 1901), pp. 139-42.

MILITARY TRAINING AND THE LANDWEHR 193

called one of the founders of the East Prussian *Landwehr* has troubled several generations of German historians. It seems futile to discuss whether any originality was shown in describing a *Landwehr,* since all the problems connected with a militia had been thoroughly aired in Prussia by more than two decades of controversy. Other armies had tried a militia and their experience was certainly not unknown to Clausewitz. The Austrians had organized a *Landwehr* in 1808-1809 and the Russian army had been reinforced by a militia since 1805. There had also been unsuccessful attempts during the 1790's to form a militia in the south German states.[44]

THE EAST PRUSSIAN *Landwehr*

When the estates assembled an official program was therefore at hand. Instead of being called upon to prepare their own plan of armament and defence, the deputies were asked to consider the draft of a law which Dohna had drawn up with the aid of Clausewitz' suggestions. By summoning the estates to consider measures for provincial defence, several grave legal problems had been raised. Foremost among these was the fact that a true *Landtag* had to be called by the king. And though special privileges had been granted to the East Prussian *Landtag* by Frederick William III its competence was limited to purely local matters, particularly those of an economic character. In South Prussia, West Prussia, and New East Prussia there was no provincial representation. To include deputies from these places in the East Prussian estates amounted to a revision of local government.[45]

These legal difficulties were of immediate concern to Auerswald, the President of the East Prussian Government and personal representative of the crown, upon whom descended the responsibility of assembling the estates. Like most of the bu-

[44] Lehmann declares Clausewitz the founder of the *Landwehr* in order to trace its intellectual origin to Scharnhorst. The rather involved proof is developed in *Knesebeck und Schön,* pp. 214-43. *Cf.* W. Wendland, *Versuche einer allgemeinen Volksbewaffnung in Süddeutschland während der Jahre 1791 bis 1794* (Berlin, 1901), p. 222.

[45] *Cf.* Lehmann, " Das alte Preussen," *op. cit.,* pp. 409-11.

reaucrats in East Prussia he hesitated to take the risk which Stein and the foremost of the East Prussian patriots were urging upon him. After considerable prodding and much correspondence with the other provincial presidents, Schön and Wissmann, who were equally dubious of the step which public opinion demanded, Auerswald issued a summons calling the deputies to a *Landtag*. This seemed unduly bold without the shadow of legality cast by York's authority as military governor and Auerswald suppressed the summons within two days. Eventually a formula satisfactory to the timid bureaucrats was found by avoiding the term *Landtag* and inviting the deputies to a free assembly. It was not made clear whether the summons was issued in General York's name or Stein's, though the authority of the latter as a plenipotentiary of the Tsar of Russia was announced in the message.[46]

In contrast to the narrow-mindedness of East Prussian officialdom, Stein and York displayed great breadth of vision. Their social and political views and the differences of opinion that had made Stein's second ministry so difficult did not permit a cordial relationship to develop, but neither man permitted his personal feelings to interfere with his public responsibility. York looked on Napoleon's defeat as a heaven-sent opportunity for Prussia to cast off the French alliance and recover its national independence. As a soldier he asked from East Prussia only those reinforcements which he needed to follow the course dictated by military honor. Stein saw the events in East Prussia against the wide horizons of European politics. Nothing would speed the advance of Russian troops into Germany more than a show of force by the German people themselves. And from the spark kindled in East Prussia might come that general revolt of the German nation for which Stein had worked for so many years. With York he shared the opinion that decisive ac-

[46] Lehmann, *Knesebeck und Schön*, pp. 182-83. Stein to Auerswald, Jan. 22, 1813, nevertheless mentions the *Herrenstände*. *Stein Denkschriften*, IV, 203. The history of the East Prussian *Landtag* is very difficult to reconstruct. Ritter's account of these events is considered to be the best. See Ritter, *op. cit.*, II, 171-81.

tion would force Frederick William to abandon the pretense of his friendship for Napoleon and come to terms with Alexander I. This common understanding of Prussia's best interests made York a willing henchman, a general who was willing to risk " another Tauroggen." [47]

The responsibility which Stein and York assumed in East Prussia was without precedent in an absolute government. That a provincial *Landtag* should be called together on command of men either in official disgrace or in the service of foreign governments was a novel element in Prussian history. Their success owed in no small degree to the deep resentment of the East Prussians for the ravishment of their province by the French. No other group responded with such enthusiasm to the opportunity for revenge afforded by the War of Liberation. To be the first to strike, the East Prussians had to reassert the old provincial control of the militia which the absolute monarchs had taken such pains to destroy. This did not prove to be as significant as the impetus which their revolution gave to the reorganization and expansion of the Prussian army.[48]

On February 7, 1813 the East Prussian *Landtag* ratified the proposals that had been made for the defence of the province.[49] Both a *Landwehr* and a *Landsturm* were approved but measures for setting up the latter were not outlined. Service in the *Landwehr* was obligatory for all men between the ages of eighteen and forty-five. Substitutes were permitted upon the pay-

[47] Lehmann, *Knesebeck und Schön*, p. 207; Lehmann, *Freiherr vom Stein*, pp. 441-55. Though Stein was the stoutest champion of German resistance to Napoleon it is interesting to note that in 1811 he had yielded to despair and had doubted the capacity of the Germans for a national revolt. *Cf. Stein Denkschriften*, III, 450-52, 457-61.

[48] Droysen, *op. cit.*, I, 443, dissolves the constitutional issues in a bath of patriotism. Ritter, *op. cit.*, II, 178, and Ide, *op. cit.*, p. 36, agree that the procedure in East Prussia was revolutionary. Boyen did not characterize the measures of 1813 as open revolution but he admitted the decisiveness of the East Prussian action.

[49] See Pertz, *op. cit.*, III, 288-94. Scharnhorst's relation to the East Prussian *Landwehr* is considered in Boyen, *Erinnerungen*, II, 331-32.

ment of a fee, but this was less an attempt to release the wealthy classes than a deference for the rights of the Mennonites, who had always been allowed to escape the regular military service by making donations to the treasury. Only infantry units were to be raised in the first levy of 20,000 men. Weapons were not abundant until the Russians dipped into their own stores and made captured French muskets available. Despite the example of Stein and York, and the more disinterested patriots, the old provincial loyalty was strong enough to enact a provision that the *Landwehr* be employed only within the province. This restriction did not prove to have any binding force, however. Universal service was now established in East Prussia and it remained for the royal government, which had removed from Berlin to Breslau in Silesia, to follow the provincial example.[50]

With the erection of a *Landwehr* in East Prussia the die was virtually cast for the royal authorities. While they were free to repudiate the action of the province, the events there strengthened the hand of the leaders who wanted to join Russia and attack the French. With the silent approval of this war party East Prussia was able to carry out its own defence measures. These in turn hastened the measures that the national military leaders had planned for the expansion and mobilization of the regular army. The action of the East Prussian *Landtag* was equally significant for Prussian foreign policy. The hesitancy and doubt of the king were at last removed, and Prussia began the military and diplomatic preparations that culminated in the War of Liberation.

[50] Chareton, *op. cit.*, pp. 79-83, 139; C. F. Velhagen, *Preussens Landwehr* (Königsberg, 1815), pp. 11-12. To provide York with cavalry replacements an official call was made for volunteers for a Prussian National Cavalry Regiment.

CHAPTER VIII
THE MOBILIZATION OF 1813

THE royal authorities in the temporary capital at Breslau were not slow in following the example set in East Prussia. Conscription of subjects for the regular army was declared on February 9, 1813, two days after the enactment of the East Prussian law.[1] While universal service had been decreed before in the Prussian canton system, its actual operation had placed the heaviest burden of military service on the serfs. In 1813 the problem of universal conscription in a class society was simplified by providing a military organization for each social group: a national militia (the *Landwehr*) for the landed peasants and the moderately well-to-do, volunteer officer training units for the upper class youths, and the regular army for the masses. So it was that in 1813-1814 most of the conscripts were still the poor and landless. Though the peasantry tended to retain its old and deep-seated aversion to military service, and the upper classes were reluctant to accept their new obligations to the state, conscription was nevertheless a success.

SIGNIFICANCE OF THE EAST PRUSSIAN EXAMPLE

The extent of the East Prussian influence on the establishment of a universal service army in Prussia has long been debated by historians. Scharnhorst's biographers would naturally tend to minimize this influence, but it cannot be denied completely.[2] In 1809-1810 the military reformers had made an earnest effort to obtain general conscription, yet in 1813 their original plans called for mobilizing the Prussian army without

---

[1] The title of the law referred only to the suspension of previous military exemptions for the duration of the war. *Gesetzsammlung für die Königlichen Preussischen Staaten 1813* (Berlin, n.d.), pp. 13-14. This collection will be cited henceforth as *Gesetzsammlung 1813*.

[2] Max Lehmann remains the outstanding defender of Scharnhorst in all the armament proceedings. See *Knesebeck und Schön*, pp. 232-33, 243-44, 260-61, 265-66. Also see Klippel, *op. cit.*, III, Chap. VIII, 652 ff.

any conscripts other than those provided by the canton system.³ That these plans were eventually redrawn in order to include national conscription may be attributed largely to the example of the East Prussian patriots. Although measures for strengthening the Prussian army had been started before the dramatic meeting of the East Prussian estates, they were at first feebly executed and were gravely hampered by the existing diplomatic relations and formal commitments with the French. Not until the revolt in East Prussia did the war party become strong enough to dominate the royal government. Their triumph made possible a bold preparation for war.⁴

The new spirit was manifested by the appointment on January 28, 1813 of an Armament Commission, made up of Hardenberg, Scharnhorst, and Hake who were to supervise the mobilization and expansion of the army. However, the decrees of the Armament Commission were of significance only for Silesia to which most of the army had been removed. The Mark Brandenburg, the principal liaison area of the *Grande Armée*, was then left free of Prussian troops. In the other provinces the local commanders, imitating York, went to work on their own initiative.⁵

Scharnhorst's biographers, on the other hand, usually date the beginning of Prussia's mobilization from December, 1812, and emphasize the measures that ended in March, 1813 with the concentration of the field army. But the armed forces were moving toward Silesia during most of this period, and elsewhere in Prussia the royal authorities had only the vaguest control over rearmament. It is hard to believe that the mobili-

3 Preuss. *Heer 1813*, pp. 33-35. See Jany, *op. cit.*, IV, 83.

4 Ide, *op. cit.*, p. 39.

5 Preuss. *Heer 1813*, pp. 27-30, 57-59, 115-16, 118-19. The opportunities for local commanders during the winter of 1812-1813 are described in Max Lehmann, "General Borstell und der Ausbruch des Krieges von 1813," *Historische Zeitschrift*, XXXVII (1877), 55-56. Lehmann concludes in this article that Borstell's action in 1812-1813 was upright, honorable, and patriotic, though confined to smaller and less important matters than those dealt with by York.

THE MOBILIZATION OF 1813   199

zation in Silesia was at first very effective because responsible leaders were not at hand. The king did not arrive there until January 25, and not until January 28 did Scharnhorst resume his old post as head of the War Department. Meanwhile Prussia gave every evidence of continuing to cooperate with the French, and negotiations with Austria and Russia for forming a new alliance against Napoleon were only beginning.[6]

MOBILIZATION AND EXPANSION OF THE REGULAR ARMY

Royal orders for mobilizing the army were issued on January 12, February 1, and March 2 and 18, 1813. The first, of January 12, 1813, came when the French request for additional troops was made the pretext for raising infantry and cavalry units to their established strength, and for drawing in cantonists of artillery and pioneers.[7] A second Cabinet Order of February 1, 1813 was intended to increase the army by 37,000 men and double the number of battalions. Thirty-nine additional reserve battalions were to be added to the infantry then only forty-six battalions strong; eleven new depot battalions were to be created also. These orders were actually carried out only in Silesia; troops of Bülow on the Vistula, Borstell in Pomerania, and York in East Prussia were not affected. The third measure which came on March 2 and 18, 1813 authorized the last phase of expansion, and by sanctioning a slight increase, raised the number of new formations to fifty-two battalions. A supplementary instruction of February 7 provided that all subalterns of the campaign of 1806-1807 might be promoted at once, and that any capable cadet, non-commissioned officer, or sergeant was to be commissioned immediately.[8]

6 Preuss. *Heer 1813*, pp. 27, 29, 118-19. Scharnhorst insisted that the army could be increased quickly if only the political indecision and paralysis could be eliminated. Prussian rearmament could be carried out under the pretext of assisting the French. Scharnhorst to Thile, Jan. 9, 1813, *Scharnhorsts Briefe*, I, 449-50.

7 Jany, *op. cit.*, IV, 70-71; Nord, *op. cit.*, pp. 60-61.

8 Preuss. *Heer 1813*, pp. 33-34, 39, 44, 68, 84. The orders of Jan. 12 and Febr. 1, 1813 are given in *ibid.*, Anlage I and II, pp. 376-81. Osten-Sacken,

These orders amounted to a mobilization of the army in three stages. At the same time the number of regiments was to be increased by distributing the trained men throughout the new formations. Whether each of the new units was complete cannot be determined, but the preponderance of reserve battalions, forty-one out of fifty-two, indicates that great numbers of short-term cantonists, depot material, and old soldiers were used.

None of these measures modified the existing means of obtaining men for the army, but on February 3 innovations began with the announcement by Hardenberg that Volunteer *Jäger* units would be formed.[9] He appealed specifically to the propertied classes, exempted under the existing laws, to relinquish their privileges and volunteer. The announcement also informed the upper classes of the impending abandonment of the canton system and at the same time offered them a new type of service. By this means it was hoped that youths of good family could be enticed into the army to train as officers.[10]

At first the *Jäger* were given special treatment befitting troops required to arm and uniform themselves. They formed in separate units and were shielded from contact with ordinary cantonists. Discipline was also administered gently at first. Eventually these provisions were changed because few commanding officers believed in them or even in the previous decrees against capital punishment. Many Volunteer *Jäger* were therefore whipped like ordinary recruits. In spite of considerable government encouragement the number of volunteers was disappointing. Although some 2,798 men volunteered in the first

op. cit., II, 86-87, 92-93. Trained men for the new units were difficult to obtain since all the officers naturally tried to hold experienced men in their own commands. Deserters and even criminal offenders were pardoned if they had seen service; old soldiers and foreigners of German origin were actively recruited. *Ibid.*, II, 93.

[9] *Gesetzsammlung 1813*, pp. 15-17. The definitive order came on Febr. 9, 1813, *ibid.*, pp. 19-20.

[10] "Die Formation der freiwilligen Jäger Detachements bei der preussischen Armee im Jahre 1813," *Militär-Wochenblatt*, Beiheft 1845, pp. 454-55, 461; H. Ulmann, "Die Detachements der freiwilligen Jäger in den Befreiungskriegen," *Historische Vierteljahrschrift*, X (1907), 484-85.

months of 1813, by the summer of that year the total had reached only 7,800.[11]

UNIVERSAL MILITARY SERVICE

These meager additions did not permit a rapid increase of the army. And in view of the freedom from military service conferred upon so many subjects by the law of 1792, it was not at all certain that the levy of 37,000 men ordered on February 1 could be raised. The Armament Commission did not hesitate to press upon the king the urgent need for a conscription law. On February 9 the exemptions from military service in the canton law of 1792 were abolished for the duration of the war.[12] This decree establishing universal service abrogated only those provisions of the canton regulations that dealt with exemptions. Five weeks before the outbreak of hostilities the reformers finally achieved the legal reform they had sought for so long. Henceforth, all able-bodied men[13] were to be enrolled in the canton lists, and the harshness of the law was modified only by the announcement that any man serving one month would be eligible for a commission. Notwithstanding, the popular press objected vehemently, declaring the land was unprepared for such a burden. People from every class asserted that the free Prussian lands had become a police-state.[14]

Yet the enforcement of the conscription law did not immediately oppress the people. The repeal of exemptions applied primarily to men from seventeen to twenty-four years, and they were given eight days in which to report to any branch of the service before being made subject to arbitrary conscription.

11 *Ibid.*, X, 485-503; "Die Formation der freiwilligen Jäger," *op. cit.*, pp. 462-65. Other volunteer units were formed: the Foreign Battalion of Reuss, Reiche's Foreign Legion, the Royal Prussian Free Corps, and various National Cavalry Regiments. The total strength of all these amounted to less than 5,000 men.

12 *Gesetzsammlung 1813*, pp. 13-14.

13 The men had to have teeth that met in front in order to bite the cartridges. *Preuss. Heer 1813*, Anlage XIII, p. 395.

14 Ide, *op. cit.*, p. 42.

Large French garrisons in Prussia as well as the slowness of negotiations with Russia restrained the hand of the Armament Commission. Frederick William was particularly apprehensive over the fate of Berlin, which was not evacuated by Eugene's troops until March 4. The concentration of the field army, which had been planned for February 12, did not begin until February 28 when the alliance with Russia was signed. By March 16 these military preparations were sufficiently advanced to declare war upon the French Empire. On the following day Frederick William made his unprecedented appeal, *An Mein Volk*, which informed the people of the necessity of the war and indicated the spirit in which it would be carried on. This address from the throne marked the change in Prussian history from dynastic to national war.[15]

THE ROYAL *Landwehr*

On the same day that the king made his appeal to the people, the *Order on the Organization of the Landwehr* announced the formation of a universal levy on the East Prussian model.[16] This was the most direct and obvious influence of that province upon the national armament program. Until February, 1813 the Armament Commission conceived military power solely in terms of an augmented standing army; there was no thought of a militia of the kind proposed by the Military Reorganization Commission in 1807 and 1808. Even the universal service law of February 9 was intended to fill the reserve units of the regular army; there was at first no intention of using universal conscription to create a national militia. All of the previous orders of the Armament Commission were intended to put only the regular army on a war footing. Boyen's memoirs make it clear that the establishment of an East Prussian and a national *Landwehr* upset the official program for rearmament. All ar-

---

15 Hintze, *Die Hohenzollern*, p. 471. *An Mein Volk* and *An Mein Kriegsheer*, Mar. 17, 1813, in *Preuss. Heer 1813*, Anlage XVII and XVIII, pp. 403-05. On March 10, 1813 the Iron Cross was established.

16 *Gesetzsammlung 1813*, pp. 36-37, 109-12. The announcement also implied royal sanction for the East Prussian *Landwehr*.

rangements had been based on equipping a small number of troops.[17]

Scharnhorst's final contribution to the reorganization of the Prussian army was the draft of the law establishing the national *Landwehr*.[18] Both the content and the form of the royal proclamation resembled the East Prussian law, but it also reflected the spirit of the order of February 9 ending the canton exemptions. Duty in the *Landwehr* was made compulsory for every man, aged seventeen to forty, though recruiting was to proceed first through volunteers and then by lot among those liable to service. Recruiting was carried out in each circle by a commission on which the *Junker* representation balanced that from the urban and peasant classes. Unlike the provincial *Landwehr* the national organization included cavalry and artillery as well as infantry.[19]

Raising the *Landwehr*

Supervision of the *Landwehr* had been vested on March 15 in the four Military Governments of Königsberg, Stargard, Berlin, and Breslau.[20] In each government military and civil

17 Boyen, *Erinnerungen*, II, 332-33. Boyen added that Scharnhorst had to rework the plans for rearming Prussia when the provincial *Landwehr* was established. Armament shortages were an immediate consequence. In the Alliance of Kalisch, signed on February 28, Prussia had agreed to form a militia, but as late as Febr. 21, 1813 the central authorities were without a well-prepared plan for a *Landwehr*. Every effort was being made to strengthen and mobilize the standing army. It may be concluded therefore that the East Prussian action was decisive for the national *Landwehr*. Jany, *op. cit.*, IV, 83.

18 See Scharnhorst's letter to his daughter, Mar. 19, 1813, in *Scharnhorsts Briefe*, I, 462. Cavaignac, *op. cit.*, II, 311-22, 335-38, traces the intellectual origins of the *Landwehr* and concludes that without the milieu of the French Revolution the Prussian army could not have been nationalized.

19 The printed announcements which made the *Landwehr* organization known to the people were a new departure in Prussian military practice as well as a symbol of the new spirit of nationalism. Copies of the *Verordnung über die Organisation der Landwehr*, are found in the *Geheimes Archiv des Kriegsministeriums*, Rep. 4, ZD15.

20 Each Military Government embraced the following territory: Königsberg, from the eastern frontier to the Vistula; Stargard, from the Vistula

officials exercised control over the training, assembly, and military use of the Landwehr. While the importance of local authorities in any successful rearmament effort was recognized in the control of recruiting, the Military Governments were intended to serve the larger interests of statecraft. This organization disposed the troops for the defence of the great rivers and made possible royal control of the militia, thus safeguarding absolutism from the interference of the estates.[21] In his proclamation on the Landwehr Frederick William had given heed to their rights, but he had also added, " The time does not permit me to consult with my loyal estates. But the development of the Landwehr will be determined by the energy of the provinces." [22] With the progress of the war and the conquest of former Prussian territories, new Military Governments were established to carry out conscription.[23]

Although the Landwehr was a realistic measure for increasing the size of the Prussian armed forces, the law did not make clear whether it was a form of compulsory militia or a reserve for the regular army. Since the canton system was now enforced on a universal service basis, the male population might be called on to train in the replacement depots of the regular army. During the spring of 1813 the Military Governments, circle commissions, and royal officials all engaged in a competitive search for recruits. Whether the Landwehr, like the eighteenth century Prussian militia, would provide a safe haven from the claim of the regiments was not clear.[24] Rühle von Lilienstern in his

to the Oder; Berlin, from the Oder to the Elbe; Breslau, Upper and Lower Silesia. Nord, *op. cit.*, p. 63.

[21] The creation of additional military authorities threw the conscription program into great disorder since the territories of the brigade cantons and the new Military Governments overlapped. Throughout the spring of 1813 numerous regulations sought to define the competence of each authority. Preuss. *Heer 1813*, pp. 349-50.

[22] *Ibid.*, Anlage XIX, pp. 405-06.

[23] Boyen, *Erinnerungen*, III, 2-5 (on the original Military Governments); Chareton, *op. cit.*, pp. 197-200.

[24] Courbière, *Heeresverfassung*, p. 178. See Preuss. *Heer 1813*, p. 302.

Kriegs-Katechismus für die Landwehrmann did not offer a solution with his vague definition of the force as the instrument for "the defence of the land in time of war."[25]

The creation of *Landwehr* by circles under the supervision of a civilian commission gave rise to many recruiting practices, and in the several Military Governments there were great variations in the handling and in the quality of the troops.[26] Certain details were administered uniformly; officers below the rank of company and squadron leaders were chosen by the circle commissions, and the nominations were approved by the Military Governments. Most of the officers were *Invaliden* from the old army, or officers retired in the reductions of 1807-1808. Some officers were transferred from the line, and others were commissioned from the Volunteer *Jäger*. A very significant number of men in *Landwehr* ranks were veterans of the pre-1806 army.

Unlike the East Prussian arrangements the national *Landwehr* undertook to form units of all three services. As the army expanded the existing supplies of arms were soon exhausted and the equal development of infantry, cavalry, and artillery became impossible. Before the summer reorganization small arms were not distributed to the *Landwehr*, except East Prussian units, until the requirements of the regular forces had been met. Since the line officers insisted upon full equipment and ample reserves, there were units of *Landwehr* infantry in which the first rank was armed with nothing more formidable than the pike.[27] During the war it was reported that some men were barefoot. The *Landwehr* wore the discarded uniforms of the old army if any were available, otherwise civilian clothes were

---

[25] J. J. R. von Lilienstern, *Kriegs-Katechismus für die Landwehrmann* (Breslau, 1813), p. 2.

[26] *Cf.* "Errichtung der Landwehr und des Landsturms in Ostpreussen, Westpreussen, am rechten Weichselufer und Litthauen im Jahre 1813," *Militär-Wochenblatt*, Beiheft 1846, pp. 1-146; "Geschichte der Organisation der Landwehr in dem Militair-Gouvernement zwischen Elbe und Weser," *Militär-Wochenblatt*, Beiheft 1857, pp. 1-49; "Geschichte der Organisation der Landwehr in dem Militair-Gouvernement zwischen Weser und Rhein im Jahre 1813 und 1814," *Militär-Wochenblatt*, Beiheft 1857, pp. 49-108.

[27] Boyen, *Erinnerungen*, II, 332.

worn. The organization by brigades, which consisted of four infantry battalions and three to four cavalry squadrons, followed the East Prussian model. This organization lost its significance when *Landwehr* regiments were included in regular army brigades during the armistice of June-August, 1813.[28]

STRENGTH OF THE ARMY ON THE OUTBREAK OF WAR

Before the armistice few *Landwehr* brigades were sufficiently trained for use against the enemy, but genuine universal service which was the basis of the *Landwehr* was an important change in Prussian military practice. At the outbreak of war on March 16, 1813, Prussia's armed forces consisted only of line troops, brought to war strength by measures proposed by the Armament Commission, and by the growth of the war reserve in the cantons since 1809. A *précis* written by Scharnhorst late in February or early in March of 1813 recorded these elements of the army's strength. Field troops, including 4,000 Volunteer *Jäger*, were reckoned at 65,675 men; troops in the process of forming amounted to 34,940; depot and garrison troops numbered 30,083. If every unit succeeded in reaching its established strength the total, together with various free corps, would reach 131,748 men.[29]

The beginning of hostilities on March 16, 1813 found the Prussians with a field army of 1,776 officers, 66,963 men, 20,105 horses, and 213 guns. Medical, train, and technical troops added 2,643 men and 3,625 horses. Second line troops included 615 officers, 32,642 men, 650 horses, and 56 guns. Lack of training made this reserve far less effective than it had been in 1806. Together with garrison troops numbering 398 officers, 22,277 men, with 1,743 horses and 148 train *Knechte*, the personnel of the army on March 16, 1813 totaled 127,394 men.[30]

[28] Courbière, *Heeresverfassung*, pp. 179-80; Chareton, *op. cit.*, pp. 122-24.

[29] *Preuss. Heer 1813*, p. 66. Boyen gave the total of mobile troops in March, 1813 as 61,671. *Erinnerungen*, III, 229-34.

[30] *Preuss. Heer 1813*, pp. 162-63, and Anlage XXVI, pp. 421-57.

In estimating the effectiveness of the Prussian rearmament effort from 1807 to 1813 it must be remembered that half the men in the armed forces in 1813 were recruits with little training. The army was weak in artillery, small arms were scarce, and horses were few and in bad condition. Before 1806 Prussia could mobilize and equip a well-disciplined army of 185,764 first line troops in less than two weeks. This force would be almost three times the size of the army that took the field on the outbreak of war in 1813.[31]

WARTIME PROBLEMS

With the beginning of the War of Liberation the Prussian military program was beset with new difficulties. There was an even greater need for the rapid development of reserves, but the central control over this important work remained ineffective. Both the raising and training of *Landwehr* militiamen was left to the independent action of the provincial authorities and the Military Governments. Another problem was the procurement of weapons and munitions for the expanding army. Enough equipment had been available to supply the reduced army, but there was insufficient armament for all the new formations of 1813.[32]

Not until the summer of that year were enough small arms at hand to equip all the troops. Purchases of muskets abroad, especially in Austria, and gifts of artillery and powder captured by the Russians, helped to satisfy Prussian requirements. The distribution of *matériel* was at first complicated by the disorder into which the army had been thrown by the attempt to mobilize the first and second line troops simultaneously. Though some English arms shipments did arrive on the Baltic coast, England's direct aid to Prussia either in the form of weapons or the "Cavalry of St. George" (gold pieces) was insignificant during the spring campaign. After June 14, 1813, when Eng-

---

31 See Boyen, *Erinnerungen*, I, 187.

32 Consult the *Bericht des Majors von Schöler vom 7. April 1813 über Angelegenheiten der Bewaffnung*, in *Preuss. Heer 1813*, Anlage XXIII, pp. 413-17.

land agreed to an annual subsidy of £666,666 if the Prussians maintained a field army of 80,000 men, large quantities of English arms were provided. By that time the army's new organization and the clarification of the *Landwehr's* relation to the line minimized the difficulties attending the distribution of weapons. In order that the number of combatants might be increased the *Landwehr* had been distributed among the brigades of the regular army. This made it impossible to carry out a policy of arming all the line troops before attending to the requirements of the *Landwehr*.[33]

In the spring of 1813 the general confusion, misunderstanding of the nature and purpose of the *Landwehr*, insufficient armament, and the lack of a coordinated plan frustrated Prussia's bold challenge. Napoleon's quick utilization of French garrison troops in Germany, and the reinforcement of the *Grande Armée* by new levies in the Empire, stopped the Prussians in their first campaign. Heavy casualties suffered by the Prussian troops in the spring battles, as well as the attempt to expand the Prussian army, soon exhausted the normal war reserve. Canton training lagged, however, and there was an increasing tendency to replace battle losses by conscription in the cantons for the depot battalions. For the purpose of expanding the armed forces the principal weight of the conscription program before the summer of 1813 was borne by the *Landwehr*.[34]

ORGANIZING THE *Landwehr* IN THE PROVINCES

Only in East Prussia could the *Landwehr* be called an unqualified success. Many peasants in the other Military Governments fled to the forests or migrated. In the east, where the land had been laid waste by the French, there was considerable

---

33 *Cf.* Chareton, *op. cit.*, pp. 94, 124. Previous negotiations between England and Prussia in the spring of 1813 had been thwarted by English fear of Prussian designs on Hanover. Prussia obtained only a small sum in comparison with the £2,000,000 granted Swedish, Hanoverian, and Hanseatic troops. *Cf.* Sorel, *op. cit.*, VIII, 96-99, 134.

34 *Cf. Preuss. Heer 1813*, p. 342 *passim*. A review of the development of *Landwehr* by provinces is given in Cavaignac, *op. cit.*, II, 458-69.

THE MOBILIZATION OF 1813

enthusiasm for war. No difficulty was experienced in making the levies and the *Landwehr* tax of one million thalers was over-subscribed. But the suffering of the people was very great, and when the French evacuated the territory east of the Oder they left behind them ruin and typhus.[35]

Undaunted, the General Commission in East Prussia began conscription on March 27, 1813. A survey based on the 1811 census had been made of the men liable to service.[36] Training began on April 28 and by the middle of May the East Prussian *Landwehr* was declared "ready." In common with most militia units, none was in action until the end of the armistice. Neither artillery nor cavalry could be raised; the few men who had horses joined one of the volunteer cavalry regiments or the *Jäger*. For lack of uniforms, cloaks of a common color were distributed. After March 17 the royal authorities delivered some small arms of French manufacture which had been captured by the Russians at Kovno.[37] In view of the limited training and the lack of equipment the rather elaborate instructions written for the tactical employment of the *Landwehr* were superfluous.[38]

East Prussia's contribution to the armed forces was very great. In the first eight months of 1813, 25,922 men were conscripted for various kinds of service. Approximately 20,000 men were taken into the *Landwehr*, while the rest went into the line regiments or York's corps. During the preceding year only 704 men had been taken. In West Prussia which had a large Polish population the conscription of *Landwehr* was resisted, but the quota of almost 7,000 men was eventually raised.[39]

---

[35] Bezzenberger, *Ostpreussen in der Franzosenzeit*, pp. 21-23, 27-28. Also see Chareton, *op. cit.*, pp. 144-45.

[36] *Cf.* Boyen, *Erinnerungen*, III, Beilage XXIII, pp. 312-15.

[37] Chareton, *op. cit.*, pp. 139-42; Bezzenberger, *Ostpreussen in der Franzosenzeit*, pp. 26-27.

[38] *Cf.* Lilienstern, *Kriegs-Katechismus*, pp. 21 ff., and Boyen, *Erinnerungen*, III, 333-49, and 349 ff., additional exercise regulations for the *Landsturm*.

[39] Bezzenberger, *Ostpreussen in der Franzosenzeit*, pp. 69, 79, 82, 95, documents on the conscription by circles in East and West Prussia. Other data in "Errichtung der Landwehr und des Landsturms in Ostpreussen," *op. cit.*, pp. 96-121; *Preuss. Heer 1813*, pp. 260, 263.

Silesia received the *Landwehr* program with great tumult. The population had always been exempt from Prussian military service and there was no love of the army. Nor did the province have East Prussia's grievance against the French. Silesia had been spared damage during the war of 1806-1807 and had not suffered at the hands of Napoleon's troops marching across Germany to Russia. During the period of the reforms Silesia had been in a state of revolt over local grievances, and in 1810 Prussian troops were billeted there in order to quiet the population.[40] When conscription was announced angry crowds rioted, and as soon as men were taken for the army thousands began to flee into Polish territory. It was necessary for the Russians to return these deserters in order to enforce the law.[41] To the king's great despair, for the conscription in Silesia was under immediate royal supervision, instead of the sixty-eight battalions and seventy-one squadrons that had been planned, only twenty-four battalions and a few squadrons were raised by the time of the armistice in June, 1813.[42]

Hardenberg on May 6 had expressed great dissatisfaction with the slow mobilization of the Silesian *Landwehr*. On March 20 he had indicated that Silesia could raise 49,974 *Landwehr* of infantry and cavalry, but his reports for June 3, 1813 showed only 25,000 men in these formations. Not even the invasion of Silesia by French troops at the end of May made the inhabitants more willing to serve. Harsh punishments for desertion, such as whipping and shooting which were still being used despite the Articles of War, did not stop the offense. Yet military requirements were distributed unequally in Silesia since some areas were not furnishing men. During the armistice, June 4 to August 10, many communities both great and small found themselves in neutral territory between the opposing armies

---

40 Boyen, *Erinnerungen*, II, 67-68, comments on the trouble in Silesia.

41 Chareton, *op. cit.*, pp. 148-50; "Organisation der Landwehr, Landwehr-Reserven und des Landsturms der Provinz Schlesien im Jahre 1813," *Militär-Wochenblatt*, Beiheft 1845, pp. 402-04.

42 *Cf.* Boyen, *Erinnerungen*, II, 440-47, III, 4-5.

and were thus able to evade their obligations under the Prussian laws. Breslau was so conspicuous in its opposition to compulsory military service that Frederick William (on July 1) warned the city of dire punishments unless conscription were resumed. The supply of muskets for the Silesian *Landwehr* was adequate at first since 10,000 or more were delivered from Austria, and an additional 20,000 were stored in the Silesian fortresses. Flints were scarce, however, and a search was made for a substitute stone; the Berlin porcelain factory was even ordered to prepare an *Ersatz*.[43] Finally, on June 8, 1813, Frederick William III made Gneisenau personally responsible for raising the full complement of Silesian *Landwehr*. By drastic methods Gneisenau was able to bring its strength to the number originally set forth by Hardenberg. Additional units of *Landwehr* were raised in the other Military Governments but with less difficulty than in Silesia.[44]

Value of the *Landwehr*

Not until the armistice of June-August, 1813 did the real value of the *Landwehr* become apparent. No one foresaw that this militia which the Armament Commission vaguely intended for limited duty, garrisons, or siege forces would provide most of the man power for rebuilding the Prussian army. Even the confusion that attended the raising of *Landwehr* in Military Governments, provinces, and circles contributed to that end by delaying the appearance of trained *Landwehr* units on the battlefield. When it became clear that this newly conscripted militia could not be organized and trained in time to fight alongside the

---

[43] "Organisation der Landwehr, Landwehr-Reserven und des Landsturms der Provinz Schlesien," *op. cit.*, pp. 401, 404-06. The commanding officers of the Silesian *Landwehr* frankly expressed their contempt for the peasantry that made up the rank and file. But the peasants feared and resented the army; many had to be trapped like animals and carried off to the regiments. *Ibid.*, Beiheft 1845, p. 412.

[44] *Ibid.*, Beiheft 1845, pp. 407-410, and Beilage I, p. 414. For an account of the *Landwehr* in other provinces see *Preuss. Heer 1813*, pp. 234-92, and *Militär-Wochenblatt*, Beiheft 1857.

line troops, military authorities began to think about combining it with the line. This decision was forced upon individual commanding officers by the exhaustion of reserves in the regular army depots. By May some badly depleted line regiments had begun to draw in men originally conscripted for the *Landwehr*. In view of this the *Landwehr* came to resemble the kind of militia which had been proposed before 1806 more than it did the militia projects of the Military Reorganization Commission. The raising of *Landwehr* in the spring of 1813 had in effect increased the framework of the regular army. Yet these hastily raised levies, rather than the meager total of trained war replacements, enabled the Prussians to rebuild their army during the armistice and carry on against Napoleon.[45]

THE *Landsturm*

A *Landsturm* or militia for boys and men not qualified for regular military service had been mentioned on March 17 in the king's message to the people. No organization was provided until April 21 when the *Landsturm* was officially created. This edict was a victory for the radical reformers who had been striving since 1808 to transform a professional service army into a citizen army.[46] Every man was made responsible for home defence; it was a real *Notwehr* (emergency defence). Nationalism triumphed in the *Landsturm;* while the regular army and the militia represented dynastic and provincial loyalty, the new force cut through those ties to the people.[47] These guerrilla bands were to assemble by districts and circles, but only on the command of army officers or royal officials. Unlawful assembly was punishable as mutiny. At the approach of the enemy the fields were to be laid waste and the invader was to be harassed

---

45 *Cf.* Preuss. *Heer 1813*, pp. 306-07; Chareton, *op. cit.*, pp. 118, 160; and Cavaignac, *op. cit.*, II, 454-55.

46 See Ferdinand Delbrück, *Erläuterungen der Königlichen Verordnungen über den Landsturm* (Königsberg, 1814), pp. 1-7; Ide, *op. cit.*, pp. 43-44. On the significance of the *Landsturm* for the new concept of national war consult Huber, *op. cit.*, pp. 143-49.

47 Boyen, *Erinnerungen*, III, 316-27, 386; *Stein Denkschriften*, IV, 611, 617.

by attacks on his communications, outposts, and encampments. Uniforms for the *Landsturm* were expressly forbidden; the weapons were to be flails, rakes, pikes, and axes.[48]

No mass organization of the *Landsturm* was ever attempted. Small units assembled only in a few places where the enemy was raiding. Strong objections to the *Landsturm* were raised by conservatives and royal officials on the ground that it endangered calm and order among civilians. There was an element of truth in this assertion and on July 17, 1813, the king ordered military supervision of *Landsturm* units, and permitted them to assemble only on command of the Military Governments. From August 8 *Landsturm* battalions were developed as replacements for the *Landwehr*. Later on, Stein's attempt to organize a militia of this type in the German lands liberated from the French encountered strong opposition from the local princes, who wished to control their own armies and were frightened at the thought of armed peasants led by officers tainted with the new national and liberal sentiment.[49]

THE SPRING CAMPAIGN OF 1813

Napoleon's enemies did not immediately form a coalition in the spring of 1813 to pursue the opportunity that the disastrous Moscow campaign offered. Without assistance from abroad the Prussian and Russian armies were greatly handicapped in their attempt to defeat Napoleon in northern Europe. Prussia had only limited resources, and the Russians were divided in council over the advisability of carrying the war into Germany. Although England professed satisfaction with the alliance between Frederick William III and Alexander I, the cost of Welling-

[48] Details in "Organisation der Landwehr, Landwehr-Reserven und des Landsturms der Provinz Schlesien," *op. cit.*, pp. 411-13. The *Landsturm* was more bother than worth; a host of violations of the civil code always followed the formation of these peasant bands. *Cf.* J. J. R. von Lilienstern, *Die Deutsche Volksbewaffnung* (Berlin, 1815), pp. 63-65, 72 ff.

[49] Jany, *op. cit.*, IV, 91; *Stein Denkschriften*, IV, 611-12 describes the reaction of typical German princes. Also see *ibid.*, IV, 532, 578-81, 585-89, 591-92. Consult E. Daniels, "Ein vergessenes Dokument zur Geschichte der Freiheitskriege," *Preussische Jahrbücher*, CXLIV (1911), 256-64.

ton's peninsular campaign as well as a lingering mistrust of Prussia for harboring designs on Hanover, deprived the two continental powers of any immediate English aid, either troops or money. Austria remained neutral, seeking a diplomatic formula that would permit Metternich to act as mediator between the warring nations. Bernadotte brought Sweden into the war against Napoleon in May, but his troops, which landed at Stralsund, the historic portal for Swedish intervention in north Germany, were too disorganized at first to give effective aid.

Napoleon, on the other hand, was still master of a great part of Europe, and as a field commander he remained incomparably superior to any allied general. He had at first planned to drive the allies back to Warsaw and raise the siege of French garrisons along the Oder and Vistula, of which the largest was the Tenth Army Corps in Danzig. Although the French army still outnumbered its opponents, Napoleon soon realized that it was inadequate for such an ambitious plan. The ranks were filled with new recruits who could not make long or rapid marches, while the cavalry was too weak to support extended operations. And since the allies were showing more energy than had been anticipated, Napoleon decided to conclude his preparations and seek battle on Saxon territory.[50]

Near Lützen a battle was forced upon Napoleon by Wittgenstein, the Russian commander of the allied forces. On May 2 Wittgenstein opened an attack on what he believed to be the weakly defended right wing of a greatly extended French army. But his calculations were in error, and when the initial allied attack had been spent, a bitter struggle developed for control of a series of villages south of Lützen. In one of these, Gross Görschen, Scharnhorst received the wound that eventually cost his life. Desperate fighting in the villages weakened the allies for the French counterattack, but they were saved by Napoleon's

[50] A number of campaign histories are listed in the bibliography; the most useful is F. L. Petre, *Napoleon's Last Campaign in Germany 1813* (London, 1912).

lack of a strong cavalry which made vigorous pursuit impossible. Lützen was a costly victory for the French, who suffered 18,000 casualties without taking any prisoners or trophies. Metternich's interests had been served more than the Emperor's: the bloody but indecisive fighting seemed to assure success for his policy of mediation.

Their defeat at Lützen obliged the allies to defend Silesia from invasion, and for this purpose they took up the strong positions around Bautzen that had been made famous during the Seven Years' War. Napoleon's first attack on May 20 was intended to hold his adversaries fast for a combined frontal and flanking attack the next day. But Ney failed to complete the flanking maneuver, and infantry eventually had to drive the Prussians from the heights. Late in the afternoon of May 21 the French strength prevailed, though the defenders drew off in good order. Once more Napoleon was victorious, but the allies had also escaped destruction for a second time.[51]

The Death of Scharnhorst

Scharnhorst's death on June 28, 1813 from the wound he had received at Gross Görschen was a great blow to the Prussians. His loss left the army without its most effective leader in the period of reorganization that followed. Since 1807 Scharnhorst had been the symbol and the moving spirit of military reform in Prussia. In a state where intrigue was valued more than political sagacity, and whose army clung to a long outmoded military system, the reformer required more than a mere technical mastery of his subject. Scharnhorst was not ideally suited to the unending and continually shifting struggle for royal favor, but his brilliance in military affairs and his resilience to the rebuffs, personal slights, and discouragements assured his eventual success.

If all of Scharnhorst's ideas for the rebirth of Prussian military power were not carried out, the failure cannot be at-

[51] Consult P. Foucart, *Bautzen, 20 et 21 mai 1813* (Paris, 1897). Frederick the Great had withdrawn to the heights of Bautzen after his defeat at Hochkirch, October 14, 1758.

tributed to lack of zeal. Nor was his legacy to the Prussian army solely a product of his military ability. Unlike so many German soldiers and statesmen, Scharnhorst's attractive personality, and his genuine humility, won him a circle of close friends. They became inspired by his example and absorbed in his conceptions of war and military power. Through the work of two of his disciples, Boyen and Clausewitz, Scharnhorst's influence upon the development of the Prussian army was assured.[52]

THE ARMISTICE OF POISCHWITZ

After two inconclusive battles both sides were weary and in need of a breathing spell. Napoleon had not succeeded either by diplomacy or war in separating the allies, nor had his victories been complete enough to impress the Austrians. His military position was nevertheless very strong. French troops held the Elbe as a secure defence line; other French columns occupied Breslau, abandoned by the allies in their retreat toward Schweidnitz. If there were a pause in the operations, the French recruits would benefit from intense training exercises and the inadequate cavalry units could be reinforced. An armistice would also permit the Emperor to play his game of wooing Austria while preparing the destruction of the Prussian and Russian armies. There was an equal need on the allied side for a military reorganization and a new agreement on the conduct of the war. Prussian leaders were especially alarmed over the Russian proposals to abandon Silesia and retire into Poland. Nonetheless, the allies adopted a bold front at Poischwitz in negotiating for an armistice that began on June 4 and lasted, with one extension, until August 10.[53]

[52] Scharnhorst was dispatched on a diplomatic journey to Vienna in the spring of 1813 in order to draw Austria into the war with France. This trip was interrupted when it became known that a Prussian officer would not be received favorably as a negotiator. Scharnhorst returned therefore to Prague where he died of the infection in his wounded knee. Letters of the last period of Scharnhorst's life are collected in Paul Wagner, " Briefe an Scharnhorst," *Historische Zeitschrift*, CXXVII (1923), 243-59.

[53] Cf. Sorel, *op. cit.*, VIII, 107-33.

This respite was of the greatest value to the Prussians, since it enabled them to gather additional weapons and munitions, and to rebuild their depleted cadres with the *Landwehr* enrolled during the spring. Great numbers of Russian reserves were also brought up to strengthen the Tsar's forces, and the Swedes used the opportunity to complete the formation of their army. Diplomatic preparations were pushed with equal success. At Reichenbach on June 14 and 15 England agreed to subsidize Prussia and Russia, whose alliance at Kalisch now supplemented by new commitments with the English formed the basis of the coalition.[54]

All those misunderstandings and grievances that had interfered with the spring campaign were aired in a great conference of the allied monarchs at Trachenberg. To impress the Austrians with the strength and resolution of the new coalition, a plan of campaign was drawn up (July 12) that had the great virtue of subordinating all measures and interests to the destruction of Napoleon's main army. Equal firmness was shown in the representations of the allies at the Congress of Prague which met during the latter part of the armistice. This attempt by Metternich to mediate between the belligerents proved futile, and after a final exchange of notes with Napoleon he concluded that war between France and Austria was unavoidable. When Austria declared war two days after the expiration of the armistice all the great powers were at last arrayed against Napoleon.[55]

54 *Ibid.*, VIII, 134-35. Before the end of June English arms began to arrive at Baltic ports. By July 15 some 40,000 muskets and 8,500,000 paper-wrapped cartridges were delivered. In addition to English cannon, powder, ball, wagons, and uniforms, not less than 113,000 English muskets were used by the Prussian army in the fall campaign of 1813. *Cf. Preuss. Heer 1813*, pp. 179-81, and Anlage XXIV, pp. 417-18.

55 Sorel, *op. cit.*, VIII, 154 ff. Consult Otto Harnack, "Die Ursachen der Niederlage Napoleons im Herbste 1813," *Historische Zeitschrift*, XIC (1902), 387-88. For the strength of the French army in Germany in 1813 see Boyen, *Erinnerungen*, III, 507-45, and the tables on pp. 519, 541.

REORGANIZATION OF THE PRUSSIAN ARMY DURING THE ARMISTICE

In June of 1813 the regular Prussian army, including newly formed depots, the fortress troops, and train personnel, numbered approximately 140-150,000 men. This made an impressive total if the great number of reserve and garrison formations were overlooked. The actual battle strength of the Prussian army was not very formidable; barely a third of these troops had been assembled for any one of the battles fought during the spring. Even with Russian assistance Prussia was too weak to mount an overpowering offensive. This lesson of the indecisive spring campaign was thoroughly assimilated by Prussian military leaders, and during the armistice they made the expansion of the army their first concern. A good picture of the Prussian army at the start of the armistice is provided by Boyen's estimate of the regular forces, in which he included new formations, depot troops, and garrisons, but not the *Landwehr*.[56]

STRENGTH OF THE REGULAR ARMY IN JUNE, 1813

Infantry		Cavalry		Artillery	Pioneers
Line	40,891	Line	12,020		
Reserve	29,637	Provincials	1,351		
Ersatz	11,414	Volunteers	2,416		
Foreigners	6,468	Depot Squadrons	3,461		
Garrison	20,422				
Volunteers	4,549				
Total	113,381		19,248	16,187	1,305

Grand total 150,121 men

Throughout the summer of 1813 men in every province were conscripted for the *Landwehr* with a vigor that often equalled the harsh recruiting of native subjects during the Seven Years' War. The very great increase in the size of the army during the armistice was accomplished by incorporating these new levies even before they could be trained or equipped properly. There were being recruited 120,000 *Landwehr* troops, who were to

---

56 Boyen, *Erinnerungen*, III, 462-63.

make up two-fifths of the combatants of the four army corps organized after July 12, a third of the garrison troops, and almost all of the siege corps. By provinces the *Landwehr* reached the following strength.[57]

Lithuania, East and West Prussia to the Vistula	20,000 men
Prussia west of the Vistula	6,620
Silesia	49,974
New Mark	7,941
Electoral Mark Brandenburg	20,560
Pomerania	15,409
Total	120,504

Several methods of combining the *Landwehr* with the line had been considered: by forming mixed battalions, adding a *Landwehr* battalion to each regiment, or adding a *Landwehr* regiment to each brigade. The first method was advocated by those officers who believed that the *Landwehr* needed more training before it could risk the hazards of battle. They argued that these civilians in uniform would become soldiers more quickly if they were treated like cantonists and added in small numbers to each battalion. There the close association of veteran and recruit would provide the most practical instruction in soldiering. This suggestion did not find favor with the crown, however. Despite the analogy with the canton method it was feared that this practice would be harmful to the spirit of the line army. Even when threatened by an enemy as resourceful as Napoleon a Hohenzollern instinctively paused before submitting the royal army to what might prove to be a dangerous experiment. That the original character of the *Landwehr* as a militia gave it a claim to a distinct identity in the army's organization appealed to the monarch and his advisers. This feeling also ruled out the addition of *Landwehr* battalions to regiments of the line. The decision to minimize administrative and organizational problems by handling the *Landwehr* in large units was hastened by Russian demands that the size of the Prussian army be increased quickly. So it was that regiments that were

[57] Chareton, *op. cit.*, pp. 167-68.

referred to and numbered as *Landwehr,* and which were clad in distinct uniforms, were incorporated in the brigades of the field army. Since two-thirds of these conscripted *Landwehr* men had received only the barest training, and many had not handled muskets before the summer of 1813, it is surprising that the expanded army had any cohesion at all.[58]

On July 27, 1813 the *Landwehr* troops were reorganized in the following units:[59]

	Infantry	Cavalry Regiments or	Battalions,	Squadrons
East Prussia	5	5	20	16
West Prussia	3	3	11	9
Pomerania	3	3	12	12
New Mark	3	2	12	8
Electoral Mark	7	7	26	28
Silesia	17	10	68	40

Together these amounted to 149 battalions and 113 squadrons. At the end of the armistice the Prussian army had almost doubled in size, and with garrison detachments being provided by the *Landwehr,* more line regiments were freed for battle. Without the *Landwehr* Prussia would have continued to fight with a great numerical disadvantage.[60]

The artillery was also reorganized during the armistice, and the effectiveness of this work probably accounts for the successful combination of *Landwehr* and line troops. The new units that were formed included one mounted battery, ten and a half unmounted batteries, and four twelve-pound batteries. These additions gave the army a total of fifty batteries, thirteen park columns, and two artillery train columns. From the spring of 1813 to the fall, thirty-three new batteries were created; not all were complete with cannon, although 300 guns and 900 wagons

---

58 *Ibid.*, pp. 168-71.

59 Jany, *op. cit.*, IV, 90. There is no agreement among the authorities on the number of battalions that were raised, or the distribution of the troops by provinces, only that the total strength was about 120,000 men.

60 Cavaignac concludes that the *Landwehr* was the dominant element in the military revival of Prussia in 1813. The preparation of reserves and the use of *Krümper* were of no more than secondary value. Cavaignac, *op. cit.*, II, 455.

captured at Leipzig helped to meet the shortages. Of the 15,000 men in the artillery about an eighth, that is the contingent which had participated in the Russian campaign of 1812, could be called fully trained. A thorough reorganization of the cavalry was not attempted during the armistice. For want of horses it was impossible to mount all the veteran cavalrymen who were available. The cavalry in every army was forced to use farm and draft horses which would have been scorned a decade earlier.[61]

Strength of the Prussian Army on August 10, 1813 [62]

Infantry Battalions

90 of the Line	72,130
39 of Reserve and Garrison	31,838
8 of *Jäger* and Foreigners	11,153
151 of *Landwehr*	109,120
Total	224,241 men

Cavalry Squadrons

89 including the National Cavalry Regiments	13,375
22 of Reserve	3,389
23 of *Jäger* and Foreigners	3,064
113 of *Landwehr*	10,952
Total	30,780 men

Artillery

50 and one-half batteries	8,749
33 companies in fortresses or in siege operations	6,566
Total	15,315 men

Technical Troops

7 Field Pioneer Companies	567
6 Fortress Pioneer Companies	738
Total	1,305
Grand Total	271,641 men

[61] *Die Preussische Artillerie von ihrer Neuformation 1809*, pp. 31-33; Rummel, *op. cit.*, pp. 6, 11, 17-19. Consult E. von Colomb, *Beiträge zur Geschichte der preussischen Kavallerie seit 1808* (Berlin, 1880), pp. 8-10.

[62] Jany, *op. cit.*, IV, 93-94. With officers Jany notes that the total man power reached 279,000 at the end of the armistice. For more detailed tables see *Preuss. Heer 1813*, Anlage XXVI, pp. 548-51.

The field troops, except the cavalry and infantry of the Royal Guard which had a separate organization, formed four army corps. Line troops were distributed through three of these, while the fourth, apart from the artillery, was made up entirely of reserve and *Landwehr* material. Each corps consisted of four brigades, and each brigade was made up of one regiment of line infantry, one regiment of reserve infantry, one regiment of *Landwehr* infantry, one regiment of cavalry, and one battery. In reserve were twenty to twenty-eight squadrons of cavalry and two or more batteries. The troops not held in reserve were used in the four siege corps which reduced the French fortresses.[63]

ORGANIZATION OF THE PRUSSIAN FIELD TROOPS AT THE END OF THE ARMISTICE, AUGUST 10, 1813

	Battalions	Squadrons	Batteries	Men	Guns
Royal Guard	6½	8	2	7,091	16
I. Army Corps	45	44	13	38,484	104
II. Army Corps	41	44	14	37,816	112
III. Army Corps	40½	42	10	41,135	80
IV. Army Corps	48½	29¼	4	33,170	32
Field troops at Wallmoden	4¼	7	1	4,068	8
Total	185¾	174¼	44	161,764	352

Included in these totals were the *Jäger* detachments and the six pioneer companies, distributed two to each of the first three Army Corps. The four siege corps included forty-three battalions, twenty-two squadrons, six batteries, and one pioneer company, a total of 30,670 men and 48 guns. There were in addition to these effectives 80,368 *Landwehr* troops still in training, formation, or serving as garrisons.[64] The *Landwehr* did much more than free regular troops from onerous duties behind the lines. Except for engagements in the first few weeks after the armistice their combat record was remarkably good. However, most commanding officers were prudent enough to adopt a battle and marching order intended to prevent panic among the *Landwehr*. These formations nevertheless proved

[63] Osten-Sacken, *op. cit.*, II, 122-23; Jany, *op. cit.*, IV, 101.
[64] Osten-Sacken, *op. cit.*, II, 123.

their worth in the heavy fighting which marked the Battle of the Nations at Leipzig (October 16-19, 1813). When it became clear that this victory had broken Napoleon's power, 36,000 *Landwehr* were detailed to garrison duty, and not less than 55,000 were added to the forces laying siege to enemy fortresses. Yet desertions among the *Landwehr* were numerous; in the first stages of the campaign 29,000 men fled from their ranks alone.[65]

CONSCRIPTING ADDITIONAL MAN POWER

The Prussian army suffered heavy losses in the great battles fought by the allies after the armistice of the summer months. But the allied victories freed Prussia from French military occupation and made possible the erection of additional Military Governments in former Prussian territory. From them it was expected that enough *Landwehr* and *Landsturm* could be raised to maintain the field army at its maximum strength.[66] And after October, 1813 a serious attempt was made to spare the old Prussian provinces further drafts of men by applying conscription to the newly regained lands. On November 19 two new Military Governments were created, both in former Prussian territory, the " Fifth " between the Elbe and the Weser, and the " Sixth " between the Weser and the Rhine where Prussia had had scattered holdings before 1807. From these governments 13,000 conscripts were immediately required, but since the French had already made excessive demands there, the organization of the *Landwehr* could not be completed until March, 1814. Free corps and volunteer units were also formed but their strength was not very great.[67]

Little enthusiasm for the war was manifested in the reconquered areas. Morale was especially low in the Sixth Military

[65] Chareton, *op. cit.*, pp. 183-85, 195-96. See Jany, *op. cit.*, IV, 95-96, 98.

[66] *Cf.* Stein *Denkschriften*, IV, 238-43, Stein's plan of Mar. 16, 1813 for organizing conscription and military contributions in conquered territory. The *Landsturm* contingents of individual states are set forth in Stein's memoir of Mar. 22, 1814. *Ibid.*, IV, 610-12.

[67] Jany, *op. cit.*, IV, 97-98. On the *Landwehr* in the Fifth and in the Sixth Military Government, consult *Militär-Wochenblatt*, Beiheft 1857.

Government. Nevertheless, 22,000 conscripts who were used primarily in siege operations came from there. The reinforcement obtained from these sources prompted the formation through 1814 of not less than twenty-five governments and three general-governments, including the Hansa cities. Rühle von Lilienstern, appointed Defence Commissar by Stein, supervised the recruiting that was carried out in these governments.[68] The formations which he raised were not enrolled in the Prussian army. Only the County of Berg was under Prussian rule and there a bitter conflict ensued over conscription.[69]

Napoleon's defeat and exile enabled the Prussian troops to march home and begin demobilization, but the character of Prussia's peacetime army was yet to be determined. To Hermann von Boyen, who took over the guidance of the newly reorganized War Ministry on June 3, 1814, fell the task of demobilizing the army and establishing the legal basis of military service. His acceptance of this post implied that strong efforts would be made to retain the military institutions which had been tested during the War of Liberation. When his administrative reforms were granted Boyen became the first Prussian War Minister to exercise the authority and prerogatives implied in that title. Both his esteem for Scharnhorst and his wartime experience with the *Landwehr* were reflected in his proposals for universal military service. The conscription law of September 3, 1814 which bore Boyen's name became the legal cornerstone of the Prussian armed forces that were eventually to unite Germany.[70]

[68] *Cf.* J. J. R. von Lilienstern, *Die Deutsche Volksbewaffnung* (Berlin, 1815), a collection of the ordinances issued by German states in 1814-1815. Details of this armament in W. Just, *Verwaltung und Bewaffnung im westlichen Deutschland nach der Leipziger Schlacht 1813 und 1814* (Göttingen, 1911).

[69] Daniels, *op. cit.*, pp. 256-58.

[70] See G. S. Ford, "Boyen's Military Law," *American Historical Review*, XX (1915), 528-38. After 1815 the legal basis of the army bore the twofold aspect of the Prussian armed forces: the standing army represented the conquest *Politik* of absolutism, while the *Landwehr* corresponded to the new relation between prince and subjects that had been established during the war. At the same time the law recognized that wars were now the concern of the people. *Cf.* Wolzendorff, *op. cit.*, p. 22; Höhn, *op. cit.*, pp. 16-18.

CONCLUSION

Conscription in Prussia

MILITARY conscription bearing equally on every class was the principal reform sought in Prussia during the Age of the French Revolution.[1] Since the early eighteenth century conscription of the lower classes had been carried out in Prussia by means of the canton system. Frederick William I had assigned each regiment a canton district from which native subjects could be conscripted for a short training period. Each regiment maintained in its canton a trained reserve for replacing battle casualties and bringing the regimental complement to its war strength. Universal conscription had never been attempted but this was not for want of legal authorization: the canton laws required every able-bodied man to perform military service. For reasons of economy, the convenience of the upper classes, and the requirements of mercantilism, only landless peasants were conscripted. By 1806 the canton system had become an administrative device for sorting out the less capable serfs whose selection for the army would not affect the productivity of agriculture. Industry, trade, and transportation were not endangered by the canton laws because all men in these occupations had been exempted from military service.

Twice during the eighteenth century the administrative machinery of the canton system was overhauled. An important change had been made in 1763 when control of conscription passed from the army to the civil bureaucracy. These officials were more concerned for the needs of the national economy than the requirements of the army, hence many additional subjects were spared military training. No radical changes in this policy were announced in the canton law of 1792, which proved more generous than any previous law in conferring exemptions. Al-

[1] The basic achievements of the military reform are summarized in Max Lehmann, ed., "Boyen's Darstellung der preussischen Kriegsverfassung," *Historische Zeitschrift*, LXVII (1891), 66-67.

though the law was introduced by a broad statement of universal service, landless peasants were virtually the only persons remaining for the conscription officials after the list of exemptions had been compiled.

The difficulties inherent in this policy had been thoroughly aired before a reform commission called in 1795 to suggest means for enlarging the army. By that date an army expansion had been made necessary by the growth of other European armies, and by the new demands imposed on the Prussian armed forces by the partition of Poland. Strained financial resources did not permit the hiring of additional mercenaries. A few officers, mindful of the native reservists who had helped to maintain the strength of Frederick's army, proposed to meet the new situation by conscripting more Prussian subjects. Ten years spent in drafting and amending proposals did not bring any fundamental change in the army's recruiting methods. The commission rejected Knesebeck's plan for a universal service army, but was sufficiently impressed by Courbière's proposal for increasing the number of native soldiers that a faster tempo of training and furloughing peasant conscripts was authorized. This program which began in 1805 might have increased the size of the army had not war with France broken out within a year.

The period of peace from 1795 to 1806 offered a great opportunity for military reform. Without royal leadership a reform effort in an absolute state was doomed but no support was forthcoming from the Prussian crown. Both Frederick William II and Frederick William III were assured by their reactionary advisers that the military methods perfected by Frederick the Great were still sound. And warnings were not lacking that any departure from the path of tradition was not only unnecessary but might also be dangerous. It would have been foolhardy to attempt conscription in the newly acquired Polish provinces. The native population was so rebellious that large forces had to be garrisoned there for police duties. Prussia's impressive territorial gains in the partitions of Poland had actually weakened the army; by removing many regiments from their canton areas the training of their reservists ceased. Conscription of the new subjects was not politically expedient, while for many regiments, conscription of the old Prussian subjects became impossible.

After the disasters of Jena and Auerstädt in 1806, another group of reformers led by Scharnhorst took up the task of rebuilding the Prussian army. It was evident to Scharnhorst that the French methods of waging war, especially the national character of their armies, had raised grave problems for the absolute monarchies. Conscription had revolutionary implications for the social structure of the old regime. One of Scharnhorst's greatest services was his skillful adaptation of the new principles of warfare and military organization to Prussian institutions without threatening the state with revolution.

Scharnhorst's first suggestions for conscripting additional Prussian subjects were more cautious than the proposals that had been made before 1806. He considered universal service suitable only for a militia which would train persons of means. Whether service was performed in the regular army along with mercenaries and serfs, or in the militia, was to be determined by a property test. Before 1806 militiamen were to have been trained by the regular army. Prussia would then have had a cadre army brought to war strength by natives trained in peacetime. This was more consistent with the principle of the canton system than Scharnhorst's plans in 1807 for establishing a militia on a separate footing from the regular army.

None of the militia projects of 1807-1808 met with Frederick William's approval and when the Treaty of Paris (September 8, 1808) imposed a limit of 42,000 men on the Prussian army, he was less disposed to consider anything so radical as a militia based on universal military service. Notwithstanding the indifference of the crown, bold proposals for a popular army were made in 1809 and 1810. These demands were the result of the reformers' conviction that a national revolt of the German people might overthrow Napoleon. It would be well for Prussia to prepare for this revolt by training a great contingent of natives as well as the regular army. This could be done by eliminating all canton exemptions and enforcing the universal service laws which had been proclaimed for more than a century. Eloquent appeals by Scharnhorst and Boyen in 1810 failed in view of the terrible poverty of the state, and the king's fear that the French would retaliate for an expansion of the Prussian army.

THE *Krümper* SYSTEM

The defeat of his conscription proposals obliged Scharnhorst to seek other means for strengthening the armed forces. A resort was made, therefore, to the canton system, the traditional Prussian organization for training reserves of native subjects. Until 1813 this *Krümper* training program, as it has become known, was governed by the canton law of 1792. *Krümper* was the military slang term for a cantonist who had received a few months' training in the army and had then been released to his civil occupation. It was recognized that canton training did not make possible the rapid growth of the armed forces, hence cantonists were intended primarily as a wartime reserve to cover losses of battle and desertion.

The only departure from previous methods was the emphasis upon the use of old soldiers. Great numbers of war prisoners who eventually found their way back to Prussia and numerous veterans of the disbanded regiments sought employment again in the army. All officers with depleted complements were quick to use these trained men. Official orders attempted to regulate the practice of accepting veterans rather than raw recruits in the training program but a system was never developed. Most of the *Krümper* were former soldiers of the army of 1806-1807. And the *Krümper* program itself was not an innovation but an expedient made necessary by the lack of a universal conscription law. It could hardly be considered a subterfuge for defeating the provisions of the Treaty of Paris, nor did it succeed in achieving a phenomenal rise in the strength of the Prussian army.

THE *Landwehr* OF 1813

The great defeats suffered by the *Grande Armée* in the winter of 1812-1813 gave the Prussian war party an opportunity to demand a more vigorous military program. Yet the first step toward real universal service was taken by East Prussia as soon as the French had been driven from that province. The example of these provincial patriots and the realization that Napoleon's army had been shattered overcame Frederick William's hesitancy, and on February 9, 1813 universal service was proclaimed in all the Prussian lands. The exemptions in the canton law were repealed and every able-bodied man became subject to conscription for the regular troops. This harsh provision was considerably modified by authorizing a *Landwehr,* or militia that was intended more or less for those subjects previously exempted from service, and by the encouragement given upper class youths to volunteer for officer training.

All trained personnel including *Krümper,* veterans, and pensioners, were mobilized in February and March, 1813 for the regular army. Replacements and reserve units for the regular army were obtained by conscription, which was also vigorously applied for the creation of the *Landwehr.* Throughout the spring of 1813 most conscripts were taken for the *Landwehr,* which had at first an organization separate from the line. This means of giving brief training to new recruits, rather than the *Krümper* system, made possible the expansion of the Prussian army. A very fortunate turn of events gave the Prussians an opportunity in the armistice of June-August, 1813 to rebuild their armed forces. *Landwehr* troops not only replaced the losses suffered during the unsuccessful spring campaign, but were added in sufficient numbers to double the size of the army. Prussia's military revival in 1813 was made possible by the addition of a conscripted and quickly trained *Landwehr* to the cadres of the regular army.

THE REFORM OF MILITARY ADMINISTRATION

A thorough reform of the Prussian army before 1806 had been made difficult by the confused administration of military affairs. Both the civil and military bureaucrats were bitterly opposed to any changes that touched their interests, and if a thorough reform had been approved it could not have been executed without reorganizing the bureaucracy. The not often recognized fact that the conduct of public affairs is never very efficient in an absolute government was borne out in Prussian military administration during the eighteenth century. The division of business was badly planned; several bureaus dealt with the same matters; and important business was referred to departments that were inadequately staffed. Each monarch without regard for existing arrangements created new offices as he saw fit. Relations between the old and the new bureaus were never set forth with any clarity, and while a bureau might report directly to the crown during one reign, in the next a new chain of command would be authorized.

The method of handling the business of the Prussian army was suited to the personalities and talents of Frederick William I and his son, Frederick the Great. Owing to their great abilities and constant devotion to the interests of the state, the complicated machinery for administering military affairs proved satisfactory. A breakdown occurred as soon as less talented rulers inherited the throne. Frederick William II and Frederick William III tried to find a way out of their difficulties by creating additional offices and entrusting more control of military affairs to their personal adjutants. By adding new bureaus to a structure which was already top-heavy, the usefulness of the existing offices was diminished.

The rise to power of the king's adjutant was a more serious defect. All business that required the king's approval passed through his hands: after Frederick the Great's death the adjutant alone among military officials could gain an immediate royal audience. If the adjutants had been talented men their authority might have been of some advantage to the army. But they were for the most part soldier-courtiers without any real knowledge of military affairs who were inclined to be pedants and drill masters. This arrangement saved the pride of Frederick the Great's successors, who lacked his military talents but were unwilling to relinquish royal control of the army to a War Minister. Because of the adjutants' personal relation to the king a spirit of cabal prevailed in military administration. The system made possible the growth of individual fortunes but was ruinous for the army.

While still a finance minister Stein had lashed out sharply against the intrigue and corruption in military affairs. He was anxious therefore to make a Ministry of War one of the principal organs of the central government. As soon as Stein began his second ministry in October, 1807, Scharnhorst drew up a program for rebuilding Prussian military administration. Stein's short tenure of office as well as other difficulties made it impossible to secure a general reorganization of the government, but the discussions in the fall of 1807 permitted Scharnhorst to make a strong plea for a unified military administration.

The Ministry of War which Stein and Scharnhorst advocated would entrust responsibility for military affairs to a single minister, and by combining functions previously exercised by numerous independent bureaus, would bring unity into military administration. Scharnhorst struggled against the influence of the king's personal military advisers both as a "foreigner" in Prussian service who had received their rebuffs and slights, and as a capable administrator who was aware of the waste and corruption that had been the consequence of their control. While a unification of military bureaus was achieved by the Ministry of War that was finally approved on December 25, 1808, a Minister of War was not named. Frederick William III preferred to divide responsibility between Scharnhorst and Count Lottum, a conservative who had opposed most of the plans for the reorganization of the army. Although the new military administration proved of great value in the army expansion of 1813, the rebuilding of the Prussian army before that date would have profited greatly from the guiding hand of a War Minister.

THE TRAINING OF THE ARMY

Without the guidance of a reform-minded minister it proved impossible to train the Prussian army completely in the new methods of warfare. After the battles of 1806 it was apparent that the army needed more experience in the use of divisions, that is units composed of all the arms. Other requirements included practice in the art of skirmishing, forming columns, and conducting *tirailleur* actions. To change the tactics of the army it was necessary to provide training instructions, since the Prussian officers knew only the linear formations perfected by Frederick the Great. All armies fought in line and that tactical method was not obsolete; what the Prussians needed was a more flexible tactical system in which columns, skirmishers, *tirailleurs*, or the line would be used as the topography and the circumstances warranted. No tactical instructions for officers appeared before 1812, and the short interval of time before the outbreak of war, as well as the turmoil in the Prussian army that resulted from the partial mobilization of that year, made these instructions of little practical use. Nor could any training be provided for the thousands of officers who were inactive from 1807 to 1813. This circumstance illustrates the reliance upon the old officers' corps in the rebuilding of the army, as well as the difficulties that prevented the introduction of wholly new tactics. There was more success in introducing an organization that permitted the several arms to cooperate. By 1808 the army had been reorganized in brigades which embraced infantry, cavalry, and artillery in a Prussian approximation of the French divisions. Maneuvers were infrequent but the officers gained some

CONCLUSION

experience in handling larger masses of troops and making the elements of the brigades work together.[2]

[2] The successful employment of several arms in single unit was entirely dependent upon the skill of the brigade commander. In 1813 some Prussian brigades were nothing more than a mass of several types of regiments which resembled the structure of a Prussian army before 1806 more than a French division. Brigades and divisions were at least comparable in size. French divisions averaged 6,000 to 8,000 men in 1813; three to five divisions made up an army corps. In 1808 the Prussian brigades were to average 7,000 men but in 1813 they were somewhat larger. Four Prussian brigades made up an army corps. *Cf.* Boyen, *Erinnerungen*, III, 512-13. When Tauentzien's and Bülow's corps joined the Army of the North, Bernadotte tried to organize these Prussian contingents in true divisions. Tauentzien's troops were reorganized in three divisions numbering about 10,000 men. There was insufficient time to recast Bülow's corps and his brigades were simply called divisions. *Cf.* Chareton, *op. cit.*, pp. 172-73.

BIBLIOGRAPHICAL ESSAY

For thirty years the interest of German scholars and military historians in the events of the War of Liberation (1813-1814) has been at low ebb. Most of the important German studies of the reorganization of Prussia and the overthrow of the Napoleonic political system in Germany were written in the period from 1871 to 1914. Between the Reformation and the organization of the German Empire the greatest experience common to the German people had been their resistance to Napoleon. When the Germans won political unity under Bismarck's leadership, historical scholarship was oriented toward the last previous epoch in which the German nation had acted as a conscious whole. At the centenary of these events, in 1913, there was a great outpouring of books and articles, intended primarily for popular consumption but including studies that reflected the best scholarship. These accounts dealt principally with the "efficiency" wrought in the Prussian government by the Stein-Hardenberg reforms; there was only an undertone of respect for the liberal and humanitarian aspirations of the Baron vom Stein. It cannot be denied that most German historians have looked upon Stein as a phenomenon of German nationalism rather than a prophet or spokesman for liberal political institutions.

Why the German historians chose to regard the revolt against Napoleonic tyranny from a nationalist rather than a liberal point of view would require a detailed explanation, involving, among other matters, the whole question of the triumph in Germany of authoritarian politics over the democratic principles of the French Revolution. Loyalty to monarchical institutions was unquestionably fortified by the almost universal admiration displayed by German historians for the Prussian army and its role in the events of 1813-1814. Scharnhorst, as the principal organizer of the new Prussian army of 1813, has emerged therefore with an historical stature equal to that of Stein.

Greatest and most important of the biographers of Scharnhorst is Max Lehmann. His masterly study, *Scharnhorst* (Leipzig, 1886-1887, 2 v.), is not only the authoritative account of the Hanoverian's life but is the model military biography. By presenting the orthodox and patriotic conception of Scharnhorst this book did not arouse the storm of controversy that greeted his subsequent biography, *Freiherr vom Stein* (Leipzig, 1902-1905, 3 v.) (all references are in the single volume edition), which attributed the political reforms in Prussia to French influence. Although Lehmann's point of view in his military studies would now be regarded as conservative and nationalist, his books and articles have nevertheless remained the most valuable accounts of the military reforms inspired by Scharnhorst.

The evolution of the Prussian army under the successors of Frederick the Great has been subjected to close scrutiny by Colmar von der Goltz. While his major work, *Von Rossbach bis Jena* (Rev. ed., Berlin, 1906), successfully reinterpreted the history of the army after the Seven Years' War, it suffered from a too obvious attempt to belabor every scrap of evidence into support of his thesis. That von der Goltz, whose writing reflected an intransigent nationalism, should have attempted to prove that the Prussian army of 1806 was one of the most formidable of Napoleon's opponents is not surprising. It was a great tribute to his skill as an historian that he was able to prove that the Prussian army was not as feeble as its subsequent defeat made it appear to be. His findings were eventually substantiated even in the impartial publications of the French General Staff.[1]

The German General Staff's valuable histories dealing with the period of the reforms owed not a little to the ability of Curt Jany, whose career as a military historian had begun with a series of monographs on the seventeenth and eighteenth century Prussian army. This mastery of detail enabled Jany to write a magnificent documentary history, *Geschichte der Königlich*

---

[1] *Cf.* Pascal Bressonnet, *Études tactiques sur la campagne de 1806* (*Saalfeld-Iéna-Auerstedt*) (Paris, 1909).

Preussischen Armee (Berlin, 1928-1933, 4 v.), which traces the development of the Prussian army from mediaeval times to the Great War of 1914. Jany's craftsmanship and scrupulous historical honesty were obvious influences upon the official General Staff histories written for the centenary celebration in 1913. Unlike the officially inspired accounts of Frederick the Great, and of the Franco-Prussian War, the General Staff historical section contributed excellent studies of the military reorganization after 1807 and the role of the Prussian army in 1812-1813.[2]

French scholars have pursued the topic of Prussia's military rebirth from the standpoint of Napoleon's triumph at Jena and his subsequent attempts to maintain his new political order in Germany. Their interpretations have generally emphasized the French influence upon the Prussian political and military reforms. Jacques M. E. Godefroy Cavaignac is without question the most distinguished of these historians. His *La formation de la Prusse contemporaine* (2nd ed., Paris, 1897-1898, 2 v.) provides a full picture of the reorganization of the state and relates the events in Prussia to contemporary European history. In his treatment of the Prussian army after 1806 Cavaignac tended to exaggerate the French influence upon the work of the military reformers. Neither Joseph M. C. Vidal de la Blache nor V. Chareton has written as comprehensively as Cavaignac, yet their works cannot be neglected by the student of the civil-military reforms in Prussia.[3]

Comparatively few English or American historians have shown an interest in the era of Stein and Scharnhorst. J. R. Seeley's *Life and Times of Stein* (London and Boston, 1879,

---

[2] *Das Preussische Heer im Jahre 1812* (Berlin, 1912); *Das Preussische Heer im Jahre 1813* (Berlin, 1914); *1806 Das Preussische Offizierkorps und die Untersuchung der Kriegsereignisse* (Berlin, 1906). Also see Major Rudolf Friedrich, *Geschichte des Herbstfeldzuges 1813* (Berlin, 1903-1906, 3 v.).

[3] Joseph M. C. Vidal de la Blache, *La régénération de la Prusse après Iéna* (Paris, 1910), and V. Chareton, *Comment la Prusse a préparé sa revanche 1806-1813* (Paris, 1903).

2 v.) was admirable in its day but it is now sadly outdated. Stein's importance has been emphasized in studies by Guy Stanton Ford, particularly his *Stein and the Era of Reform in Prussia, 1807-1815* (Princeton, 1922) which reveals a masterly understanding of a complex period of German history. Another American historian, Eugene N. Anderson, in his *Nationalism and the Cultural Crisis in Prussia, 1806-1815* (New York, 1939) has brought a penetrating analysis to bear on the personalities who carried out the military and civil reforms.

Printed sources for the reappraisal of Prussian history from 1807 to 1813 exist in considerable abundance. Before the present war the Prussian state archives had begun the publication of the documents upon which the history of the Stein-Scharnhorst reforms must henceforth be based.[4] This work was done with great care and honesty, and the volumes on the reorganization of the army were intended to supplant the original collection which was based only on the General Staff archives and was first published as a supplement to the *Militär-Wochenblatt*. This older edition of sources, *Die Reorganisation der Preussischen Armee nach dem Tilsiter Frieden* (Scherbening and Willisen, eds., Berlin, 1862-1866, 2 v.), has not lost its usefulness, however, especially in view of the fact that since the outbreak of war in 1939 the work of the archivists on the new project has been curtailed. Whether the series can ever be completed is now a matter for speculation. Next to the collected documents the memoirs of Hermann von Boyen, *Erinnerungen* (Friedrich Nippold, ed., Leipzig, 1889-1890, 3 v.) contain the most useful material. Boyen's description of the first reform years was drawn largely from memory, consequently there are inaccuracies and inconsistencies in this portion of his account. Nevertheless, his memoirs provide an extraordinary insight into the court intrigue, personal issues, disappointments, and

[4] *Die Reorganisation des Preussischen Staates unter Stein und Hardenberg. Part one. Allgemeine Verwaltungs- und Behördenreform* (Georg Winter, ed., Leipzig, 1931), and *Die Reorganisation des Preussischen Staates unter Stein und Hardenberg. Part two. Das Preussische Heer vom Tilsiter Frieden bis zur Befreiung 1807-1814* (Rudolf Vaupel, ed., Leipzig, 1938).

triumphs of the reformers. The memoirs are rewarding too for the flashes of criticism which Boyen leveled from time to time against the old army system.

Scharnhorst's activity as a military journalist left his biographers a great number of professional papers, articles, and books which set forth his conception of the art of war. For the critical period of Scharnhorst's life, from 1807 to 1813, there are relatively few documents; only the official memoranda proposing military reforms, some letters, and Scharnhorst's edition of the laws and orders for the organization of the Prussian army are available to document his career as a public servant.[5] Scharnhorst's private reflections and his own occasional doubts and fears are mirrored in his letters, *Scharnhorsts Briefe* (Karl Linnebach, ed., Munich and Leipzig, 1914). For want of a substantial mass of private papers there is no edition comparable to that for the Stein material now available to the historian in the handsome series, *Freiherr vom Stein. Briefwechsel, Denkschriften, und Aufzeichnungen* (Erich Botzenhart, ed., Berlin, 1931-1937, 7 v.). The historian's understanding of the causes of Prussia's defeat is enriched by the report, *Nachrichten über Preussen in seiner grossen Katastrophe* (Berlin, 1888), from the pen of Scharnhorst's gifted disciple and close friend, Carl von Clausewitz.

Documents pertaining to the legal structure of the Prussian army in the eighteenth century are collected in *Das Heerwesen in der Zeit des Absolutismus* (Eugen von Frauenholz, ed., Munich, 1940), a volume in the series devoted to the sources of German military history. The reports of the commissions, and the memoranda of the officers who tried to remake the Prussian army after the death of Frederick the Great, may be found in the *Mittheilungen aus dem Archiv des Königlichen Kriegsministeriums* (Berlin, 1891-1895, 3 v.). The interest in military

---

[5] See the main bibliography for the Scharnhorst material; note his edition of the important Prussian military laws and orders enacted from 1807 to 1810, *Auszug aus den Verordnungen über die Verfassung der Königlich Preussischen Armee* (Berlin, 1810).

affairs before 1806 is made evident by the abundance of periodical literature; a convenient list of titles with comments on the editors and contents will be found in Chapter III.

The collection of monographs and sources of Prussian history found in the *Acta borussica: Denkmäler der Preussischen Staatsverwaltung im 18. Jahrhundert* (Gustav F. von Schmoller, ed., Berlin, 1892 ff.) has not been cited in the bibliography since the material did not provide any immediate reference for the present work. However, the administrative and economic studies to be found in this great series are of obvious importance for the student of Prussian military history.

BIBLIOGRAPHY

Guides and Bibliographical Aids

Dahlmann, Friedrich C., and Waitz, Georg. Quellenkunde der Deutschen Geschichte. 8th rev. ed., Leipzig, 1912.
Pohler, Johann. Bibliotheca historico-militaris. Cassel, 1887-1899, 4 v.
Scharfenort, Louis von. Quellenkunde der Kriegswissenschaften für den Zeitraum 1740-1910. Berlin, 1910.

Sources: Documents

Aus dem Garnisonleben von Berlin und Potsdam 1803 bis 1806. Urkundliche Beiträge und Forschungen zur Geschichte des Preussischen Heeres, II, Heft 9. Berlin, 1906.
Bezzenberger, A., ed. Urkunden des Provinzial-Archivs in Königsberg und des gräflich Dohnaschen Majorats-Archivs in Schlobitten betreffend die Erhebung Ostpreussens im Jahre 1813 und die Errichtung der Landwehr. Königsberg, 1894.
Botzenhart, Erich, ed. Freiherr vom Stein. Briefwechsel, Denkschriften, und Aufzeichnungen. Berlin, 1931-1937, 7 v.
Boyen, Hermann von. Beiträge zur Kenntniss des General von Scharnhorst und seiner amtlichen Thätigkeit in den Jahren 1808 bis 1813. Berlin, 1833.
——. Darstellung der Grundsätze der alten und der gegenwärtigen Preussischen Kriegsverfassung. Berlin, 1817.
Clausewitz, Carl von. Nachrichten über Preussen in seiner grossen Katastrophe. Kriegsgeschichtliche Einzelschriften, II, Heft 10. Berlin, 1888.
Frauenholz, Eugen von, ed. Das Heerwesen in der Zeit des Absolutismus. Munich, 1940.
Gesetzsammlung für die Königlichen Preussischen Staaten 1813. Berlin, n. d.
Granier, H., ed. Berichte aus der Berliner Franzosenzeit 1807-1809. Publikationen aus den Königlich Preussischen Staatsarchiven, LXXXVIII. Leipzig, 1913.
Griewank, Karl, ed. Gneisenau; Ein Leben in Briefen. Leipzig, 1939.
Knesebeck, Karl Friedrich Freiherr von dem. Bruckstücke aus den hinterlassenen Papieren. Magdeburg, 1850.
Lilienstern, J. J. R. von. Die Deutsche Volksbewaffnung in einer Sammlung der darüber in sämmtlichen Deutschen Staaten ergangenen Verordnungen. Berlin, 1815.
Linnebach, Karl, ed. Scharnhorsts Briefe. Erster Band. Privatbriefe. Munich and Leipzig, 1914.
Lionnet, Albert. Die Erhebungspläne preussischer Patrioten Ende 1806 und Frühjahr 1807. Historische Studien, Heft 120, Berlin, 1914.
Martens, Georg F. von. Nouveau recueil de traités. Göttingen, 1817-1842, 16 v.
——. Recueil des principaux traités. 2nd ed., Göttingen, 1817-1835, 8 v.

Miller, David Hunter. My Diary at the Conference of Paris. New York, 1924, 21 v.
Mittheilungen aus dem Archiv des Königlichen Kriegsministeriums. Berlin, 1891-1895, 3 v.
Recueil des traités de la France, publié sous les auspices du ministère des affaires étrangères. Paris, 1864-1907, 23 v. in 24.
Ribbentrop. Sammlung von Vorschriften, Anweisungen und sonstigen Aufsätzen in Beziehung auf den Dienst der Militair-Ökonomie-Beamten. Berlin, 1814-1821.
——. Sammlung von Vorschriften, Anweisungen und sonstigen Aufsätzen über das Etats, Kassen und Rechnungswesen bei der Königlich Preussischen Armee. Berlin, 1815.
Sammlung der für die Königlichen Preussischen Staaten erschienenen Gesetze und Verordnungen von 1806 bis zum 27ten Oktober 1810. Berlin, 1822.
Scharnhorst, David G. von. Auszug aus den Verordnungen über die Verfassung der Königlich Preussischen Armee, welche seit dem Tilsiter Frieden ergangen sind. Auf allerhöchsten Befehl zum Gebrauch für die betreffenden Königlichen Behörden zusammengetragen. Berlin, 1810.
Scherbening and Willisen, eds. Die Reorganisation der Preussischen Armee nach dem Tilsiter Frieden. Berlin, 1862-1866, 2 v.
Schulze, Friedrich, ed. Die Franzosenzeit in deutschen Landen 1806-1815. Leipzig, 1908, 2 v.
——. Urkunden der deutschen Erhebung. Leipzig, 1913.
Stägemann, F. A. von. Briefe und Aktenstücke zur Geschichte Preussens unter Friedrich Wilhelm III. F. Rühl, ed., Leipzig, 1899-1902, 3 v.
Stern, A. Abhandlungen und Aktenstücke zur Geschichte der Preussischen Reformzeit 1807-1815. Leipzig, 1885.
Treuenfeld, Bruno von, ed. Das Jahr 1813 bis zur Schlacht von Gross Görschen. Leipzig, 1901.
Vaupel, Rudolf, ed. Die Reorganisation des Preussischen Staates unter Stein und Hardenberg. Part two. Das Preussische Heer vom Tilsiter Frieden bis zur Befreiung 1807-1814. Publikationen aus den Preussischen Archiven, XCIV, Leipzig, 1938.
Winter, Georg, ed. Die Reorganisation des Preussischen Staates unter Stein und Hardenberg. Part one. Allgemeine Verwaltungs- und Behördenreform. Volume one. Vom Beginn des Kampfes gegen die Kabinettsregierung bis zum Wiederantritt des Ministers vom Stein. Publikationen aus den Preussischen Staatsarchiven, XCIII. Leipzig, 1931.

SOURCES: BOOKS

Anmerkungen zu der Schrift des Herrn von Lindenau über die höhere preussische Taktik und ihre zeitherige Unrichtigkeit und Unzweckmässigkeit. Berlin, 1790.
Arndt, E. M. Das Preussische Volk und Heer ins Jahr 1813. Leipzig, 1813.
Arnim, ——. Über die Canton-Verfassung in den Preussischen Staaten. Frankfort and Leipzig, 1788.

Berenhorst, Georg H. von. Aus dem Nachlasse. Edward Bülow, ed., Leipzig, 1845-1847.
——. Betrachtungen über die Kriegskunst. 3rd ed., Leipzig, 1827.
Bülow, Heinrich Dietrich von. Annalen des Krieges. Berlin, 1806.
——. Der Geist des neueren Kriegssystems. Hamburg, 1805.
——. Neue Taktik der Neuern, wie sie seyn sollte. Leipzig, 1805.
——. Kritik des Feldzuges in Deutschland im Jahre 1806. Berlin and Leipzig, 1808.
——. Militärische und vermischte Schriften von Heinrich Dietrich von Bülow. Edward Bülow and Wilhelm Rüstow, eds., Leipzig, 1853.
Clausewitz, Carl von. Der Feldzug 1812 in Russland und die Befreiungskriege von 1813-15. 3rd ed., Berlin, 1906.
Decken, F. von. Betrachtungen über das Verhältnis des Kriegsstandes zu dem Zwecke der Staaten. Hanover, 1800.
Delbrück, Ferdinand. Erläuterungen der Königlichen Verordnungen über den Landsturm. Königsberg, 1814. A thirty page pamphlet.
Die wahrscheinlichen Hauptursachen der Unglücksfälle bei den deutschen Waffen im Jahre 1806. Aus den Bemerkungen eines Augenzeugen. Jena, 1807.
Eichhorn, J. A. F. Die Zentralverwaltung der Verbündeten unter dem Freiherrn vom Stein. Deutschland (sic), 1814.
Faber, Gotthelf Theodor von. Bemerkungen über die französische Armee der neuesten Zeit oder der Epoche von 1792 bis 1807. Königsberg, 1808.
Guibert, J. A. H. de. Bemerkungen über die Kriegsverfassung der Preussischen Armeen. Cologne, 1778.
——. Journal d'un voyage militaire en Prusse en 1789. Paris, 1790.
Kleist, Franz Alexander von. Über die eigenthümlichen Vollkommenheiten des Preussischen Heeres. Berlin, 1791.
Leipziger, August Wilhelm von. Kritische Beleuchtung der Lindenauschen Bemerkungen über die höhere preussische Taktik. Breslau, 1793.
Lilienstern, J. J. R. von. Berichte eines Augenzeugen von dem Feldzuge... 1806. Tübingen, 1807.
——. Kriegs-Katechismus für die Landwehrmann. Breslau, 1813.
Lindenau, K. F. von. Beleuchtung der Anmerkungen eines Ungenannten zu der Schrift über die höhere Preussische Taktik. Leipzig, 1790.
——. Über die höhere Preussische Taktik, deren Mangel und zeitherige Unzweckmässigkeit. Leipzig, 1790.
Miller, F. von. Reine Taktik der Infanterie, Cavallerie und Artillerie. Stuttgart, 1787-1788, 2 v.
Müffling, F. C. F. Freiherr von. Die preussisch-russische Kampagne im Jahre 1813. Vienna, 1813.
——. Operationsplan der preussisch-sächsischen Armee im Jahre 1806. Weimar, 1807.
Ribbentrop, Kriegs und Domänen Rath. Verfassung des preussischen Canton-Wesens historisch bearbeitet und mit einigen Bemerkungen versehen. Minden, 1798.

Rohde, ——. Über die Schrift des k. k. Oberleutnants Herrn von Lindenau betreffend die preussische Taktik. Potsdam, 1791.

Saldern, Friedrich Christoph von. Taktische Grundsätze und Anweisung zu militärischen Evolutionen. Dresden, 1786.

Scharnhorst, David G. von. Handbuch der Artillerie. Hanover, 1804-1814, 3 v.

——. Handbuch für Offiziere in den Anwendbaren Theilen der Krieges-Wissenschaften. Hanover, 1787-1790, 3 v.

——. Militärische Schriften. Freiherr von der Goltz, ed., Berlin, 1881.

——. Militairisches Taschenbuch zum Gebrauch im Felde. 2nd ed., Hanover, 1793.

——. Über die Wirkung des Feuergewehrs. Berlin, 1813.

——. Unterricht des Königs von Preussen an die Generale seiner Armee. Hanover, 1794.

Schilderung der Preussischen Kriegsverfassung. Schwerin, 1776.

Toulongeon, Jean Réné d'Emskerque de. Une mission militaire en Prusse en 1786. Jules Finot and Roger Galmiche-Bouvier, eds., Paris, 1881.

Venturini, G. Lehrbuch der angewandten Taktik oder eigentlichen Kriegswissenschaft. Schleswig, 1798-1801, 5 v.

Voss, Julius von. Was war nach der Schlacht bei Jena zur Rettung des preussischen Staates zu tun? Berlin, 1807.

Wilke, F. F. Handbuch zur Kenntnis des preussischen Cantonwesens. Stettin, 1802.

Sources: Memoirs

Boyen, Hermann von. Erinnerungen aus dem Leben des General-Feldmarschalls Hermann von Boyen. Friedrich Nippold, ed., Leipzig, 1889-1890, 3 v.

Donnersmarck, Wilhelm Ludwig Victor, Graf Henckel von. Erinnerungen aus meinem Leben. Zerbst, 1846.

Hardenberg, Karl August, Fürst von. Denkwürdigkeiten des Staatskanzlers Fürsten von Hardenberg. Leopold von Ranke, ed., Leipzig, 1877, 5 v.

Lloyd George, David. Memoirs of the Peace Conference. New Haven, 1939, 2 v.

Marwitz, F. A. L. von der. Der Preussischer Adel. Friedrich Schinkel, ed., Breslau, 1932.

——. Preussens Verfall und Aufsteig. Friedrich Schinkel, ed., Breslau, 1936.

Massenbach, Christian von. Betrachtungen und Aufschlüsse über die Ereignisse der Jahre 1805 und 1806. Frankfort, 1808.

——. Historische Denkwürdigkeiten zur Geschichte des Verfalls des Preussischen Staats seit dem Jahre 1794. Amsterdam, 1809.

——. Memoiren zur Geschichte des Preussischen Staates unter der Regierung Friedrich Wilhelm II und Friedrich Wilhelm III. Amsterdam, 1809, 3 v.

Reiche, Ludwig von. Memoiren des Königlich Preussischen Generals der Infanterie Ludwig von Reiche. Louis von Weltzien, ed., Leipzig, 1857, 3 v.

Schmidt, Generalleutnant Friedrich Karl von. Erinnerungen aus dem Leben des Generalleutnants Friedrich Karl von Schmidt. Urkundliche Beiträge und Forschungen zur Geschichte des Preussischen Heeres, III, Heft 11-13. Berlin, 1909.

Sources: Periodicals

Bailleu, Paul. "Die Schlacht von Auerstedt. Eigenhändige Relation König Friedrich Wilhelm's III.," *Deutsche Rundschau*, CI (1899), 382-399.
Brinkmann, Carl. "Eine neue Quelle zur Preussischen Geschichte nach dem Tilsiter Frieden," *Forschungen zur Brandenburgischen und Preussischen Geschichte*, XXIV (1911), 371-445.
Geiger, Ludwig. "Charakteristik Gneisenau's durch eine Zeitgenossin," *Historische Zeitschrift*, LXXXVI (1901), 270-272.
——. "Zur Charakteristik Gneisenaus," *Historische Zeitschrift*, LXXXXII (1904), 472-473.
Granier, H., ed. "Aktenstücke zur Geschichte des Krieges von 1806/07," *Forschungen zur Brandenburgischen und Preussischen Geschichte*, XIII (1900), 514-541.
Knesebeck, Carl Friedrich von dem. "Mittheilungen aus dem Nachlasse des Feldmarschalls von dem Knesebeck über den russischen Operationsplan von 1812," *Militär-Wochenblatt*, Beiheft 1848, 101-109.
Lehmann, Max, ed. "Boyen's Darstellung der preussischen Kriegsverfassung," *Historische Zeitschrift*, LXVII (1891), 55-80.
——. "Eine militärische Verfügung Friedrich Wilhelm's I," *Historische Zeitschrift*, LXVIII (1892), 83-84.
——. "Ein Regierungsprogramm Friedrich Wilhelm's III," *Historische Zeitschrift*, LXI (1889), 441-460.
——. "Preussen und die allgemeine Wehrpflicht im Jahre 1809," *Historische Zeitschrift*, LXI (1889), 97-109.
——. "Preussen und die allgemeine Wehrpflicht im Jahre 1810," *Historische Zeitschrift*, LXIX (1892), 431-461.
——. "Vier Denkschriften Scharnhorst's aus dem Jahre 1810," *Historische Zeitschrift*, LVIII (1887), 54-105.
Meinecke, Friedrich, ed. "Aus den Akten der Militärreorganisations-Kommission von 1808," *Forschungen zur Brandenburgischen und Preussischen Geschichte*, V (1892), 487-495.
——. "Die preussischen Geldmittel während des Feldzuges 1813/14. Eine Aufzeichnung Rothers," *Historische Zeitschrift*, LXXXXIII (1904), 255-259.
Meusel, Friedrich, ed. "Aus Marwitz' Memoiren: Der Zusammenbruch des preussischen Staates 1806," *Deutsche Rundschau*, CLXII (1915), 426-449; CLXIII (1915), 114-127, 248-281, 357-396.
——. "Marwitz' Schilderung der altpreussischen Armee," *Preussische Jahrbücher*, CXXXI (1908), 460-484.
Scharnhorst, David G. von. "Prüfung des Werks: *Ueber die höhere Preussische Taktik*," *Neues militärisches Journal*, III (1790), 239-265.
——. "Recensionen. *Anmerkung zu der Schrift des Herrn von Lindenau*," *Neues militärisches Journal*, IV (1790), 262-267.
——. "Ueber die Schlacht bei Marengo," *Denkwürdigkeiten der militärischen Gesellschaft in Berlin*, I (1802), 52-59.

Thimme, Friedrich, ed. "Zu den Erhebungsplänen der preussischen Patrioten im Sommer 1808. Ungedruckte Denkschriften Gneisenau's und Scharnhorst's," *Historische Zeitschrift*, LXXXVI (1901), 78-110.
Wagner, Paul, ed. "Briefe an Scharnhorst," *Historische Zeitschrift*, CXXVII (1923), 243-259.

SECONDARY MATERIAL

THE PRUSSIAN ARMY, ITS HISTORY, ORGANIZATION, AND ADMINISTRATION

1806 Das Preussische Offizierkorps und die Untersuchung der Kriegsereignisse. Herausgegeben vom Grossen Generalstabe, Berlin, 1906.
Alt, ——. Das Königliche Preussische stehende Heer. Berlin, 1869-1870, 2 v.
Apel, Hauptmann. Der Werdegang des Preussischen Offizierkorps bis 1806 und seine Reorganisation. Oldenburg in Gr., n. d.
Blumenthal, M. Der preussische Landsturm von 1813. Berlin, 1900.
Boguslawski, A. von. Armee und Volk im Jahre 1806. Berlin, 1900.
Bräuner, P. Geschichte der preussischen Landwehr. Berlin, 1863.
Caraman, Victor Marie. Essai sur l'organisation militaire de la Prusse. Paris, 1831.
Chareton, Captain V. Comment la Prusse a préparé sa revanche 1806-1813. Paris, 1903.
Ciriacy, F. von. Chronologische Übersicht der Geschichte des preussischen Heeres dessen Stärke Verfassung und Kriege seit dem letzten Kurfürsten von Brandenburg bis auf die jetzigen Zeit. Berlin and Posen, 1820.
Closen, Karl. Die preussische Landwehr. Munich, 1855.
Cochenhausen, Generalleutnant Friedrich von. Friedrichs Geist im Heer der Befreiungskriege. Berlin, 1927.
——, ed. Von Scharnhorst zu Schlieffen. 1806-1906. 100 Jahre preussisch-deutscher Generalstab. Berlin, 1933.
Courbière, R. de l'Homme de. Grundzüge der Deutschen Militärverwaltung. Berlin, 1882.
——. Geschichte der brandenburgisch-preussischen Heeresverfassung. Berlin, 1852.
Crousaz, Adolph von. Das Offiziercorps der Preussischen Armee. Halle a. S., 1876.
——. Die Organisation des brandenburgischen und preussischen Heeres seit 1640. 2nd ed., Berlin, 1873, 2 v. in 3.
——. Geschichte des Königlich Preussischen Kadetten-Corps. Berlin, 1857.
Das Königlich Preussische Kriegsministerium 1809—1. März. 1909. Herausgegeben vom Kriegsministerium, Berlin, 1909.
Das Preussische Heer im Jahre 1812. Herausgegeben vom Grossen Generalstabe, Berlin, 1912.
Das Preussische Heer im Jahre 1813. Herausgegeben vom Grossen Generalstabe, Berlin, 1914.
Duparcq, E. de la Barre. Historische und militairische Studien über Preussen. Leipzig, 1854.
Friccius, Karl. Zur Geschichte der Errichtung der Landwehr in Ost- Westpreussen und Litthauen im Jahre 1813. Königsberg, 1863.

Friedlaender, Gottlieb. Die königliche allgemeine Kriegsschule und das höhere Militär-Bildungswesen 1765-1813. Berlin, 1854.
Goltz, Colmar von der. Von Rossbach bis Jena. Rev. ed., Berlin, 1906.
Gragert, Wilhelm. Allgemeine Wehrpflicht und Staatsverfassung. Düsseldorf, 1937.
Gumtau, C. F. Jäger und Schützen des preussischen Heeres. Berlin, 1834-1838, 3 v.
Helfritz, Hans. Geschichte der Preussischen Heeresverwaltung. Berlin, 1938.
Höhn, Reinhard. Verfassungskampf und Heereseid. Der Kampf des Bürgertums um das Heer 1815-1850. Leipzig, 1938.
Huber, Ernst R. Heer und Staat in der deutschen Geschichte. Hamburg, 1938.
Ide, Justus. Die Entwicklung der preussischen Armee als Verfassungsbestandteil vom Tode Friedrichs II. bis zur Gründung des Norddeutschen Bundes. Kiel, 1936.
Jany, Curt. Die alte Armee von 1655 bis 1740. Urkundliche Beiträge und Forschungen zur Geschichte des Preussischen Heeres, II, Heft 7. Berlin, 1905.
———. Die Anfänge der alten Armee. Urkundliche Beiträge und Forschungen zur Geschichte des Preussischen Heeres, I, Heft 1. Berlin, 1901.
———. Geschichte der Königlich Preussischen Armee. Berlin, 1928-1933, 4 v.
Kalkoff, Paul. Die Vorgeschichte der allgemeinen Wehrpflicht in Preussen. Breslau, 1913.
Knorr, Emil. Von 1807 bis 1893. Zur Entwicklungsgeschichte unserer Heeresverfassung. Berlin, 1893.
Lyncker, Alexander. Der altpreussische Armee 1714-1806 und ihre Militärkirchenbücher. Berlin, 1937.
Meisner, Heinrich Otto. Der Kriegsminister 1814-1914. Berlin, 1940.
Meynen, Arthur. Die staatsrechtliche Stellung des preussischen Kriegsministers. Breslau, 1910.
Nord, Reinhold. Die Deutsche Heeresverfassung nach den Gewaltfrieden von Tilsit und Versailles 1806-1935. Berlin, 1936.
Osten-Sacken und von Rhein, Ottomar Frhrn. von der. Preussens Heer von seinen Anfängen bis zur Gegenwart. Berlin, 1911-1914, 3 v.
Rosinski, Herbert. The German Army. Rev. ed., Washington, D. C., 1944.
Scharfenort, Louis von. Die Königlich Preussische Kriegsakademie 1810-1910. Berlin, 1910.
———. Kulturbilder aus der Vergangenheit des altpreussischen Heeres. Berlin, 1914.
Schmidt, Paul. Der Werdegang des preussischen Heeres. Berlin, 1903.
Schmidt-Bückeburg, R. Das Militärkabinett der preussischen Könige und deutschen Kaiser; seine geschichtliche Entwicklung und staatsrechtliche Stellung 1787-1918. Berlin, 1933.
Schnackenburg, E. Das Invaliden und Versorgungswesen des brandenburgpreussischen Heeres bis zum Jahre 1806. Berlin, 1889.
Schultz, W. von. Die preussischen Werbungen unter Friedrich Wilhelm I. und Friedrich dem Grossen. Schwerin, 1887.

Schwartz, Franz. Organisation und Verpflegung der Preussischen Landmilizen im siebenjährigen Kriege. Leipzig, 1888.
Velhagen, C. F. Preussens Landwehr. Königsberg, 1815.
Wohlers, Günther. Die staatsrechtliche Stellung des Generalstabes in Preussen und dem Deutschen Reich. Bonn and Leipzig, 1921.
Wolzendorff, Kurt. Der Gedanke des Volksheeres im Deutschen Staatsrecht. Tübingen, 1914.

TECHNICAL ACCOUNTS OF WARFARE, WEAPONS, UNIFORMS, AND TACTICS

Boguslawski, A. von. Die Entwickelung der Taktik vom 1793 bis zur Gegenwart. Berlin, 1873, 4 v.
Bressonnet, Pascal. Études tactiques sur la campagne de 1806 (Saalfeld-Iéna-Auerstedt). Paris, 1909.
Colomb, E. von. Beiträge zur Geschichte der preussischen Kavallerie seit 1808. Berlin, 1880.
Die Preussische Artillerie von ihrer Neuformation 1809 bis zum Jahre 1816. Urkundliche Beiträge und Forschungen zur Geschichte des Preussischen Heeres, III, Heft 14-15. Berlin, 1909.
Jany, Curt. Die Gefechtsausbildung der Preussischen Infanterie von 1806. Urkundliche Beiträge und Forschungen zur Geschichte des Preussischen Heeres, I, Heft 5. Berlin, 1903.
———. Der Preussische Kavalleriedienst vor 1806. Urkundliche Beiträge und Forschungen zur Geschichte des Preussischen Heeres, II, Heft 6. Berlin, 1904.
Kaehler, D. A. J. Die Preussische Reiterei von 1806 bis 1876 in ihrer inneren Entwicklung. Berlin, 1879.
Kiesling,———. Geschichte der Organisation und Bekleidung des Trains der Königlich Preussischen Armee 1740-1888. Berlin, 1889.
Kling, C. Geschichte der Bekleidung, Bewaffnung, und Ausrüstung des Königlich Preussischen Heeres. Herausgegeben vom Kriegsministerium. Weimar, 1906-1911, 3 v.
Malinowski, L. von, and Bonin, K. von. Geschichte der brandenburgisch-preussischen Artillerie. Berlin, 1840-1842, 3 v.
Mila, Adalbert. Geschichte der Bekleidung und Ausrüstung der Königlich Preussischen Armee in dem Jahren 1808 bis 1878. Berlin, 1878.
Müller, Hermann von. Die Entwickelung der Feldartillerie in Bezug auf Material, Organisation und Taktik 1815-1892. Berlin, 1893-1894, 3 v.
Ollech, R. Historische Entwickelung der taktischen Uebungen der Preussischen Infanterie. Berlin, 1848.
Pelet-Narbonne, G. von. Geschichte der Brandenburg-Preussischen Reiterei von den Zeiten des Grossen Kurfürsten bis zur Gegenwart. Berlin, 1905, 2 v.
Rummel, Paul. Ueber die Organisation und Mobilmachung der preussischen Artillerie im Jahre 1813. Berlin, 1863.
Sautermeister, Reinhard. Die taktische Reform der preussischen Armee nach 1806. Tübingen, 1935.

Schöning, Kurd Wolfgang von. Historisch-Biographische Nachrichten zur Geschichte der brandenburgisch-preussischen Artillerie. Berlin, 1844-1845, 3 v.

BIOGRAPHIES

Bahn, Rudolf. Georg Heinrich von Berenhorst der Verfasser der "Betrachtungen über die Kriegskunst." Halle a. S., 1911.
Caemmerer, R. von. Clausewitz. Oldenburg i. Gr., 1905.
Conrady, E. von. Leben und Wirken des Generals der Infanterie . . . Carl von Grolman. Berlin, 1894-1896, 3 v.
Delbrück, Hans. Das Leben des Feldmarschalls Grafen Neidhardt von Gneisenau. 3rd ed., Berlin, 1908, 2 v.
Droysen, Johann G. Das Leben des Feldmarschalls Grafen Yorck von Wartenburg. 11th ed., Leipzig, 1913, 2 v.
Ford, Guy Stanton. Stein and the Era of Reform in Prussia, 1807-1815. Princeton, 1922.
Fouqué, Friedrich Baron de la Motte. Ernst Friedrich Wilhelm Philipp von Rüchel, militärische Biographie. Berlin, 1828, 2 v.
Henderson, E. F. Blücher and the Uprising of Prussia against Napoleon, 1806-1815. New York and London, 1911.
Klippel, G. H. Das Leben des Generals von Scharnhorst. Leipzig, 1869-1871, 3 v.
Lehmann, Max. Freiherr vom Stein. New edition in one volume, Leipzig, 1921.
——. Knesebeck und Schön. Leipzig, 1875.
——. Scharnhorst. Leipzig, 1886-1887, 2 v.
——. Stein, Scharnhorst und Schön. Leipzig, 1877.
Meinecke, Friedrich. Das Leben des Generalfeldmarschalls Hermann von Boyen. Stuttgart, 1895-1899, 2 v.
Pertz, Georg H. Das Leben des Feldmarschalls Grafen Neithardt von Gneisenau. Berlin, 1864-1880, 5 v.
——. Das Leben des Ministers Freiherrn vom Stein. Berlin, 1849-1855, 6 v.
Ritter, Gerhard. Stein. Eine politische Biographie. Berlin, 1931, 2 v.
Seeley, J. R. Life and Times of Stein, or Germany and Prussia in the Napoleonic Age. London and Boston, 1879, 2 v.
Unger, W. von. Blücher. Berlin, 1907-1908, 2 v.
Wohlauer, Albert. Stein und Schön in der Provinz Preussen zu Anfang des Jahres 1813. Breslau, 1882.

CAMPAIGN HISTORIES

Die preussischen Kriegsvorbereitungen und Operationspläne von 1805. Kriegsgeschichtliche Einzelschriften, Heft 1. 1st ed., Berlin, 1883.
Die Teilnahme des preussischen Hülfskorps an den Feldzug gegen Russland im Jahre 1812. Kriegsgeschichtliche Einzelschriften, Heft 24. Berlin, 1898.
Foucart, P. Bautzen, 20 et 21 mai 1813. Paris, 1897.
——. Campagne de Prusse 1806. Paris, 1890.

Goltz, Colmar von der. Von Jena bis Eylau. Berlin, 1907.
Holzhausen, Paul. Die Deutschen in Russland 1812. Berlin, 1912.
Lettow-Vorbeck, Oscar von. Der Krieg von 1806 und 1807. Berlin, 1892-1899, 4 v.
Maude, F. N. 1806, the Jena Campaign. London, 1909.
Müller-Bohn, H. Die deutschen Befreiungskriege. Deutschlands Geschichte von 1806-1815. Berlin, 1907-1908, 2 v.
Osten-Sacken und von Rhein, Ottomar Freiherr von der. Militärische-politische Geschichte des Befreiungskrieges im Jahre 1813. Berlin, 1902-1906, 2 v.
Petre, F. L. Napoleon's Campaigns in Poland 1806-1807. London, 1906.
———. Napoleon's Conquest of Prussia-1806. London, 1907.
———. Napoleon's Last Campaign in Germany 1813. London, 1912.
Ulmann, Heinrich. Geschichte der Befreiungs-Kriege 1813 und 1814. Munich, 1914-1915, 2 v.
Zelle, Walter. Geschichte der Freiheitskriege 1812-1815. Brunswick, 1903-1906, 4 v.

Periodical Literature

Boguslawski, A. von. "Soldatenhandel und Subsidienverträge," *Militär-Wochenblatt*, Beiheft 1885, 297-304.
Daniels, Emil. "Ein vergessenes Dokument zur Geschichte der Freiheitskriege," *Preussische Jahrbücher*, CXLIV (1911), 256-64.
"Die Formation der freiwilligen Jäger-Detachements bei der preussischen Armee im Jahre 1813," *Militär-Wochenblatt*, Beiheft 1845, 449-515.
Dorn, Walter. "The Prussian Bureaucracy in the Eighteenth Century," *Political Science Quarterly*, XLVI (1931), 403-423; XLVII (1932), 75-94, 259-273.
"Entwickelung der Preussischen Kriegsartikel," *Militär-Wochenblatt*, Beiheft 1890, 351-394.
"Errichtung der Landwehr und des Landsturms in Ostpreussen, Westpreussen, am rechten Weichselufer und Litthauen im Jahre 1813," *Militär-Wochenblatt*, Beiheft 1846, 1-146.
Ford, G. S., "Boyen's Military Law," *American Historical Review*, XX (1915), 528-538.
Friedrich, Major von. "Die Auffassung der strategischen Lage seitens der Verbündeten am Schlusse des Waffenstillstandes von Poischwitz 1813," *Militär-Wochenbatt*, Beiheft 1902, 1-27.
———. "Die strategische Lage Napoleons am Schlusse des Waffenstillstandes von Poischwitz," *Militär-Wochenblatt*, Beiheft 1901, 1-36.
"Geschichte der Organisation der Landwehr in dem Militair-Gouvernement zwischen Elbe und Weser," *Militär-Wochenblatt*, Beiheft 1857, 1-49.
"Geschichte der Organisation der Landwehr in dem Militair-Gouvernement zwischen Weser und Rhein im Jahre 1813 und 1814," *Militär-Wochenblatt*, Beiheft 1857, 49-108.

Glover, Richard. "The Battle of Valmy: A Reconsideration," *Army Quarterly*, XXXIV (1937), 337-348.
Gossler, Major von. "Beitrag zur Geschichte unserer Heeresverfassung," *Militär-Wochenblatt*, Beiheft 1885, 269-296.
Harnack, Otto. "Die Ursachen der Niederlage Napoleons im Herbste 1813," *Historische Zeitschrift*, XIC (1902), 385-400.
Haussherr, H. "Hardenbergs Reformdenkschrift Riga 1807," *Historische Zeitschrift*, CLVII (1938), 267-308.
Herrmann, Alfred. "Friedrich Wilhelm III. und sein Anteil an der Heeresreform bis 1813," *Historische Vierteljahrschrift*, XI (1908), 484-516.
Hintze, Otto. "Der österreichische und der preussische Beamtenstaat im 17. und 18. Jahrhundert," *Historische Zeitschrift*, LXXXVI (1901), 401-444.
——. "Preussische Reformbestrebungen vor 1806," *Historische Zeitschrift*, LXXVI (1896), 413-443.
Hubrich, Eduard. "Zur Entstehung der preussischen Staatseinheit," *Forschungen zur Brandenburgischen und Preussischen Geschichte*, XX (1907), 347-427.
Hülsen, Walter von. "Yorck als Erzieher unseres Heeres," *Militär-Wochenblatt*, Beiheft 1908, 435-451.
Janson, Generalleutnant von. "Scharnhorsts militärisches Testament und sein Verhältnis zu Knesebeck," *Militär-Wochenblatt*, Beiheft 1906, 407-418.
Jany, Curt. "Die Kantonverfassung Friedrich Wilhelms I.," *Forschungen zur Brandenburgischen und Preussischen Geschichte*, XXXVIII (1925), 225-272.
Kessel, Eberhard. "Die Wandlung der Kriegskunst im Zeitalter der französischen Revolution," *Historische Zeitschrift*, CIIL (1933), 248-276.
Lehmann, Max. "Boyen's Denkwürdigkeiten," *Historische Zeitschrift*, LXVII (1891), 40-54.
——. "Das alte Preussen," *Historische Zeitschrift*, XC (1903), 385-421.
——. "General Borstell und der Ausbruch des Krieges von 1813," *Historische Zeitschrift*, XXXVII (1877), 55-76.
——. "Scharnhorst's Kampf für die stehenden Heere," *Historische Zeitschrift*, LIII (1885), 276-299.
——. "Werbung, Wehrpflicht und Beurlaubung im Heere Friedrich Wilhelm's I," *Historische Zeitschrift*, LXVII (1891), 254-289.
——. "Zur Geschichte der preussischen Heeresreform von 1808," *Historische Zeitschrift*, CXXVI (1922), 436-457.
Liebert, Major. "Die Rüstungen Napoleons für den Feldzug 1812," *Militär-Wochenblatt*, Beiheft 1888, 355-392.
Meerheimb, F. von. "Berenhorst und Bülow," *Historische Zeitschrift*, VI (1861), 46-74.
Meusel, Friedrich. "Die Besoldung der Armee im alten Preussen und ihre Reform 1808," *Forschungen zur Brandenburgischen und Preussischen Geschichte*, XXI (1908), 243-249.

"Organisation der Landwehr, Landwehr-Reserven und des Landsturms der Provinz Schlesien im Jahre 1813," *Militär-Wochenblatt*, Beiheft 1845, 397-420.

Poten, B. von. "Das Preussische Heer vor hundert Jahren," *Militär-Wochenblatt*, Beiheft 1900, 1-62.

Schmidt, Kunhardt von. "Statistische Nachrichten über das Preussische Offizierkorps von 1806 und seine Opfer für die Befreiung Deutschlands," *Militär-Wochenblatt*, Beiheft 1901, 431-482.

Schmoller, Gustav von. "Die Entstehung des preussischen Heeres von 1640-1740," *Deutsche Rundschau*, XII (1877), 248-273.

Schrötter, Robert Freiherr von. "Die Ergänzung des preussischen Heeres unter dem ersten Könige," *Forschungen zur Brandenburgischen und Preussischen Geschichte*, XXIII (1910), 81-145.

Schwertfeger, Major von. "Die Neugestaltung der Preussischen Armee in den Jahren 1807 bis 1812," *Militär-Wochenblatt*, Beiheft 1909, 445-476.

Stadelmann, R. "Das Duell zwischen Scharnhorst und Borstell im Dezember 1807," *Historische Zeitschrift*, CLXI (1940), 263-276.

Stetten-Buchenbach, Freiherr von. "Rekrutenwerbungen in reichsritterschaftlichem Gebiet im 18. Jahrhundert," *Militär-Wochenblatt*, Beiheft 1903, 451-466.

Thimme, Friedrich. "König Friedrich Wilhelm III., sein Anteil an der Konvention von Tauroggen und an der Reform von 1807-1812," *Forschungen zur Brandenburgischen und Preussischen Geschichte*, XVIII (1905), 1-59.

———. "Zur Geschichte Friedrich Wilhelms III. und der Krisis von 1811," *Historische Zeitschrift*, IXC (1903), 65-80.

Ulmann, H. "Die Detachements der freiwilligen Jäger in den Befreiungskriegen," *Historische Vierteljahrschrift*, X (1907), 483-505.

Villate, R. "Le mouvement des idées militaires en France au XVIIIe siècle," *Revue d'Histoire Moderne*, X (1935), 226-260.

Waas, Christian. "Napoleon I. und die Feldzugspläne der Verbündeten von 1813," *Historische Vierteljahrschrift*, III (1900), 216-233.

Ziekursch, Johannes. "Die preussischen Landreservebataillone 1805/06—eine Reform vor der Reform?" *Historische Zeitschrift*, CIII (1909), 85-94.

GENERAL ACCOUNTS

Anderson, Eugene N. Nationalism and the Cultural Crisis in Prussia, 1806-1815. New York, 1939.

Bezzenberger, A. Ostpreussen in der Franzosenzeit seine Verluste und Opfer an Gut und Blut. Königsberg, 1913.

Bornhak, C. Geschichte des Preussischen Verwaltungsrechts. Berlin, 1884-1886, 3 v.

Bronsart von Schellendorff, General Paul Leopold. The Duties of the General Staff. 3rd ed., London, 1895.

Cavaignac, Jacques M. E. Godefroy. La formation de la Prusse contemporaine. 2nd ed., Paris, 1897-1898, 2 v.

Criste, Oskar. Erzherzog Carl von Österreich. Vienna and Leipzig, 1912, 3 v.
Earle, Edward Mead, ed. Makers of Modern Strategy; Military Thought from Machiavelli to Hitler. Princeton, 1943.
Ergang, Robert. The Potsdam Führer, Frederick William I, Father of Prussian Militarism. New York, 1941.
Fisher, Herbert A. L. Studies in Napoleonic Statesmanship: Germany. Oxford, 1903.
Ford, Guy Stanton. Hanover and Prussia, 1795-1803: A Study in Neutrality. New York, 1903.
Gooch, G. P. Germany and the French Revolution. London and New York, 1920.
Hintze, Otto. Die Hohenzollern und ihr Werk. Fünfhundert Jahre vaterländischer Geschichte. 4th ed., Berlin, 1915.
Jähns, Max. Geschichte der Kriegswissenschaften vornehmlich in Deutschland. Munich and Leipzig, 1889-1891, 3 v.
Just, Wilhelm. Verwaltung und Bewaffnung im westlichen Deutschland nach der Leipziger Schlacht 1813 und 1814. Göttingen, 1911.
Meier, Ernst von. Französische Einflüsse auf die Staats und Rechtsentwicklung Preussens im XIX. Jahrhundert. Leipzig, 1908, 2 v.
Meinecke, Friedrich. Das Zeitalter der deutschen Erhebung, 1795-1815. 2nd ed., Bielefeld and Leipzig, 1913.
Oncken, Wilhelm. Das Zeitalter der Revolution, des Kaiserreiches, und der Befreiungskriege. Berlin, 1884-1886, 2 v.
Philippson, Martin. Geschichte des Preussischen Staatswesens vom Tode Friedrichs des Grossen bis zu den Freiheitskriegen. Leipzig, 1880-1882, 2 v.
Poten, B. von. Geschichte des Militairerziehungs und Bildungswesens in den Landen Deutscher Zunge. Berlin, 1889-1900, 6 v.
Rüstow, Wilhelm. Untersuchungen über die Organisation der Heere. 2nd ed., Basel, 1868.
Sorel, Albert. L'Europe et la Révolution Française. Paris, 1885-1904, 8 v.
Vagts, Alfred. A History of Militarism; Romance and Realities of a Profession. New York, 1937.
Vidal de la Blache, Joseph Marie Casimir. La régénération de la Prusse après Iéna. Paris, 1910.
Wendland, Wilhelm. Versuche einer allgemeinen Volksbewaffnung in Süddeutschland während der Jahre 1791 bis 1794. Historische Studien, Heft 24, Berlin, 1901.

INDEX

Absolutism, 195, 204; administration under, 26; and the army, 36; military needs, 87; military problems, 87; and class interests, 119; weakness of, 125; and military reform, 226, 227; and efficiency, 230; triumph in Germany, 235; and military history, 239
Academies for Artillery and Engineering, 134
Academy for Officers, 29, 64, 133, 134, 135
Acta borussica, 240
Adjutants, see General Adjutants
Age, of officers in 1806, 29-30
Alexander I, 96, 98, 149, 191, 194, 195, 213
Allgemeine Kriegs Department, 144
Alliances, 186, 189, 191, 194, 195, 198, 213; between Prussia and France, 89, 173; between Prussia and Russia, 91, 202; negotiations with Austria and Russia, 199; between Prussia and England, 217
Allied Military Committee, 13-14
Altenstein, Minister von, reform proposals, 103-04; objects to conscription, 156, 157
American historians, 237
Anderson, Eugene N., 238
An Mein Volk, 202
Ansbach-Bayreuth, 59
Archduke Charles, 69, 87
Archenholz, J. W. von, 106
Archiv für Aufklärung über das Soldatenwesen, 63
Armament Commission, 198, 201, 202, 206, 211
Armament manufacture, in Prussia, 179-80
Armed Neutrality, 88
Armistice, 191, 206, 209, 210, 211, 218; at Tauroggen, 189; arranged at Poischwitz, 216; and reorganization of the army, 218; and the *Landwehr*, 219-20; and the artillery, 220; and the cavalry, 221; Prussian strength at conclusion of, 221; Prussian organization at end of, 222; significance of, 229
Army corps, recommended in 1807, 110; strength in 1808, 129; artillery of, 130; of 1813, 222

Arndt, Ernst Moritz, 190
Articles of War, 25, 103, 138, 140, 210; revision of, 136-37; statement of universal service, 137
Artillery, 149, 185, 207; in 1806, 20; during mobilization, 59; effect on mobility, 83; reduction of, 83, 84; in divisions, 85; fate in 1806, 113; in brigades, 130; number of *Krümper*, 171; rebuilding of, 180; new tactics for, 184; reorganized during armistice, 220
Artillery Testing Commission, 180
Aspern, battle of, 154
Attitude of officers toward army, 30
Auerstädt, battle of, 92, 94, 108, 109, 123, 135, 151, 227; description of, 93; lessons of, 95
Auerswald, Minister President von, 193, 194
Augereau, Marshal, 92
August, Prince, 180
Austerlitz, battle of, 89
Austria, 87, 88, 89, 90, 98, 149, 154, 157, 199, 207, 211, 214, 216, 217
Austrian army, 87, 120, 193
Austrian military reforms, 87

Baggage, 84, 142
Balance of power, shift of, 189
Baltic coast, 207; training center in 1811, 172-73
Basel, Peace of, 58, 88
Bataillon quarré, 91
Battalions, 69, 129-30, 219; as tactical units, 18, 22; fail to cooperate, 34, 131; the basis of mobilization, 59; newly created in 1813, 199, 200. See Third battalions
Batteries, number in summer, 1813, 220. See Artillery
Battle of the Nations, 223
Bautzen, battle of, 215
Bellona, 63
Bennigsen, General, 97
Berenhorst, Georg Heinrich von, 62, 63, 65, 66, 67, 125; military theories of, 65-66
Berg, County of, 224
Berlin, 52, 89, 91, 94, 132, 135, 142, 152, 174, 182, 189, 196, 202, 203, 211
Bernadotte, King of Sweden, 214

255

INDEX

Betrachtungen über die Kriegskunst, 66
Beurlaubten, 166, 167, 174, 175, 176; and supplementary training, 164; number in 1810, 169, 176; number in 1811 and 1812, 170, 176; assembled on the coast, 172; extra men in 1811, 172. *See Krümper*
Beurlaubung, 78, 160, 161; orders issued in 1808, 162; applied to the entire army in 1809, 163; instructions of 1809, 166; restraining factors, 166; importance of old soldiers, 169-70; as a "system," 171; faster rate in 1811, 171-72; effect of training depots on, 173; revised in 1812, 174; legend of, 177-78. See *Krümper* system
Beurlaubungs-System, 160
Beyme, High Chancellor, 156-57
Bibliothek für Offiziere, 62
Biographers, of Scharnhorst, 197, 198, 236; of Stein, 235-36
Bismarck, 235
Blücher, General von, 94, 107
Bohn, Andreas, 63
Borstell, General von, 64, 102, 147; dispute with Scharnhorst, 127
Botzenhart, Erich, 239
Boyen, Hermann von, 30, 101, 147, 154, 216; joins reform commission, 102; conscription appeal of 1810, 155-56, 228; and idea of national revolt, 187; on the rearmament program, 202; estimate of Prussian forces in June, 1813, 218; named War Minister, 224; memoirs of, 238-39
Boyen Law, 155-56, 224
Brandenburg, city of, 52
Brandenburg, the Mark, 21, 29, 77; as liaison area for French army, 198
Breslau, 135, 142, 152, 196, 197, 203, 211, 216
Brigades, 149, 154, 164, 166, 206, 208, 232, 233; organization of, 129-30; in battle, 131; significance of, 131; and military administration, 141; and conscription, 141; sent to the coast, 172; and the mobilization of 1812, 173-74; and surplus troops, 129, 176; as counterpart of divisions, 185, 232; organization in summer 1813, 222
Brigadier generals, 133; and canton administration, 168; and uniform training measures, 172

Bronikowsky, Lt. Col. von, 102
Brunswick, Duke of, 75, 81, 84, 85, 86, 91, 189; and the campaign of 1806, 90; at Auerstädt, 93
Buchenröder, the editor, 63
Bülow, General von, 199
Bülow, Heinrich Dietrich von, 62, 63, 65, 125; military theories of, 67
Bureaucracy, use of officers in, 70; and military reform, 230. *See* Civil officials, and Military officials
Bürgergarde, 152

Cabal, spirit of, 147
Cadet Institutes, 133, 134
Cadets, 132, 133, 134, 199
Cadres, 15, 59, 76, 80, 82, 121, 217, 227, 230; in the German army, 14; and creation of a mass army, 16
Campaigns, of 1806, 34, 90-94; of 1807, 96-98; of 1813 (spring), 213-15
Cannon, types of, 20, 83; number of, 20, 180; manufacture of, 180; captured at Leipzig, 220-21. *See* Artillery
Cantonists, 49, 80, 121, 162, 165, 200, 219; period of training, 17, 21, 24, 43, 44; and the guilds, 52; numbers in 1799-1805, 58; in the military vocabulary, 160; and change of garrisons, 169; number left untrained in 1810, 169-70; inductions in 1812, 174; supervised by inactive officers, 176; removed from East Prussia, 190; conscripted by York, 191; mobilized in 1813, 199, 200. *See Krümper*, and *Beurlaubten*
Canton boundaries, 166, 169
Canton laws, 78, 81, 156, 191; of 1732-1733, 40-41, 154; supplementary orders, 41; of 1763, 45; of 1792, 46-48; a barrier to universal service, 150, 225; from 1807-1813, 150-51
Canton lists, 40, 56, 201; nature of, 49; administration of, 50; and the *Knechte*, 51; for old soldiers, 166; after 1807, 168
Canton regulations of 1792, 117, 138, 149, 150, 177, 225; enactment of, 46-47; character of, 47-48; and statements of universal service, 47, 226; and exemptions, 47, 58-59, 225-26; declared valid in 1807, 168; modified in 1813, 201, 229
Canton revision, 49-50, 76; after 1807, 168

INDEX

Cantons, 48, 162, 208; first established, 40; size of, 40, 59; disputes over, 48; enlargement of, 59; and mobilization, 59; in ceded territory, 113; officers distributed throughout, 176
Canton service, evasion of, 55-56
Canton system, 17, 35, 56, 128, 156, 197, 198, 204; principal features of, 17, 60, 225; orders of 1732-1735, 40; basis of, 42-43; evolution of, 44; attempts to reform, 45, 46, 47, 117, 150, 152, 154, 156, 228; and Polish subjects, 45, 227; Möllendorf's comments on, 46; operation of, 48-51; attacked by reformers, 152, 153, 227; unchanged before 1813, 159; administration 1807-1813, 168-69; and *Jäger* of 1813, 200; altered in 1813, 201; shortcomings of, 225
Capital punishments, 25, 200, 210
Capitulations, 95, 105, 106, 187; in 1806, 93-94; punishment for, 107
Captains, role in administration, 27-28; revenues of, 28; and *Freiwächter*, 32; and recruiting, 35; and pay accounts, 43; end of personal profits, 142
Cashiering, of officers, 108
Casualties, in 1807, 97; replaced by *Krümper*, 116, 228; and Prussian army in 1812, 177; and French army in 1812, 189; of 1813, 208; at Lützen, 215; and death of Scharnhorst, 215
Cavaignac, J. M. E. Godefroy, 12, 185, 237
Cavalry, in 1806, 19; training and tactics of, 23, 184; at Jena, 23; and mobilization, 59; in divisions, 85; training reserves, 111; reductions of 1807, 112; organization in 1807, 113; complements in 1808, 115; and *Krümper* training, 161; use of veterans, 171, 221; arms for, 179; regulations of 1812, 184; Napoleon's lack of, 214-15; during armistice, 221
"Cavalry of St. George," 207
Centenary of War of Liberation, 235, 237
Chambers of War and Domains, 50, 54, 78, 81, 146
Chareton, V., 237
Charles, Archduke, 69, 87
Chief of the General Staff, 71, 145
Church lands, secularized, 88

Civil guards, 152
Civil officials, 125, 204, 205, 212; assist with conscription, 44; carry out conscription, 50, 225; conflict with military, 56, 83, 117; lethargy of, 60, 230; and reform, 68, 230; oppose Land Reserve, 81; and mobilization, 82-83; consulted about militia, 119-20; relation to military bureaucracy, 131; reaction to conscription proposals, 156; and use of old soldiers, 162, 166; and canton conscription after 1807, 168; and Russian campaign 1812, 189; and Stein in East Prussia, 191-92; of East Prussia, 192, 193-94; and the *Landsturm*, 212-13
Classes, and universal service in 1813, 197
Clausewitz, Carl von, 33, 101, 147, 183, 216, 239; and East Prussian *Landwehr*, 192-93
Clemenceau, 14; on long enlistments, 15
Clergymen, and canton records, 49, 50, 52
Coalition, 213; the First, 88; formed in 1813, 217
Coast defence, in 1811-1812, 172, 173, 177
Colberg, 98, 113, 142
Colonels, 49, 113, 168; role in administration, 27-28; money-minded, 30; age of, 30; and canton service, 48-49
Columns, use of, 181, 183, 184, 232
Combining *Landwehr* and line, methods of, 219-20
Commissariat officers, 59
Commission of Canton Revision, 49, 50, 51
"Company economy," in 1806, 27-28; abolished, 142
Complements, in 1806, 18, 19, 20; in 1807, 112-13; reduced in 1808, 115; established in 1809, 130; raised in 1809, 163-64
Confederation of the Rhine, 90
Confusion in *Krümper* system, 166-67
Congress of Prague, 217
Conscription, 104, 119, 123, 198, 208; dislike of, 36, 39, 210, 211; under Frederick I, 37-38; under Frederick William I, 38-40, 40-41; legal basis of, 41-42; and national economy, 42-43; by civil officials, 44, 50, 168, 225; by army officers, 44-45; of Poles, 45, 60, 227; civil-

ians' demand for, 123; and the brigades, 141; Stein approves, 151; reformers demand for, 153-54; rejected in 1808, 154; a "French swindle," 155; and Boyen's appeal in 1810, 155-56; the "grave of culture," 156; opposed by civil officials, 156-57; and Scharnhorst's memoir of 1810, 157; effect of Scharnhorst's dismissal on, 158; Frederick William III comments on, 158-59; in the cantons after 1807, 168; new provisions in 1812, 174; in East Prussia, 195-96; enacted in 1813, 197, 201, 229; purpose of in 1813, 202; for the *Landwehr*, 204, 218; in Silesia, 210, 211; in reconquered areas, 223-24; sought in Prussia, 225

Conscription commission, 154, 155, 157

Conservatives, oppose the militia, 119; withdrawn from Military Reorganization Commission, 127; and Articles of War, 137; opposition to reform, 146-48; and divisions, 185; object to *Landsturm*, 213

Continental system, 191

Contributions (to French), 112

Cooperation in battle, 23, 34, 181, 185, 232, 233

Cornets, 132, 134

Cosel, 99; desertion from, 168

Courbière, General von, 77, 78, 79, 80, 82, 115, 226

Courts-martial, 139-40

Cuirassiers, 19

Cüstrin, 94, 95

Danzig, 52, 54, 97, 188, 214

Davout, Marshal, 93

Death of Scharnhorst, 215

Decken, F. von, 63

Declaration of war, in 1806, 90; in 1813, 202; and strength of army in 1813, 206

Demobilization, in 1807, 112-13; of coastal regiments, 173; in 1814, 224

Denkwürdigkeiten der militärischen Gesellschaft, 64

Deployed order, 23, 70, 184, 232

Depots, 79, 116, 199, 200, 204, 206, 208, 212, 218

Der Geist des neueren Kriegssystems, 67

Der Soldat, 63

Der Veteran, 62

Desertion, 31, 56, 138, 210, 228; and growth of the army, 167-68; among *Landwehr*, 223

Devastation, suffered in East Prussia, 208-09

Diaz, General, 15

Discipline, before 1806, 24-25; reforms of 1808, 136-38; and milder punishments, 138; of the *Jäger*, 200

Dissolution, of historic regiments, 113-14

Divisions, adopted in 1806, 85; a failure in the Prussian army, 85-86; Scharnhorst's responsibility for, 85-86; in regulations of 1812, 185; compared with the French, 232-33

Divisions, of War Department, 145-46; of Military Economy Department, 146

Dohna, Minister Count, opposes conscription, 156, 157; in East Prussia, 192, 193

Dörnberg, F. W., Frhr. von, 192

Dragoons, 19

Drill, emphasis on, 21, 24, 27; relation to tactics, 22; simplified in 1812, 184

Duke of Brunswick. See Brunswick

East Frisia, 52, 54

East Prussia, 29, 34, 77, 94, 113, 149, 175, 188, 190, 210; revolution in, 190, 195; arrival of Stein and York, 191; military needs, 191; assembling the *Landtag*, 192-94; and Stein and York, 194-95; and the *Landwehr* law, 195-96; example of, 197-98; organizing the *Landwehr*, 208-09; raising the *Landwehr*, 209; significance of measures taken there, 229; and universal service, 195, 196, 229

East Prussian *Landwehr*, and Clausewitz, 192-93; law establishing, 195; significance of, 196, 197, 198; influence of, 202-03, 229

Echelon attack, perfected by Frederick the Great, 22; for the cavalry, 184

Economy, under Hardenberg, 158

Elbe, the, 21, 112, 188, 216

Emergency Commission, 73, 74, 76, 77, 78, 79, 81

Engineers. See Pioneers

England, and Hanover, 88; and events of 1807, 98; and German revolt, 187; and arms shipments, 207, 208; policy in spring of 1813,

213-14; and aid to Prussia, 214; subsidizes Prussia, 217
English historians, 237
English landing, fear of in 1812, 172
Enrollee, 49
Entrepreneurs, in garrisons, 32; exemptions for, 53
Ersatz battalions, plans for establishing, 116; and reserve training in 1809, 163
Ersatz flints, 211
Estates, the provincial, 29, 116; dislike conscription, 39, 155; of East Prussia and Lithuania, 192; assembled in East Prussia, 193-94, 195, 198
Eugene, Beauharnais, 202
Evasion of canton service, 55-56
Exemptions, 42, 47, 104, 117, 150, 191, 200, 210, 225, 226, 228; general basis for, 51; by royal decree, 51-52; based on residence, 52; by occupation, 52-54; based on property, 54-55; for physical defects, 55; based on religion, 55; number conferred, 58; Knesebeck on, 76; proposed by Military Reorganization Commission, 118; based on wealth, 122; in East Prussia, 196; abolished in 1813, 201, 229
Exercise Regulations for the Cavalry, 184
Exercise Regulations for the Infantry, 183
Expeditionary force, of 1812, 173-74, 177, 189
Eylau, battle of, 97

Fatherland, 158
Fatherland Reserve, 75, 76, 77
Fees, 50, 55; to release cantonists, 56
Ferdinand, Prince Louis, 91
Finances, strained, 32, 98, 99, 116, 117, 155, 156, 157, 178, 185, 226; and reductions of 1807, 111-12; and crisis of 1809-1810, 159; and new artillery, 180
First Coalition, 88
Fishermen, exemption of, 54
Foch, Marshal, proposals for German army, 14
Ford, Guy Stanton, 238
Foreigners, exemption of, 52; number in service, 56
Foreign policy, Prussian, 88-90, 97, 188, 189, 195, 196, 199, 202, 213, 216, 217
Foreign recruiting, end of, 103, 124

France, 11, 88, 157, 173, 178, 191, 196, 226; and war of 1806, 88; and war of 1809, 154; and invasion of Russia, 189
Franco-Prussian War, 237
Frankfort on the Main, enlistment headquarters, 56
Frauenholz, Eugen von, 239
Frederick I, 35, 36, 37, 38, 40, 44
Frederick the Great, 13, 19, 22, 25, 26, 61, 65, 66, 67, 69, 70, 72, 78, 102, 116, 119, 138, 183, 184, 226, 231, 232, 236, 237, 239; and cavalry, 19; and artillery, 20; and line tactics, 22; and military administration, 25-26, 230
Frederick William I, 36, 38, 39, 40, 44, 47, 119, 138, 225; regulates conscription, 40-43; regulates furloughing, 43; and military administration, 230
Frederick William II, 26, 46, 61, 70, 226; and military administration, 25, 230
Frederick William III, 26, 61, 70, 72, 75, 84, 88, 94, 97, 99, 100, 106, 119, 135, 137, 139, 152, 166, 176, 182, 201, 213, 226, 227, 229; and military administration, 25-26, 230, 231-32; interest in reform, 61; as Crown Prince, 74; on divisions, 85; indifference to reform, 86; diplomacy in 1805-1806, 89-90; and campaign of 1806, 90; at Auerstädt, 93; reform decrees of 1806, 94-95; disgust for his officers, 96; at Tilsit, 98; and confidential advisers, 102; and reform program of 1807, 103; irresolution of, 105; overlooks reserve training, 111; considers the Provincial Troops, 119-20; rejects the militia, 123; swamped with work, 125; displeased with reformers, 125-26; supports Scharnhorst, 127; and military justice, 136; and nation in arms, 138; and direct command of army, 143; and unified administration, 143-44; refuses to name War Minister, 144; and new military administration, 148; opposed to national army, 151; rejects National Watch, 153; establishes Conscription Commission, 154; rejects conscription proposal, 154, 155; meets French indemnity terms, 157; comments on conscription, 158-59; and training on Sunday, 164; approves Hake's plans,

174; and uniforms, 180-81; rejects plan for national revolt, 188; and Convention of Tauroggen, 189, 191; and East Prussian *Landtag*, 193; and French alliance, 195; and East Prussian *Landwehr*, 196; arrives in Silesia, 199; and fate of Berlin, 202; appeals to people, 202; and estates' rights, 204; warns Breslau, 211; revises *Landsturm* edict, 213; and use of *Landwehr*, 219; fears French retaliation, 228
Free corps, 206, 209, 223
Freiheit des Rückens, 137
Freiwächter, 31, 32, 103; abolition of, 142
French army, 34, 65, 68, 85, 115, 120, 149, 174, 176, 190, 208, 210, 217; alteration after 1763, 11; superiority of, 69; concentrates in Germany, 89; leadership in 1806, 91; strength at Jena, 92; strength at Auerstädt, 93; Prussian contingent for, 174; and its artillery, 184; and German revolt, 187, 188; strength in Prussia, 188; shattered in 1812, 189; evacuates the east, 209; and spring campaign of 1813, 214-15; methods of, 227
French Empire, 158, 202, 208; and recruiting, 124
French garrisons, 98, 99, 164, 202, 208, 214; strength of, 188
French historians, 237
French Revolution, 58, 189, 225, 235
French soldiers, enlistment of, 57
Friedland, battle of, 97
Fusiliers, 17, 23, 69, 171, 183
Fortresses, 20, 21, 66, 83, 95, 97, 105, 107, 110, 111, 116, 130, 172, 175, 179, 187, 191, 211, 222; and operations, 83; artillery of, 113; and national revolt, 188
Furloughing, 44, 74, 116, 121, 142, 175, 177, 226; of professionals, 31-32; advantages of, 43-44; and need for economy, 107; of officers, 108; recommended by Scharnhorst, 110; ceases for professionals, 142; as compromise measure, 150; of *Krümper*, 162; confusion in, 166-67. See *Beurlaubung*

Garde du Corps, 19, 110, 113, 167, 175
Garrison life, 31, 32
Garrisons, Prussian, 28, 31, 111, 130, 166, 175, 177, 206, 211, 218, 219, 220, 222; in Polish territory, 45; continually moved after 1807, 169;
used as police, 173. See French garrisons
Garrison troops, trained in the reserves, 116, 121
Gassenlaufen, 25, 135, 136
Gaudi, Minister von, 46
General Adjutants, 84, 86, 102, 143; role in military administration, 26; effect of War Ministry on, 146; defects of, 230-31
Generalauditoriat, 107, 140
General Canton Extract of 1811, 168-69
General Commission, 209
General Directory, 81
General Governments of the Provinces, 131
General Inspectors, 27, 131, 143
General Intendant, 28
General Kommandos, 131
General Military Treasury, 146
General Quartermaster, 59
General Quartermaster Staff, 59, 73
General Recruiting Treasury, 58
General Staff, 71, 87, 145; and historical studies, 236, 237; archives of, 238
General Staff, Chief of, 71, 145
General State Treasury, 146
General War Treasury, 146
Gentz, Friedrich von, 151
German army, 7, 115; limitations proposed in 1919, 13-15; rebirth of, 15
German Empire, 235
German historians, 70; and East Prussian *Landwehr*, 193; and War of Liberation, 235; estimate of Stein and Scharnhorst, 235
German militarism, 7
German officers and non-commissioned officers, 14, 15
German princes, and the *Landsturm*, 213
German revolt, 186, 187, 188, 194, 228; and French defences, 188
Germany, 14, 15, 90, 186, 191, 194, 208, 210, 213, 224, 235, 237; despoiling of, 88
Giant soldiers, 43, 56, 167
Glatz, 98
Gnadenthaler, 32
Gneisenau, Neidhardt von, member of Military Reorganization Commission, 101; on capital punishments, 136, 137; and national revolt, 186; and Silesian *Landwehr*, 211

INDEX

Goldbeck, High Chancellor von, 136
Goltz, Colmar von der, 236
Goltz, Minister, 157
Götzen, Count, 101, 102
Graft, of officers, 28; in canton administration, 55
Grande Armée, 97, 173, 190, 198, 208, 229; shattered in 1812, 189. *See* French army
Graudenz, 98, 113
Great War of 1914, 237
Grenadiers, 17, 171
Groeben, Georg D. von dem, 62, 63
Grolman, Carl von, 64, 101; and selection of officers, 131-32; proposes National Watch, 153
Gross Görschen, 214, 215
Guerrilla warfare, 186, 187, 188, 212-13
Guibert, J. A. H. de, 63
Guilds, dislike garrisons, 31; members exempted, 52
Guionneau, Minister, 77, 78
Gun carriages, 180
Guns. *See* Artillery, and Cannon

Haig, General, 15
Hake, General von, 64, 174, 198
Hameln, 94
Handbuch für Offiziere, 63, 67
Hanover, 88, 89-90, 214
Hardenberg, Karl August, Prince von, 104, 147, 198, 211, 235; and reform proposals, 103-04; and exemptions, 151; and national revolt, 158; assumes office in 1810, 157, 158; and the *Jäger*, 200; dissatisfied with Silesian *Landwehr*, 210
Haugwitz, C. A. H., Count, 89
Hearths, in the cantons, 40, 48
Henderson, Ernest F., 12
Henry, Prince, 72
High Council of War, 26-27, 28, 48, 73, 81, 145
Historians, responsibility of, 7
Hitler, Adolf, 15
Hohenlohe, Prince, 85, 90, 92, 93, 95
Hohenzollerns, 219
Honor courts, 140
Honor Legions, 75, 76
House, Col. E. M., 14
Hussars, 19

Impressment, of foreigners, 58
Inactive duty, for officers, 81, 108, 176, 232; for men, 175. *See* Furloughing

Indemnity, the French, 185, 190; and strong demands of 1810, 157; effect on growth of Prussian army, 178
Infantry, 184, 185; types of, 17; complements of, 18, 112-13, 115; and tactics of, 22-23, 183-84, 232; and mobilization, 59; in divisions, 85; training the reserves, 111; selects veterans, 170; arms for, 179; and target practice, 180; new regulations for, 183-84; in East Prussia, 196
Infantry regulations, the informal, 69-70; of 1787, 70; of 1812, 183-84
Inspection Schools, 134
Inspector of Light Troops, 182, 183
Inspectors. *See* General Inspectors
Instruction, in new tactics, 70, 182, 232
Instruction for the Use of the Third Rank, 181
Intendants, 59
Interpretation, of *Krümper* system, 12-13, 15, 16, 150, 163, 177-78, 228-29
Intrigue, against reform, 147
Invaliden, 32, 70, 79, 146, 176, 205; number in 1806, 34
Invasion of Russia, 177, 188, 189, 213
Investigation, of officers' corps, 104, 105, 106, 107, 108

Jäger, 200, 205, 206, 209; training and discipline of, 200; use in 1813, 222
Jany, Curt, 12-13, 175, 236, 237
Jena, battle of, 7, 11, 68, 71, 81, 92, 106, 108, 109, 123, 135, 150, 151, 227, 237; referred to by Lloyd George, 15; description of, 90-93; lessons of, 95
Jews, and the canton system, 55
Jomini, Antoine Henri, 66
Journalists, attack officers, 106
Junker, 132, 203
Jurisdiction, of military courts, 140
Justice, in army of 1806, 24-25; and new Articles of War, 136-38; and reform of courts-martial, 139-40
Justice administration, after 1808, 140

Kalckreuth, F. A., General von, 93
Kalisch, Alliance of, 202, 217
Kleist. *See* Kleist von Nollendorf
Kleist von Nollendorf, Friedrich, Count, 64, 84, 86, 102
Knechte, 20, 51, 55, 206; number in 1806, 21

Knesebeck, Freiherr von dem, 75, 76, 79, 80, 82, 115; and reform proposals, 75, 226; and national patriotism, 77; rejection of his plan, 77, 226
Könen, General Auditor von, 101, 137; revises the Articles of War, 136-37
Königsberg, 105, 106, 113, 135, 142, 152, 155, 175, 190, 191, 203
Kovno, 209
Kriegs-Augmentation, 116
Kriegsbibliothek, 63
Kriegsherr, 139
Kriegs-Katechismus, 205
Kriegs und Domänen Kammern. See Chambers of War and Domains
Kritische Beleuchtung, 65
Krümper, 99, 116, 163, 177; in historical literature, 11-13; discussed at Paris, 1919, 13-15; significance of, 16; before 1806, 81; first suggestion of, 110; proposals for infantry and cavalry, 111; legend of, 150, 177-78, 228; meaning of term, 159-60, 228; supplementary training for, 164; number before 1809, 166; number in 1810, 169, 176; importance of old soldiers for, 169-70, 228; number in 1811 and 1812, 170, 176; in infantry, 171; in artillery, 171; in cavalry, 171; and increased tempo of 1811, 171-72; additional number trained in 1811, 172; assembled on the coast, 172; in unmobilized regiments, 173; mobilized in 1813, 200. See *Beurlaubten*
Krümper system, traditional explanation of, 12; Cavaignac and Jany interpret the, 12-13; discussed at Paris Peace Conference, 13-15; revised interpretations of, 121, 163, 177-78, 228-29; as a substitute program, 159, 228-29; origins of, 160-61; purpose of, 161; use of old soldiers in, 161-62, 170; and orders of 1808, 162; applied to entire army in 1809, 163; restraining factors, 166; confusion in, 166-67; secrecy of, 164-65, 167; followed in the infantry, 171; additional measures, 171-72; legend of, 177-78; used by the reformers, 178, 228-29; character and significance of, 228-29. See *Beurlaubung*
Krümper training, effectiveness in 1811, 173; interrupted in 1812, 174

Labor brigades of 1811, 172
Lances, supply of, 179
Land and Tax Councillors, 49, 50, 54, 162, 169
Landesherr, 139
Landgrafenberg, the, 92
Land Reserve Troops, 78, 79; in Silesia, 81
Landsturm, 108, 190, 213; in the East Prussian law, 195-96; character and organization of, 212-13; raised in reconquered areas, 223
Landtag, East Prussian, 190, 192, 193, 194, 195
Landwehr, 108, 116, 190, 197, 217, 218; Clausewitz' suggestions for, 192-93; in East Prussia, 193; East Prussian law on, 195-96; significance of East Prussian, 197-98, 202; establishment of a national, 202-03, 229; Scharnhorst's relation to the, 203; nature and organization of, 204-06; and relation to the line, 208, 219-20; and conscription in spring of 1813, 208; raising and organizing the East Prussian, 208-09; raised in Silesia, 210-11; value of, 211-12, 229-30; and relation to *Landsturm*, 213; conscripted vigorously, 218, 229; strength by provinces, 219; combined with the line, 219-20; organization in July, 1813, 220; combat record of, 222-23; after October, 1813, 223; from reconquered areas, 223; and the Boyen Law, 224
Landwehr tax, 209
Lannes, Marshal, 91, 92
Leadership, of reform movement, 127
Lecoq, Lt. Col. von, 64, 72
Legend, of *Krümper* training, 150, 177-78, 228-29
Lehmann, Max, 236
Leipzig, battle of, 108, 221, 223
Leipziger, A. W. von, 65
L'Estocq's corps, 96, 97
Liberalism, and Baron vom Stein, 235
Liberation, War of. See War of Liberation
Lieutenants, selection of, 132
Light infantry, 17-18, 22-23, 69, 181, 182, 183
Lindenau, Karl F. von, 65
Line combined with *Landwehr*, 219-20
Line tactics, 22, 24, 70, 96, 181, 183-84, 232
Line troops, of 1806, 17; relation to

INDEX 263

Landwehr, 212, 219-20; as distributed in 1813, 222
Linnebach, Karl, 239
Lithuania, 74
Lloyd, General, 63
Lloyd George, 14; comments on *Krümper* system, 15
Lottum, Count, 64, 100, 102, 232; as conservative leader, 144
Louise, Queen of Prussia, 98
Lübeck, 107
Lunéville, Treaty of, 56
Lützen, battle of, 214-15

Magazin der neuesten merkwürdigen Kriegsbegebenheiten, 62
Magazin für Ingenieur und Artilleristen, 62
Magazines, of food and munitions, 21, 28, 66, 83, 141, 143
Magdeburg, city of, 52
Magdeburg, fortress of, 93, 94, 188
Man power, before 1806, 58-59; needed after 1807, 149, 150, 211; in East Prussia, 191, 192
Mark Brandenburg. *See* Brandenburg
Massenbach, Col. Christian von, 64, 66; and staff reforms, 72-73
Massenbach, Maj. Gen. von, 101-02
Mennonites, exemptions for, 55, 196
Mercantilism, 42, 55, 60, 225; and military service, 53, 55
Mercenaries, 121, 135, 226; recruiting the, 56-57, 58; methods of hiring, 57-58. *See* Professional soldiers
Mercenary army, justice in the, 25, 140; the argument for the, 120
Merchants, exemption for, 53; and East Prussian revolution, 191
Metternich, Prince, 214, 215, 217
Middle class, in officers' corps, 20; exemption of, 42
Migration, of Prussian subjects, 38, 39, 48, 156, 208
Militair-Bibliothek, 62, 67
Militärische Monatschrift, 62
Militärischen Gesellschaft, 64
Militärisches Taschenbuch, 63
Militarism, 7, 13
Militär Ökonomie Department, 144
Militär-Wochenblatt, 238
Military administration, before 1806, 25-27; and reforms of 1808, 143; character of the Prussian, 230-32
Military budget, 28, 141; and soldiers' families, 32; reductions in, 159

Military commissions, use of, 68
Military courts, 138; and purge of officers' corps, 106-07; procedure and jurisdiction of, 139-40. *See* Courts-martial
Military Department, 26-27, 48
Military discipline, character of, 25, 138, 140. *See* Capital punishments
Military Economy Department, 144, 146
Military education, 29, 71, 133-35; director of, 135
Military Governments, 203-04, 205, 207, 211, 213, 223
Military officials, before 1806, 26-27; and conscription in Seven Years' War, 44; recruiting the mercenaries, 56-58; and mobilization, 59; swamped with work, 125; in supply services, 142; object to reform, 230
Military Orphans' Home, 133, 134
Military periodicals, 29, 64, 125, 240; titles of, 61-63
Military Reorganization Commission, 103, 104, 105, 111-12, 121, 125, 128, 144, 152, 181-82, 202, 212; establishment of, 100; membership of, 100-02; first plans of, 109; achievements to Sept., 1807, 110-12; and militia plans of 1807, 116-17; proposes the Reserve Army, 118; proposes the Provincial Troops, 119-20; recommends conscription and a militia, 122; a "clique of radicals," 123; and reforms of 1808, 124-25; criticized by Frederick William III, 125-26; threatened by quarrels, 127; and brigades of 1808, 129; and reform of military justice, 135-36; revises the Articles of War, 136-37; reforms the supply services, 141-42; comes to an end, 149, 154; proposes the National Watch, 153; and last appeal for conscription, 153-54
Military roads, 188
Military schools, 67, 71; before 1806, 133-34; after 1806, 134-35
Military societies, 29, 64, 125, 134
Militia, 115, 116, 118, 123, 152, 165, 190, 191, 192, 193, 195, 197, 202, 209, 211, 212, 219; significance for canton system, 36; of 1701, 37; under Frederick William I, 38; of 1796, 74; Brunswick's, 75; Schroetter's, 77; of 1806, 81; Scharnhorst's in 1806, 82; Scharnhorst's idea of, 115-16, 227; suggested by Scharn-

264   INDEX

horst in 1807, 117; used as police, 117; known as Provincial Troops, 119-20; and danger of arming the masses, 120; relation to standing army, 121-22; alarming to other states, 122; for upper classes, 122; Stein's criticisms, 122-23; Schön's criticisms, 123; and Treaty of Paris, 129; failure of proposals for, 150; proposals of 1807-1808, 152; cannot equal the line in number, 172; royal control of, 204
Miller, F. von, 63
Miners, company of, 21, 30, 113
Minister of War, 27, 86, 143-44, 148, 224, 231, 232
Ministry of Finance, 145
Ministry of War, 128, 145, 148, 149; lack of, 27, 86; establishment of, 143-44, 224, 231-32; organization in 1808, 145-46; frictions in, 148; begins to function, 149, 154; Scharnhorst removed from, 158
Mobility, attempts to improve, 82-83, 84; of artillery in 1812, 184
Mobilization, 199, 207; administration of, 28-29, 82-83, 142; of 1805, 58-59, 69, 82; method of, 59; of 1806, 90, 96; instructions of 1809, 133; anticipated, 163, 165; of 1812, 170, 177, 232; for coast defence, 172, 177; of 1813, 176, 197-98, 199, 200, 202, 229; confusion in 1813, 207; of Silesian *Landwehr*, 210
Möllendorf, Field Marshal von, 46, 73, 77, 78, 86, 94
Moravian Brethren, 55
Müffling, Freiherr von, 64
Murat, Marshal, 94
Musketeers, 17, 171
Muskets, 22, 23, 196, 207, 211, 220; the Nothardt, 71, 179; supply of, 179, 207, 209, 211
Musketry, 22, 180, 182, 183

Napoleon, 7, 12, 15, 16, 67, 70, 78, 87, 88, 89, 90, 93, 121, 151, 177, 178, 185, 187, 188, 194, 195, 199, 210, 212, 213, 219, 228, 229, 235, 236, 237; and Prussian diplomacy, 1805-1806, 89-90; strategy in 1806, 91; at Jena, 92; and peace offer of 1807, 97; at Friedland, 97; at Tilsit, 98; and Stein, 148; establishes a civil guard, 152; defeat at Aspern, 154; and Wagram, 155; demands indemnity payments, 157; opposed by Scharnhorst, 158; and coast defence measures, 172; demands for Prussian assistance, 173; and reverses of 1812, 189; in the spring of 1813, 208; and spring campaign of 1813, 214; at Lützen, 214; at Bautzen, 215; and armistice of Poischwitz, 216; faces the great powers, 217; and battle of Leipzig, 223; defeat of, 224
Narbonne, Count, 174
Nationalism, and military service, 87, 124; and war, 202; and the *Landsturm*, 212; and German historians, 235, 236
National regiments, 75
National revolt, 187, 188, 194, 228; plans for, 185; and French defences, 188. *See* German revolt
National Watch, 153
Nation in arms, 150
Native subjects, as cantonists, 17, 35, 225; as *Knechte*, 21; conscripted as youths, 39; and canton conscription under Frederick William I, 40-41; number of, 58, 98; and plans of 1805, 76-77, 79, 226; and the Land Reserve, 79; and Stein's reforms, 118-19; as mercenaries, 124; and *Krümper* training, 162, 168-69, 228; oppressed by the French, 190, 195; and conscription in Silesia, 210; and the *Landsturm*, 212
Neisse, 97
Neue Kriegsbibliothek, 63
Neue Taktik der Neuern, 67
Neues militärische Bibliothek, 62
Neues militärisches Journal, 62
Neutrality. *See* Prussian neutrality
New East Prussia, 193
New formations, of Febr.-Mar., 1813, 199, 200
"New Prussian Model," 179
Newton, Sir Isaac, 66
Ney, Marshal, 92, 94, 215
Niebuhr, Barthold, 151
Nippold, Friedrich, 238
Nobles, exempt from military service, 42
Non-commissioned officers, 182, 199; punishments for, 25; for Land Reserve, 81; eligible for commissions, 96, 132, 199; to drill *Krümper*, 164; for the artillery, 171
Normal Troops, 182
Nothardt musket, 71, 179

Oath, military, 138-39

Occupational deferments, 52-54, 225
Oder, the, 21, 188, 214
Officers, 24, 107, 124; and ideas about tactics, 21, 65, 69-70, 181-82, 232; honor of, 25, 93; social class of, 29, 96, 132, 139-40; education of, 29, 71, 131, 133-35; age of, 29-30; attitudes of, 30; and reform leadership, 69; used in the bureaucracy, 70; on inactive lists, 81, 108, 176, 232; for the Land Reserve, 81; and personal horses, 83-84, 142; for divisions, 85, 185, 232-33; and summary reform in 1806, 95; and commissioning of commoners, 96, 103, 131, 139, 199, 201; cashiering of, 103; investigation of, 104; public outcry against, 105; and regimental trials, 106; number of, 107, 108, 175; number guilty in 1806-1807, 108; for the Provincial Troops, 120; selection and promotion of, 131-32; and the oath, 138; and courts-martial, 139-40; end of profits, 142; object to first *Krümper* measures, 162; to drill *Krümper*, 164; prefer veterans, 167, 170; for the artillery, 171; favor an insurrection, 187; discouraged, 188; from the *Jäger*, 200; for the *Landwehr*, 205; summary of role of, 232-33
Old soldiers, care of, 32, 70; used as *Krümper*, 161-62, 169-70, 228; additional orders for use of, 166; preferred by the regiments, 167; number in 1810, 169, 176; and the *Landwehr*, 205
Oppen, Lt. Gen. A. F. von, 147
Order on the Organization of the Landwehr, 202
Orders on Military Punishments, 137
Origins of word, *Krümper*, 160
Ortelsburg, 95
Ortelsburger Publicandum, 95-96
Osterode, 94

Pamphlets, war of, 65; on tactics, 181; by Arndt, 190
Paris Peace Conference, 13; significance of *Krümper* system for, 14-15
Paris, Treaty of, 11, 12, 99, 109, 115, 123, 150, 161, 165, 174, 227, 229; terms of, 128-29; secret clauses of, 152, 178
Partition of Poland, 11, 45, 60, 73, 226, 227; effect on recruiting, 58

Patriotism, among retired officers, 81; of militiamen, 121; in reconquered areas, 223-24
Patriots, 196; in 1805-1806, 88-89; and national revolt, 185-86, 187; in East Prussia, 192, 194, 195, 198
Pay, 28, 31, 43, 141, 142, 176
Peace Commission, informed by Stein, 165
Peasants, military obligation, 39, 41, 44; injustice to, 46; and canton system, 52, 225, 226; property and exemptions, 54; learning trades, 55; dislike military service, 197. *See* Native subjects
Penalties for canton evasion, 55-56
Pensions, 27, 70, 146
Peoples' war, 82, 120, 186, 187, 194, 212-13
Pershing, General, 15
Petain, Marshal, 15
Phull, General, 64
Physical defects, exemption based on, 55
Pikes, for the *Landwehr*, 205
Pillau, 98, 113
Pioneers, 130, 206
Pistols, supply of, 179
Poischwitz, armistice of, 216. *See* Armistice
Poland, 11, 22, 30, 45, 58, 60, 73, 216, 226, 227. *See* Partition of Poland
Police troops, 226; in South Prussia, 34; militia useful as, 120; for cities, 152; in Silesia, 210
Polish subjects, 60, 209, 227; in the Towarczys, 19; guarded in 1806, 34; need policing, 45, 226
Pomerania, 29, 77, 112, 113, 155, 165, 175
Pontoons, 21, 113
Portpeefähnriche, 132
Potsdam, 21, 52, 133
Potsdam, Treaty of, 89
Powder reserve, 23-24, 179, 180, 185, 207
Powdered hair, 181
Prenzlau, 94, 95
Presidents, of provinces, 193, 194
Prince Henry, 72
Prisoners of war, return of, 166; in *Krümper* system, 228
Professional men, exemption of, 53
Professional soldiers, 35, 44; length of service, 17; recruiting costs, 28; life of, 31-32; after 1792, 47; ratio to natives, 50; replacements for, 56; method of hiring, 56-57; re-

cruiting of, 58, 124. *See* Mercenaries
Professors, exemption of, 53
Promotions, requirements for officers, 132
Property, as condition for exemption, 54-55
Provincial loyalty, 77, 196
Provincial Troops, 119-20, 122, 152, 153
Prussia, 91, 179, 181, 188, 189, 191, 194, 214, 217; and diplomacy in 1805-1806, 88-90; and losses at Tilsit, 98; financial condition of, 98, 100, 109; to lead German revolt, 186; challenge of 1813, 208; military weakness in 1813, 218; and end of French occupation, 223; and War Minister of, 224; and national revolt, 228; military revival of, 229-30
Prussian army, trials of, 11; characterized by canton system, 17, 35; administration before 1806, 25-27; supply services in 1806, 27-29; strength in 1806, 32-33, 34; shortcomings of, 34, 69, 86; obtaining mercenaries for, 57-58; expansion before 1806, 73, 77; and reforms of 1805, 79-80, 81, 82; mobility of, 82-83; and divisions of 1806, 85; strength at Jena, 92; strength at Auerstädt, 93; rout of, 93; royal reform proposals, 94-95, 103; weakness after Jena, 96; demobilization of 1807, 100; Hardenberg and Altenstein suggest reforms for, 103-04; and reductions of summer, 1807, 109; structure in 1807, 110-12; strength in 1807, 114; strength in 1808, 115, 175, 176; building a reserve for, 115; reorganization of 1807-1808, 124-25; phases of its reform, 128; limited by Treaty of Paris, 128-29; and brigade organization, 129-30; strength in 1809, 130-31; reserve training in 1809, 163-64; use of *Krümper* after 1807, 159, 161; rumors of military preparations, 165; its nadir, 166; false data on, 174; contingent in French army, 174; annual growth of, 174; after reductions of 1808, 176; strength in 1810, 176; size in 1811, 176; size in 1812, 177; arms supply for, 179; tactical needs of, 184; slow growth of, 185; and Tauroggen, 189; and East Prussian example, 195, 196, 197-98; removed to Silesia, 198; expansion in 1813, 199-200, 220; strength in March, 1813, 206; role of *Landwehr*, 208; billeted in Silesia, 210; and spring campaign, 213-15; Scharnhorst's influence on, 216; advantages of armistice for, 217; reorganized during armistice, 218, 229; strength in June, 1813, 218; strength in August, 1813, 221; organization in August, 1813, 222; reinforced from former provinces, 223-24; and Boyen's reforms, 224; new needs in 1790's, 226; as interpreted by von der Goltz, 236
Prussian archives, publications of, 238
Prussian diplomacy, and war of 1806, 88-90
Prussian neutrality, 24, 82, 88, 89, 161
Public criticism of officers, 131
Punishments. *See* Discipline, and Capital punishments
Purge of officers' corps, 107-08
Purpose of author, 13

Quick-loading, 22, 180

Rauch, G. J. G. von, 147
Ravensberg, County of, 54
Rearmament, effectiveness of, 207
Rechnungsführer, 141
Reconnaissance, before Jena, 23; after Jena, 95
Recruiting the mercenaries, 35-36, 56-58
Reductions, 158, 175-76, 177; of 1807, 111-12; of 1808, 115
Reform, opportunity for, 68-69, 226; of tactics, 69-70, 95, 181-82, 183-84, 232-33; of staff organization, 72-73; of 1805, 80-81, 226; initiated by the crown, 94-96, 103; opponents of, 102, 146-47; proposed by Hardenberg, 103-04; proposed by Altenstein, 103-04; and Scharnhorst's first memoir, 109-10; obstacles to, 123; achieved in 1807-1808, 124-25; private suggestions for, 125; and impasse of 1807, 126, 127; resumed in 1808, 128; of military schools, 134-35; of military justice, 135-36, 140; of punishments, 138; of supply services, 141-42; of military administration, 143, 230; in 1809, 149; and failure to change canton law, 150-51; effect of East Prussia on, 195; Boyen's,

224; goals of, 225; French influence on, 237; historical sources for, 238-39
Reform movement, importance of tradition for, 60; spirit of, 64; continuity and leadership of, 68
Reform spirit, 61; waning of, 123
Reformers, literary activity of, 64; and proposals of 1805, 80-81; and establishment of the Military Reorganization Commission, 100-01; idea of a militia, 115-16; compromise on universal service, 118-19; and improved military education, 133-34; and soldiers' oath, 138-39; opposition to, 147; and attempt to provide man power, 150; urge broader service, 152; make use of the *Krümper* system, 178, 228; disliked by York, 182; zeal of, 185; and the East Prussian example, 197-98; and the *Landsturm*, 212; and loss of Scharnhorst, 215
Regimental artillery, 20, 184
Regimental tribunals, 106, 107, 140
Regiments, and the supply services, 27, 141; assigned their cantons, 40, 59; and canton administration, 48, 50, 51, 168-69; end of the historic, 113-14; and *Krümper* training, 162; preference for veterans, 167; and the brigades of 1813, 222
Regulated militia, 38
Regulations, for infantry in 1787, 70; for recruiting, 56-57; for selection of officers, 131-32; and tactical revisions of 1812, 183-85. See Canton regulations
Reichenbach, Treaties of, 217
Religion, basis for exemption, 55
Remounts, 23, 28, 84, 185, 190, 207; dearth in 1813, 221
Requisitions, 83, 93
Reserve Army, the, 118, 122, 123, 153
Reserve on the Vistula, 190, 191
Reserve training, 175; by unmobilized regiments, 173; checked in 1811-1812, 173-74, 177; revised by Hake, 174; resumed in 1813, 178. See *Krümper* system
Reserves, 192, 202, 207; Prussian method of developing, 17, 35, 225; paper strength in 1805, 79-80; plans of 1807-1808, 115-16, 117-18; not trained in the standing army, 120-21; slow development of, 121, 165-66; confusion over categories of,

167; cannot equal the line, 169, 172; in 1808, 175; in 1810, 176; in 1811 and 1812, 176; table of strength for 1807-1813, 178; increases of Febr.-Mar., 1813, 199; and new battalions in 1813, 200; and the *Landwehr*, 204, 208, 212, 229; in Mar., 1813, 206; in spring, 1813, 208; exhaustion of, 212; the Russian, 217; in June, 1813, 218; conclusions about the, 228-29. See Canton system
Reservists. See *Krümper*, and *Beurlaubten*
Resistance, to conscription measures, 209, 210, 223
Reviews, 24, 43
Revolt, plans for, 185-88. See German revolt, and National revolt
Rhine, the, 22, 30, 223
Ribbentrop, F. W. von, 154
Riga, 177
Roedlich, Lt. Col. Hieronymus, 100
Royal Engineering Academy, 21
Royal government, and disasters of 1812, 189-90; and East Prussian example, 196, 197; and control of rearmament, 198; mobilizes the army, 199; and the Silesian *Landwehr*, 210; its administration, 230; loyalty to, 235. See Frederick William III
Royal Guard, 129, 130, 157, 222
Royal instructions, in 1806, 94-96; to the Military Reorganization Commission, 103, 181-82; to the Superior Investigating Commission, 105; on target practice, 180
Rüchel, General von, 64, 74, 75, 76, 78, 80, 93, 115; at Jena, 92-93
Rühle von Lilienstern, 64, 204-05, 224
Rumors of military preparations, 165
Russia, 34, 73, 89, 91, 149, 170, 173, 177, 183, 189, 191, 196, 199, 202, 210, 217; and German revolt, 188; demands more Prussian troops, 219
Russian army, 11, 89, 94, 96, 149, 190, 191, 192, 193, 194, 209, 213, 216, 217; at Eylau and Friedland, 97; and uniforms, 180; provides muskets, 196; at Lützen, 214-15

Saalfeld, battle of, 91
Sabers, supply of, 179
Saldern, Friedrich von, 66
Saxon troops, 90

Saxony, 188, 214; King of, 99
Scharnhorst, 11, 12, 13, 29, 30, 63, 67, 68, 71, 72, 75, 82, 85, 86, 87, 90, 100, 118, 135, 136, 137, 144, 145, 147, 148, 154, 155, 161, 174, 198, 224, 232, 237; and the *Krümper* system, 12, 110, 160-61, 163, 228; influence of, 23, 216, 227; and military education, 29, 64, 133, 134, 135; as an editor, 62, 239; and military societies, 64; as a staff officer, 64, 101, 133; relation to Knesebeck, 75; and the militia, 81-82, 115-16, 117, 121, 186-87; advocates divisions, 85-86, 185; uses traditions, 87; leader of reform party, 100-01; relation to Borstell, 102, 127; first reform memoir, 109-10; and conscription, 118, 154, 155, 227, 228; criticism of, 123; relation to Stein, 128; and staff training, 133; on capital punishments, 137; and a War Ministry, 143, 231; head of War Department, 144; forced from office, 145, 158; and *Krümper* legend, 150; proposes civil guards, 152-53; attacks privilege of substitutes, 157; as secret organizer, 158; and the military budget, 159; and size of army in 1808, 174-75; and arms, 179; and artillery, 180; and new tactics, 183, 184; and national revolt, 186-87; hesitates in 1812, 189; and East Prussia, 197; and mobilization of 1812-1813, 198; resumes post in War Department, 199; and the *Landwehr*, 203; *précis* of 1813, 206; at Lützen (Gross Görschen), 214; death of, 215; principal services of, 227; historical stature of, 235; historical material about, 236, 239
Scharnhorst plan, the, 163, 166, 169, 172
Scherbening, Major von, 238
Schill, Ferdinand von, 186, 187
Schleicher, F. K., 62
Schmoller, Gustav von, 240
Schön, H. T. von, 122, 123, 154, 194
Schönbrunn, Treaty of, 155
Schroetter, F. L., Frhr. von, 74, 77
Schweidnitz, 216
Seafarers, exemption of, 54
Secrecy, for officers' trials, 106; and *Krümper* system, 164-65, 167
Secret military cabinet, 147, 148
Secret War Chancellory, 145
Seeley, J. R., 237-38

Seidl, K. von, 63
Seven Years' War, 30, 64, 77, 120, 215, 218, 236; conscription during, 44-45
Sharpshooters, 17, 23, 113, 125, 182
Siege corps, the Prussian, 219, 222, 224
Siege operations, the French, 94, 97, 179, 214
Silberburg, 99; desertion from, 168
Silesia, 34, 45, 52, 78, 81, 112, 129, 152, 157, 167, 178, 196, 198, 199, 215, 216; and the Land Reserve, 78-79, 81; invaded in 1813, 210; raising the *Landwehr*, 210-11
Skirmishing, 22-23, 69-70, 182, 232. *See* Light infantry, and *Tirailleurs*
Small arms, before 1806, 71; supplies after 1806, 179; for the East Prussian *Landwehr*, 196, 209; for the *Landwehr*, 205, 211; from England, 207-08
Soldiers' oath, 138-39
Soult, Marshal, 92
Sources of Prussian history, 238-39
South German militia, 193
South Prussia, 34, 193
Spandau, 94
Spaniards, revolt of the, 186
Spiessruthenlaufen, 25, 55
Spring campaign, of 1813, 207, 208, 213-15; lessons of, 218
Staegemann, F. A., 151
Staff officers, 67; better training for, 71-73, 133; complements and assignment, 132-33
Stamford, H. W. von, 62
Standing army, the need for a, 120; relation to militia, 121-22
Stargard, 203
Stettin, 94
Stralsund, 214
Students, exemption of, 53
Subsidy, from England, 208, 217
Substitutes, for conscripts, 56, 156; attacked by Scharnhorst, 157; in East Prussia, 195-96
Superior Investigating Commission, instructions for, 105; work of, 106
Supply, services in 1806, 27-28; in the field, 29, 83; administrative changes in 1808, 141-43; of arms, 179, 205, 207, 211, 217; of artillery, 180; of war material in East Prussia, 190-91
Supreme War Council, 14
Stein, Baron vom, 11, 72, 102, 119, 137, 187, 196, 224; and the reform

commission, 101; emancipation of serfs, 118-19; criticizes reformers' militia, 122-23; relation to Scharnhorst, 128; and capital punishments, 136-37; criticizes oath, 139; and the War Ministry, 143, 144, 231; complains of plots, 147; dismissed, 148; in Russian service, 149; approves conscription, 151; discounts Prussian military preparations, 165; and German revolt, 186, 187, 194; in East Prussia, 191, 192, 194, 195; relation to York, 194; and the *Landsturm*, 213; and German nationalism, 235; biography of, 236, 237-38; historical sources, 239
Swenden, 214
Sylva, 63

Tactics, in 1806, 22-23; and criticism of Frederick the Great, 65; Bülow on, 67; improvements before 1806, 70; Frederick William III on, 95, 181-82; improvements, 1806-1812, 181-82; and regulations of 1812, 183-84, 232; spirit of in 1812-1813, 185; for the *Landwehr*, 209; for the *Landsturm*, 212-13; summary of changes in, 232
Taktische Grundsätze, 66
Target practice, 22, 23-24, 180
Tauroggen, Convention of, 189, 190, 191, 195
Technical troops, 21. *See* Miners, and Pontoons
Templehoff, G. F. von, 65
Territorial expansion, effect on army, 11, 45-46, 73, 226-27
Third battalions, 18, 33, 34, 78, 79
Third rank, 69, 113, 125, 181
Thirty Years' War, 36
Thorn, 52
Tilsit, Peace of, 98-99, 166, 168, 169, 177; military clauses in, 99
Tirailleurs, 67, 70, 96, 181, 182, 232
Towarczys, 19, 113
Trachenberg, conference of, 217
Training, before 1806, 21-24; unofficial instructions for, 69-70; of staff officers, 72-73, 133; of reserves in 1805, 80; of *Krümper*, 162, 164; confusion in, 166-67; interrupted in 1811-1812, 173-74; and legend of *Krümper*, 177-78; curtailed in 1810, 180, 182; and the new tactics, 181, 183-84, 185; by Normal Troops, 182; in the winter, 182; of Light Infantry, 183; of *Landwehr*, 219, 220; not completely reformed, 232-33
Trains, the, 28, 84, 142, 143, 206, 220; and mobility, 83; attempts to simplify, 83-84
Transport, after 1808, 142
Treasuries, reorganized, 146
Turkey, 90
Typhus, 209
Tyrol, revolt of, 154

Ueber die höhere preussische Taktik, 65
Uhlans, 19, 113
Uniforms, 71, 124, 180-81; for the *Landwehr*, 205, 209, 220; and the *Landsturm*, 213
Universal service, 41-42, 46, 64, 68, 74, 116, 118, 120, 122, 206, 228; significance of the militia for, 38-39; in eighteenth century Prussia, 41-43, 46, 60, 225; and the canton system, 42-43, 150, 225; in canton law of 1792, 47, 225-26; proposed by Knesebeck, 76, 226; and nationalism, 87; in Austria, 87; compromised in 1807, 118-19; Scharnhorst's idea of, 118-19, 122, 227; not secured in 1808, 128, 153-54; and military punishments, 135, 137; stated in Articles of War, 137; and the National Watch, 153; studied in 1809, 154; disliked by Frederick William III, 155; urged by the reformers, 1808-1810, 155, 227-28; in East Prussia, 195-96; decreed in 1813, 197, 201, 229; and the *Landwehr*, 204; in the Boyen Law, 224
Urban classes, exemption of, 52

Valentini, 64
Valmy, battle of, 84, 189
Value of the *Landwehr*, 211-12, 220
Vaterland, in oath, 139
Venturini, Georg, 63, 66
Veterans, preferred by officers, 170; available in cavalry, 171; as *Krümper*, 228. *See* Old soldiers
Vidal de la Blache, Jos. M. C., 237
Vincke, Ludwig, Frhr. von, 151
Vistula, the, 21, 98, 214
Volunteers, 35, 169, 201, 223; for officer training, 197, 200, 229; for the *Jäger*, 200-01
Volunteer *Jäger*. *See Jäger*

Wagram, battle of, 155
War Commissariat, 141, 142, 146
War commissars, 141, 142
War Department, 144, 145, 167, 168; organization of, 145-46
War Magazine Administration, 28
War Minister, 27, 86, 143-44, 148, 224, 231, 232
War Ministry, 141, 146, 224, 239; proposed by Stein, 143; established provisionally, 144; relation to General Adjutants, 146-47
War of 1806, origins of, 88-90
War of Liberation, 44, 140, 161, 195, 196, 207; number of Prussian officers, 108; and the German historians, 235
War of Spanish Succession, 160
War party, the, 90, 196, 198, 229
War plans, 73, 90; for revolt, 188; in spring of 1813, 214, 216; of Trachenberg, 217
Warsaw, 188, 214
Warsaw, Duchy of, 188

War Schools, 134-35
Wartime problems, 207-08
War Treasury, 55, 146
Was bedeutet Landwehr und Landsturm, 190
Wellington, Duke of, 213-14
Weser, the, 223
Westphalia, 88, 188
West Prussia, 167, 175, 190, 193, 209
Willisen, W. von, 238
Winter exercises, 182
Wissmann, President, 194
Wittgenstein, General, 214
Wittgenstein, Count zu Sayn-, 148
Workers, exemption of skilled, 42, 53-54

York von Wartenburg, 183, 196, 198, 199, 209; and the *Beurlaubten*, 170; hostile to reformers, 182; and the Light Troops, 182, 183; and Tauroggen, 189; in East Prussia, 190, 191, 194, 195; relation to Stein, 194

UA
718
.P9S5

UA 718 .P9S5   Shanahan, William

Prussian Military Reforms,
1786-1813